image® COMICS PRESENTS

NOBLE CAUSES

FAM... ...TS

D1284018

Written and Created by

Jay Faerber

Cover by

Ian Richardson & Ken Wolak

Trade Paperback Design by

Ray Dillon
Golden Goat Studios, Inc.

For Image Comics

Jim Valentino - Publisher
Brent Braun - Director of Production
Eric Stephenson - Director of Marketing
Traci Hale - Controller/Foreign Licensing
Brett Evans - Art Director
Allen Hui - Web Developer
Tim Hegarty - Book Trade Coordinator
Cindie Espinoza - Accounting Assistant
Jon Malin - Production Assistant

Noble Causes Vol. 2: Family Secrets, copyright 2004. First Printing. Published by Image Comics Inc. Office of Publication: 1071 N. Batavia St. Suite A, Orange CA 92867.

Portions of this novel were previously printed in Noble Causes: Family Secrets 1-4.
Visit www.jayfaerber.com Printed in Korea

WWW.IMAGECOMICS.COM

Introduction BY RICK ALEXANDER

GOOD GRIEF

Jay Faerber knows grief. The deep kind. The cathartic kind.

And "*Grief*," to paraphrase a phrase (my apologies to Mr. Stone), "is good."

At least, when it's grief as done by Jay Faerber.

And as well as I think I know him (which, I'm starting to suspect, might be more along the lines of "not that well -- at all"), the easygoing, seemingly sunny-dispositioned comics creator clearly has an "inner drama queen" that's been dying to come out; er, I mean, *get* out.

And *she* has gotten out -- of Jay -- and spilled her traumatized guts all over the cleverly crafted pages (by Jay and a posse of talented collaborators too numerous to waste my allotted word count naming -- *READ THE CREDITS, DAMN YOU!*) that follow this introduction to the collected "Family Secrets" arc of Jay's overheated, intentionally melodramatic, camp (or, rather, "camping" -- thank you, Ms. Sontag) brainchild NOBLE CAUSES.

But amusing -- and often, hilarious -- as the continuing saga of the Noble family and its in-laws and outlaws may be, this second collection of the family history, both present and past, is suffused with grief, and a palpable sense of loss; for Race, the Noble who seemed the most noble Noble of all the Nobles (whew!) -- and there's no getting around this -- is still quite dead, thank you very much (Jay, this is where I plug the *first* trade paperback, NOBLE CAUSES, VOL 1: IN SICKNESS AND IN HEALTH, right? -- Jay? Hmm, where's Jay?).

And his absence is tearing the family apart. As Race's widow, Liz, tries to cope with having been thrust into this world of super-celebrities without her murdered husband's super-powered shoulder to lean on, *later* Doc turns to the bottle while Earth-mother Gaia's attempts to micromanage the PR machine that keeps the family in the chips alienates the rest of the clan: Rusty -- his brain now encased in a robot body; Frost -- the illegitimate odd man out; and Zephyr -- whose tryst with family arch-enemy Draconis, um, "complicates" her relationship with the evil demon's Noble-loving son, Krennick (There, Jay, I didn't leave anyone out, did I? -- *Jay*? Y'know, I think Jay's busy fielding offers from Hollywood, now that -- full disclosure of my former vested interest here -- well, now that *I'm* no longer "attached" as a producer to a failed attempt to sell a network TV series based on these damned books).

So, why all the "acting out" from these characters, who ought to know better, who have *larger responsibilities* to their public, to the wider world? If I had to bet – and mind you, I'm not a betting man – I'd bet on "survivors' guilt" as the root cause. All I know for sure is, largely unspoken memories of Race tower over this collection like the never-seen (and very dead) Skipper does over Williams' "Cat On A Hot Tin Roof" (in many ways, the mother of all the Spelling-produced prime-time soaps that Jay lays claim to as his *ur*-inspiration for NCs).

And those memories of a fallen hero – someone's son, someone's brother, someone's lover – they hurt. Through all the superhuman antics. Through all the over-the-top attitudes (and behavior). Through all the fun of it all.

And that means something.

It means Jay Faerber's let his "inner drama queen" out.

And, "Good grief!" (Let us now pause for a moment in memory of the dear, departed Mr. Schulz…)…

Comics are a bit better for it.

Rick Alexander
Los Angeles, CA
December 1, 2003

Afterword: Man, that Geoff ("Introduction to Vol. 1") Johns is a hard act to follow.

- Rick Alexander writes and produces the Sony Pictures Television series STRONG MEDICINE, and is one of the phalanx of producers on the new feature film version of CONAN for Warner Bros. He can't believe he left his comics at home when he moved to Hollywood.

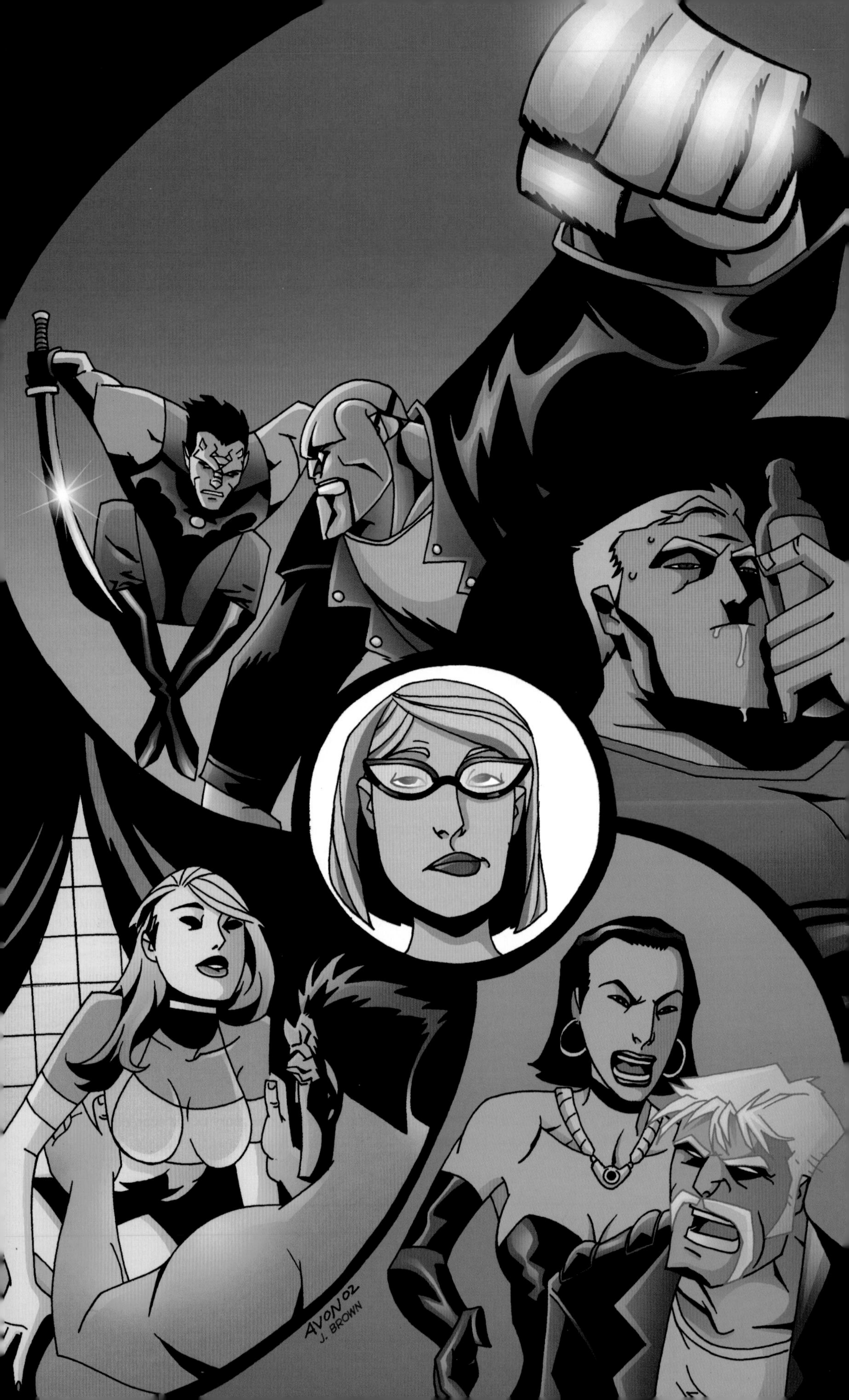
AVON 02
J. BROWN

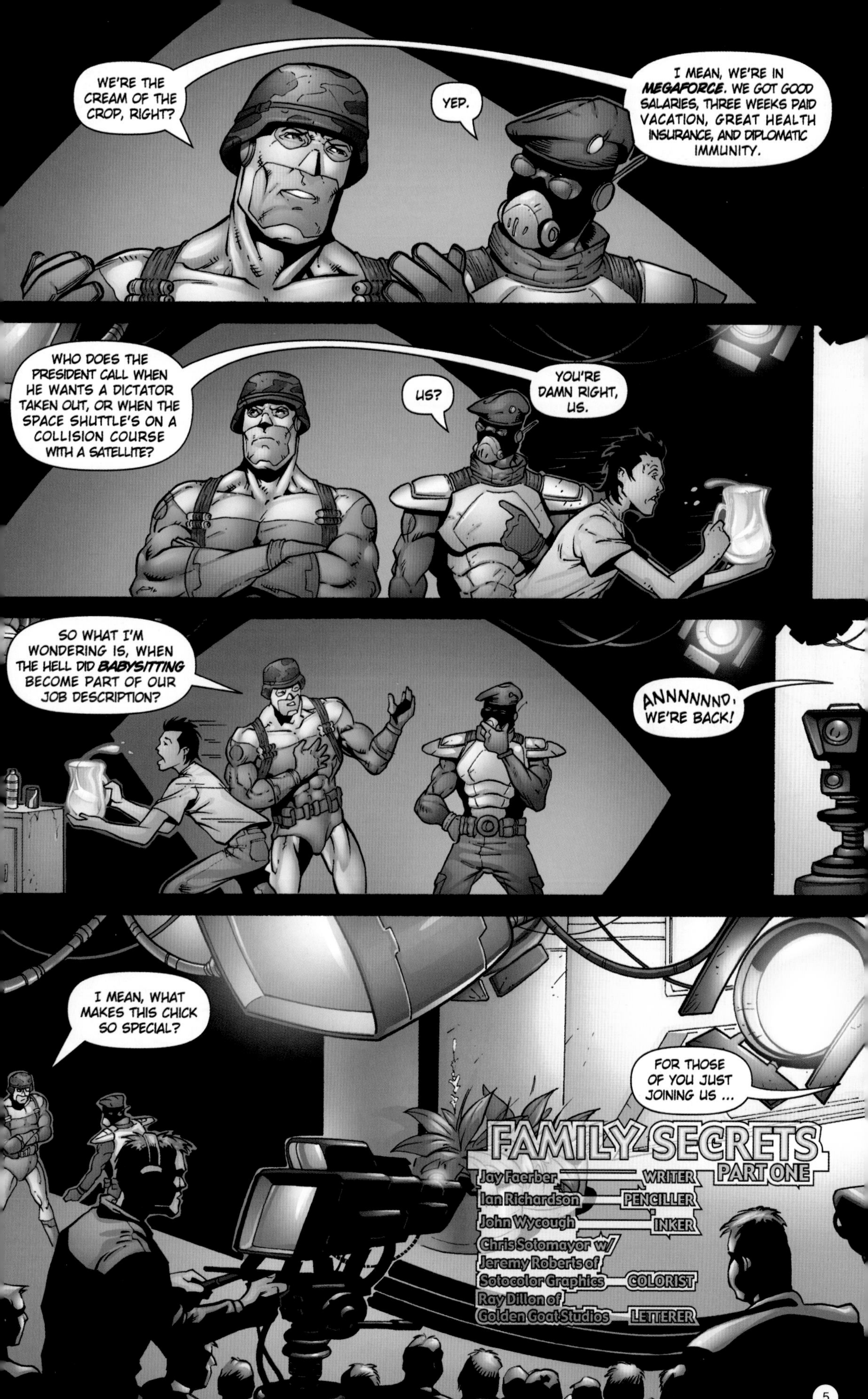
WE'RE THE CREAM OF THE CROP, RIGHT?
YEP.
I MEAN, WE'RE IN MEGAFORCE. WE GOT GOOD SALARIES, THREE WEEKS PAID VACATION, GREAT HEALTH INSURANCE, AND DIPLOMATIC IMMUNITY.
WHO DOES THE PRESIDENT CALL WHEN HE WANTS A DICTATOR TAKEN OUT, OR WHEN THE SPACE SHUTTLE'S ON A COLLISION COURSE WITH A SATELLITE?
US?
YOU'RE DAMN RIGHT, US.
SO WHAT I'M WONDERING IS, WHEN THE HELL DID BABYSITTING BECOME PART OF OUR JOB DESCRIPTION?
ANNNNNND, WE'RE BACK!
I MEAN, WHAT MAKES THIS CHICK SO SPECIAL?
FOR THOSE OF YOU JUST JOINING US ...
FAMILY SECRETS
PART ONE
Jay Faerber WRITER
Ian Richardson PENCILLER
John Wycough INKER
Chris Sotomayor w/ Jeremy Roberts of Sotocolor Graphics COLORIST
Ray Dillon of Golden Goat Studios LETTERER

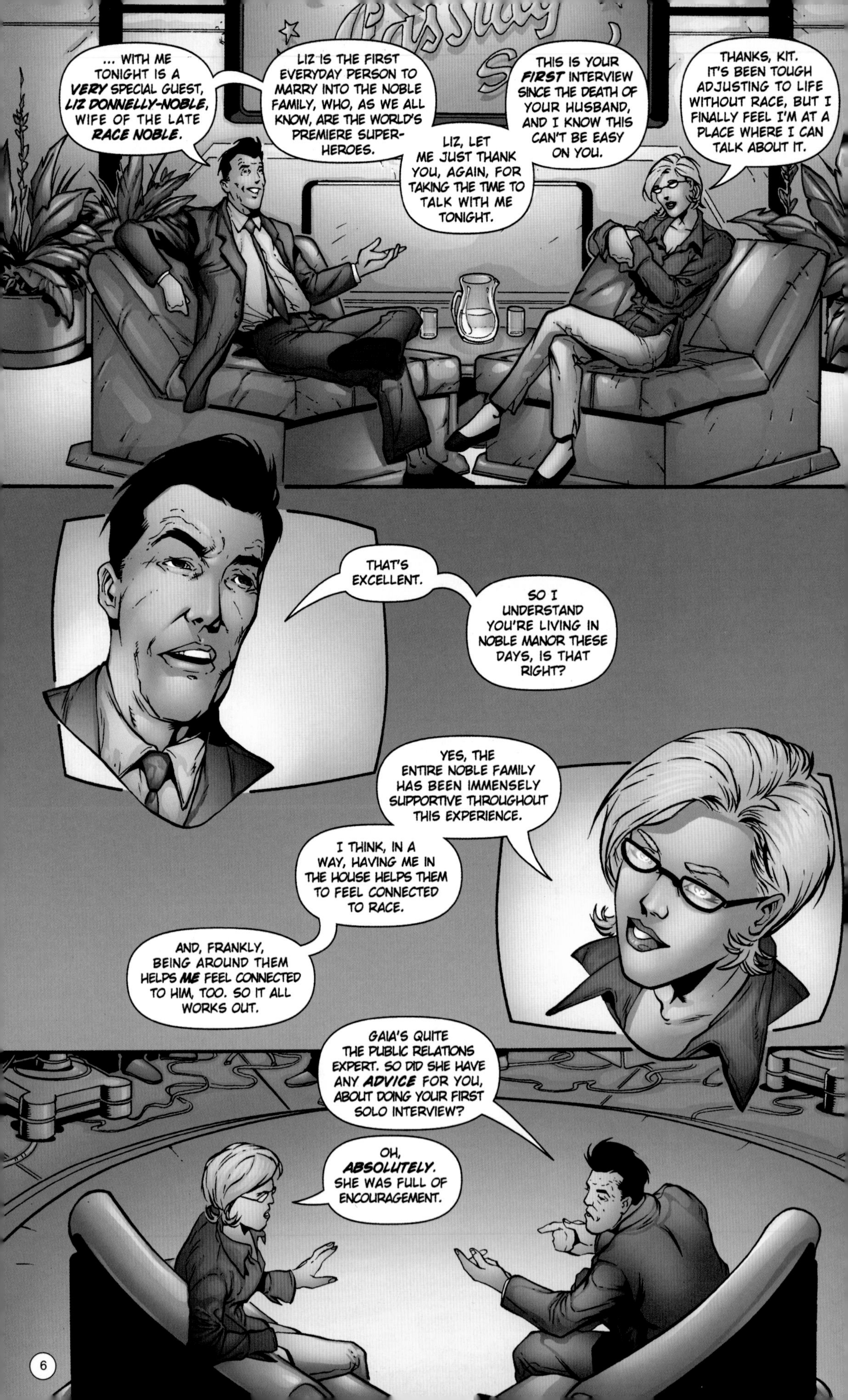
... WITH ME TONIGHT IS A *VERY* SPECIAL GUEST, *LIZ DONNELLY-NOBLE*, WIFE OF THE LATE *RACE NOBLE*.
LIZ IS THE FIRST EVERYDAY PERSON TO MARRY INTO THE NOBLE FAMILY, WHO, AS WE ALL KNOW, ARE THE WORLD'S PREMIERE SUPER-HEROES.
LIZ, LET ME JUST THANK YOU, AGAIN, FOR TAKING THE TIME TO TALK WITH ME TONIGHT.
THIS IS YOUR *FIRST* INTERVIEW SINCE THE DEATH OF YOUR HUSBAND, AND I KNOW THIS CAN'T BE EASY ON YOU.
THANKS, KIT. IT'S BEEN TOUGH ADJUSTING TO LIFE WITHOUT RACE, BUT I FINALLY FEEL I'M AT A PLACE WHERE I CAN TALK ABOUT IT.
THAT'S EXCELLENT.
SO I UNDERSTAND YOU'RE LIVING IN NOBLE MANOR THESE DAYS, IS THAT RIGHT?
YES, THE ENTIRE NOBLE FAMILY HAS BEEN IMMENSELY SUPPORTIVE THROUGHOUT THIS EXPERIENCE.
I THINK, IN A WAY, HAVING ME IN THE HOUSE HELPS THEM TO FEEL CONNECTED TO RACE.
AND, FRANKLY, BEING AROUND THEM HELPS *ME* FEEL CONNECTED TO HIM, TOO. SO IT ALL WORKS OUT.
GAIA'S QUITE THE PUBLIC RELATIONS EXPERT. SO DID SHE HAVE ANY *ADVICE* FOR YOU, ABOUT DOING YOUR FIRST SOLO INTERVIEW?
OH, *ABSOLUTELY*. SHE WAS FULL OF ENCOURAGEMENT.

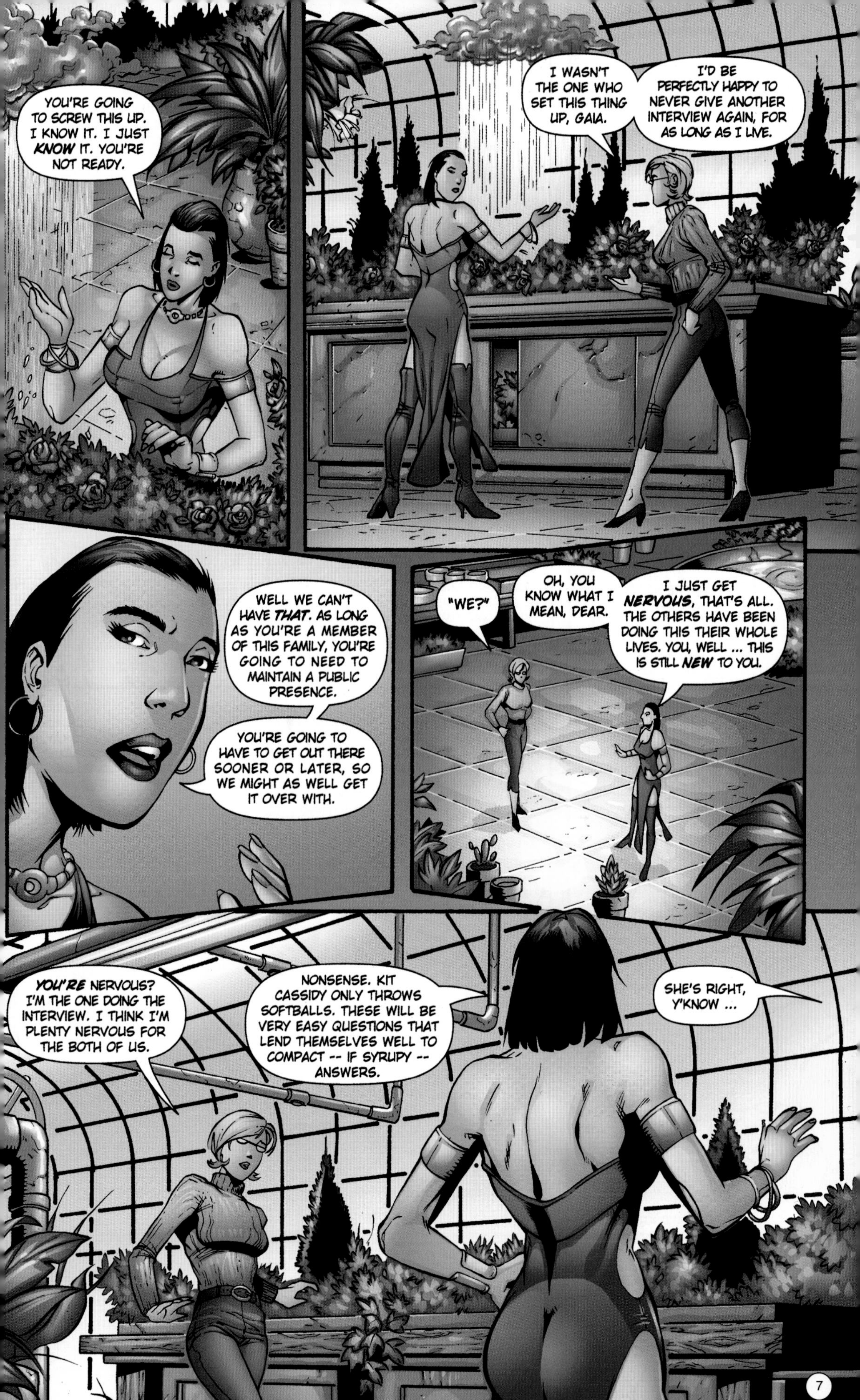
YOU'RE GOING TO SCREW THIS UP. I KNOW IT. I JUST *KNOW* IT. YOU'RE NOT READY.
I WASN'T THE ONE WHO SET THIS THING UP, GAIA.
I'D BE PERFECTLY HAPPY TO NEVER GIVE ANOTHER INTERVIEW AGAIN, FOR AS LONG AS I LIVE.
WELL WE CAN'T HAVE *THAT*. AS LONG AS YOU'RE A MEMBER OF THIS FAMILY, YOU'RE GOING TO NEED TO MAINTAIN A PUBLIC PRESENCE.
YOU'RE GOING TO HAVE TO GET OUT THERE SOONER OR LATER, SO WE MIGHT AS WELL GET IT OVER WITH.
"WE?"
OH, YOU KNOW WHAT I MEAN, DEAR.
I JUST GET *NERVOUS*, THAT'S ALL. THE OTHERS HAVE BEEN DOING THIS THEIR WHOLE LIVES. YOU, WELL ... THIS IS STILL *NEW* TO YOU.
YOU'RE NERVOUS? I'M THE ONE DOING THE INTERVIEW. I THINK I'M PLENTY NERVOUS FOR THE BOTH OF US.
NONSENSE. KIT CASSIDY ONLY THROWS SOFTBALLS. THESE WILL BE VERY EASY QUESTIONS THAT LEND THEMSELVES WELL TO COMPACT -- IF SYRUPY -- ANSWERS.
SHE'S RIGHT, Y'KNOW ...

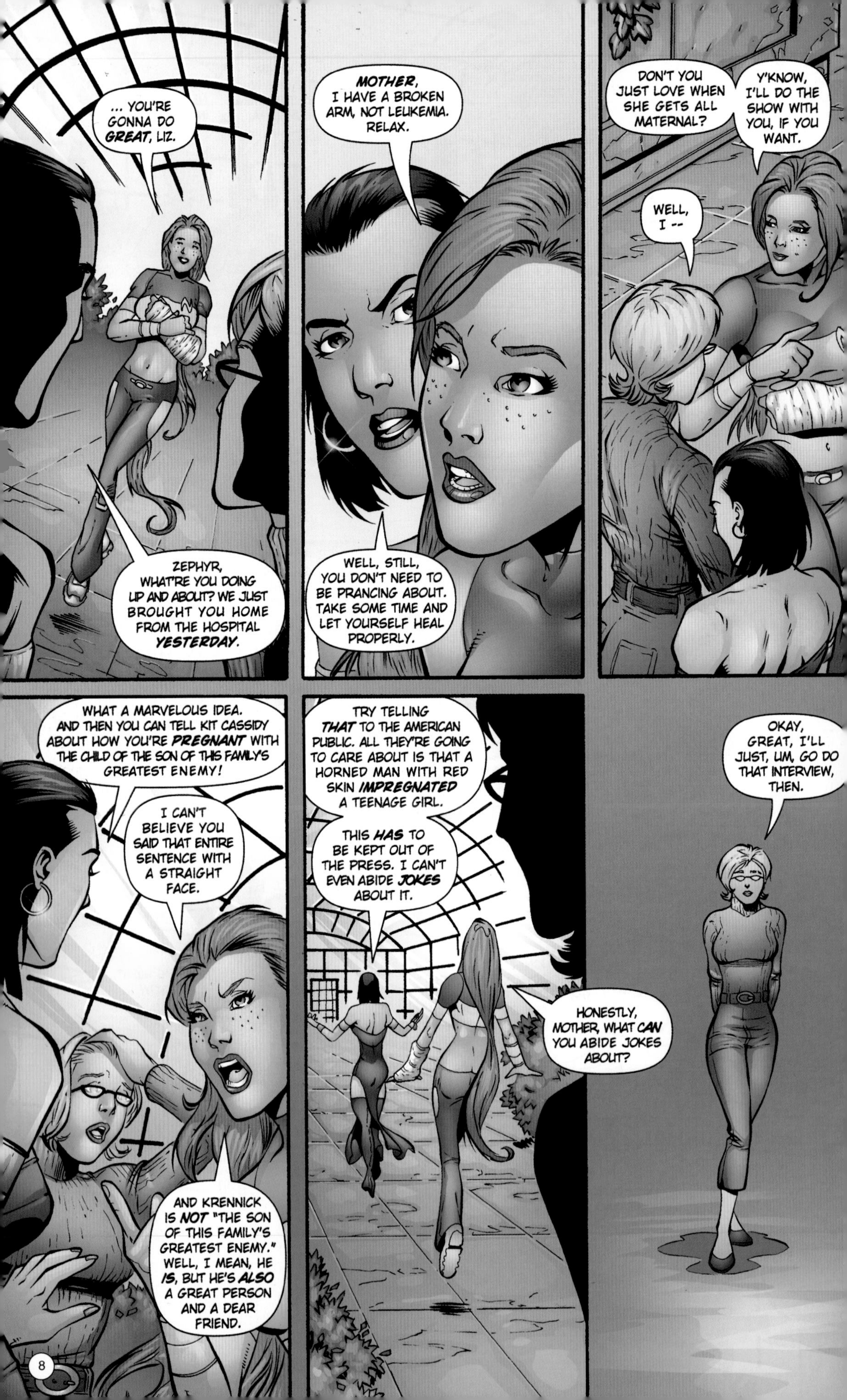
... YOU'RE GONNA DO GREAT, LIZ.
ZEPHYR, WHAT'RE YOU DOING UP AND ABOUT? WE JUST BROUGHT YOU HOME FROM THE HOSPITAL YESTERDAY.
MOTHER, I HAVE A BROKEN ARM, NOT LEUKEMIA. RELAX.
WELL, STILL, YOU DON'T NEED TO BE PRANCING ABOUT. TAKE SOME TIME AND LET YOURSELF HEAL PROPERLY.
DON'T YOU JUST LOVE WHEN SHE GETS ALL MATERNAL?
Y'KNOW, I'LL DO THE SHOW WITH YOU, IF YOU WANT.
WELL, I --
WHAT A MARVELOUS IDEA. AND THEN YOU CAN TELL KIT CASSIDY ABOUT HOW YOU'RE PREGNANT WITH THE CHILD OF THE SON OF THIS FAMILY'S GREATEST ENEMY!
I CAN'T BELIEVE YOU SAID THAT ENTIRE SENTENCE WITH A STRAIGHT FACE.
AND KRENNICK IS NOT "THE SON OF THIS FAMILY'S GREATEST ENEMY." WELL, I MEAN, HE IS, BUT HE'S ALSO A GREAT PERSON AND A DEAR FRIEND.
TRY TELLING THAT TO THE AMERICAN PUBLIC. ALL THEY'RE GOING TO CARE ABOUT IS THAT A HORNED MAN WITH RED SKIN IMPREGNATED A TEENAGE GIRL.
THIS HAS TO BE KEPT OUT OF THE PRESS. I CAN'T EVEN ABIDE JOKES ABOUT IT.
HONESTLY, MOTHER, WHAT CAN YOU ABIDE JOKES ABOUT?
OKAY, GREAT, I'LL JUST, UM, GO DO THAT INTERVIEW, THEN.

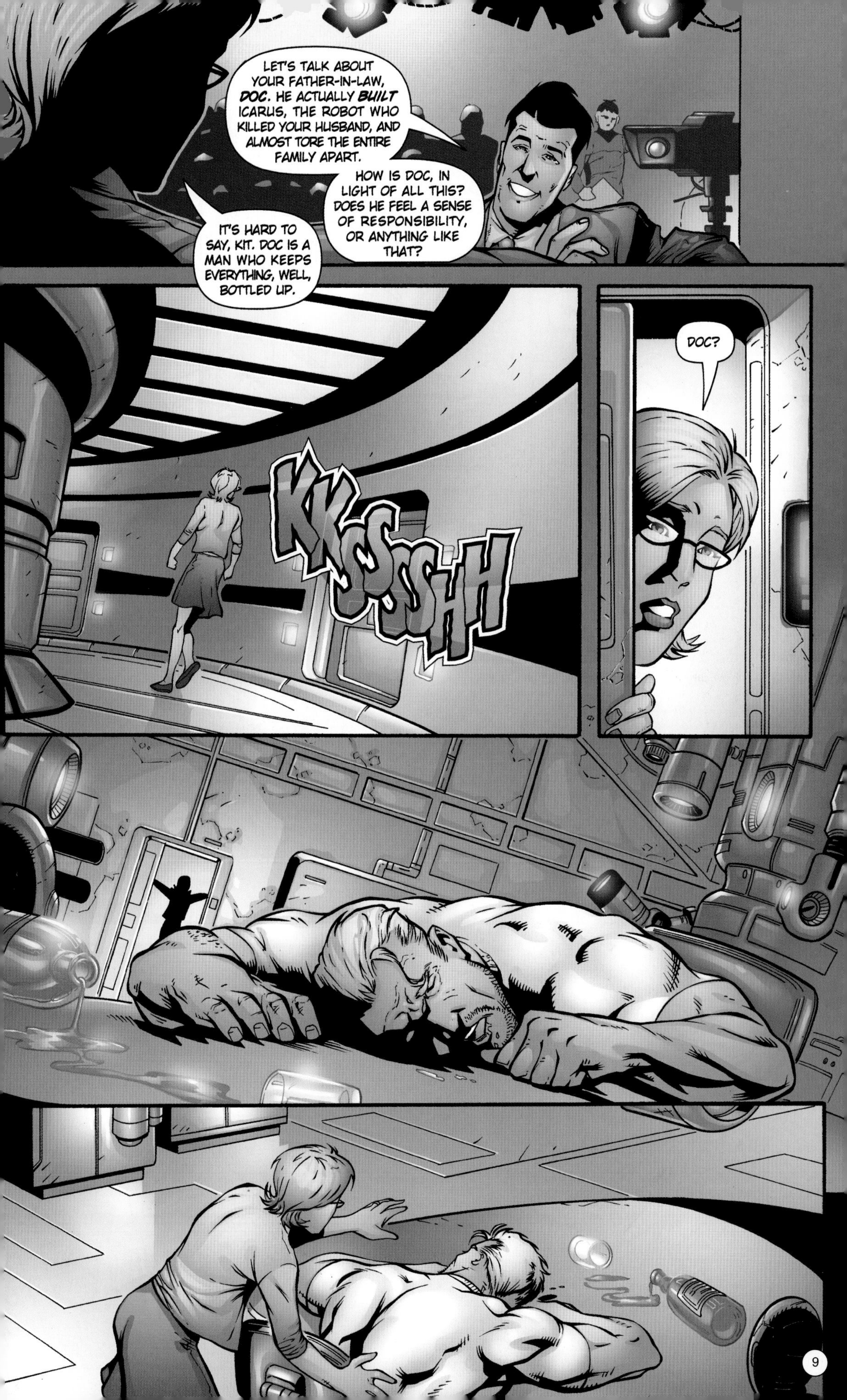
LET'S TALK ABOUT YOUR FATHER-IN-LAW, DOC. HE ACTUALLY BUILT ICARUS, THE ROBOT WHO KILLED YOUR HUSBAND, AND ALMOST TORE THE ENTIRE FAMILY APART.
HOW IS DOC, IN LIGHT OF ALL THIS? DOES HE FEEL A SENSE OF RESPONSIBILITY, OR ANYTHING LIKE THAT?
IT'S HARD TO SAY, KIT. DOC IS A MAN WHO KEEPS EVERYTHING, WELL, BOTTLED UP.
KKSSSHH
DOC?

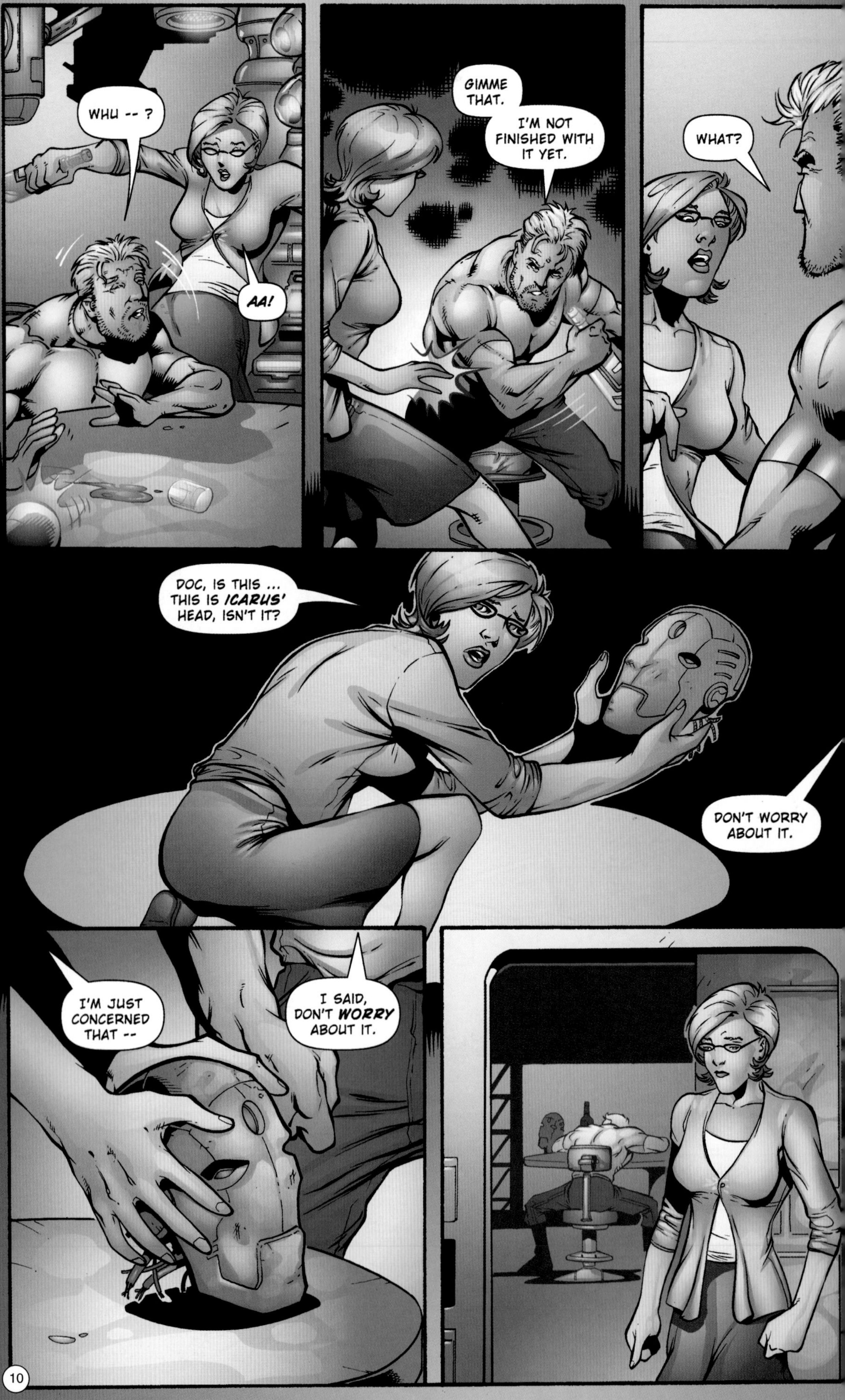
WHU -- ?
AA!
GIMME THAT.
I'M NOT FINISHED WITH IT YET.
WHAT?
DOC, IS THIS ... THIS IS ICARUS' HEAD, ISN'T IT?
DON'T WORRY ABOUT IT.
I'M JUST CONCERNED THAT --
I SAID, DON'T WORRY ABOUT IT.

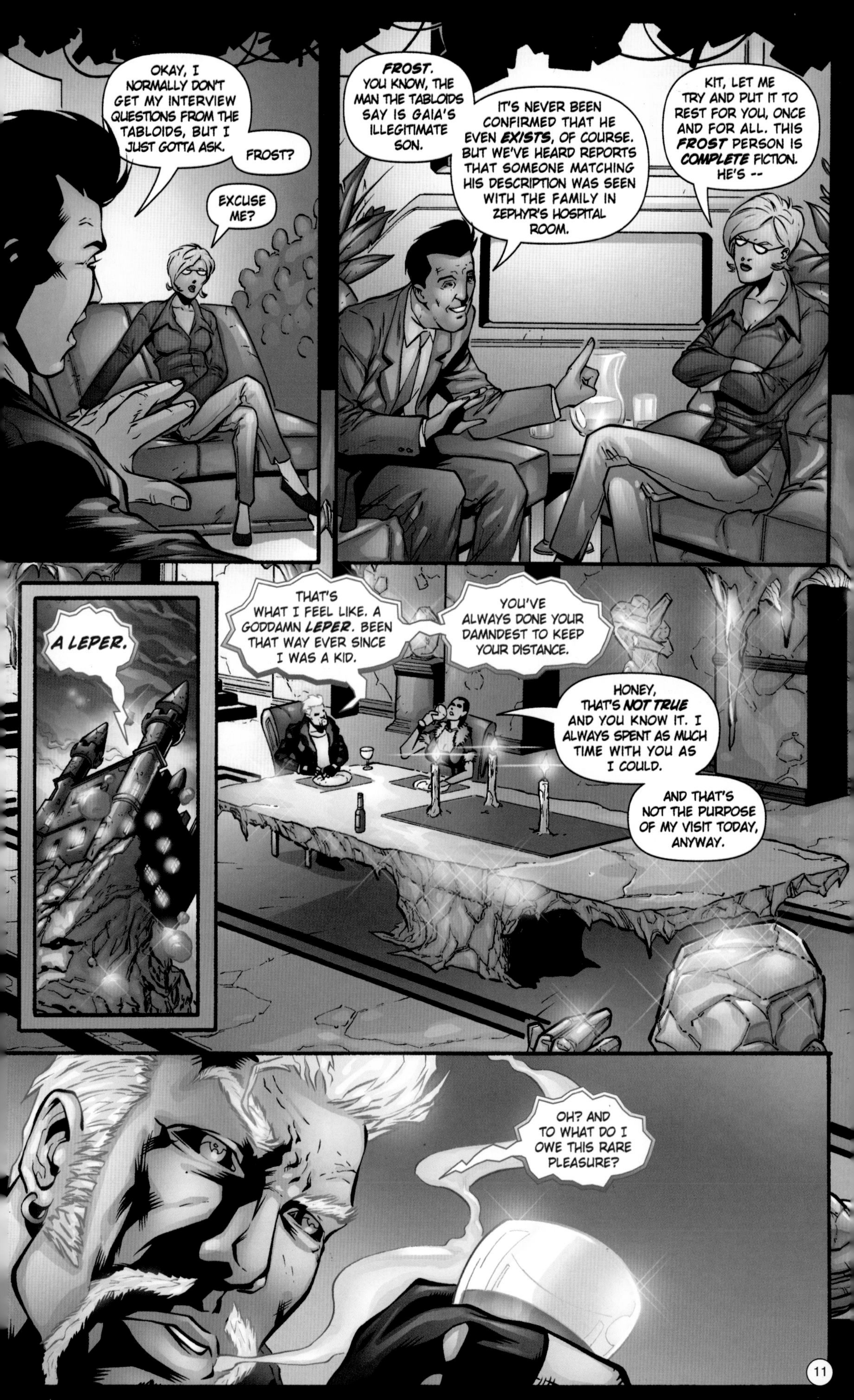
OKAY, I NORMALLY DON'T GET MY INTERVIEW QUESTIONS FROM THE TABLOIDS, BUT I JUST GOTTA ASK.
FROST?
EXCUSE ME?
FROST. YOU KNOW, THE MAN THE TABLOIDS SAY IS GAIA'S ILLEGITIMATE SON.
IT'S NEVER BEEN CONFIRMED THAT HE EVEN EXISTS, OF COURSE. BUT WE'VE HEARD REPORTS THAT SOMEONE MATCHING HIS DESCRIPTION WAS SEEN WITH THE FAMILY IN ZEPHYR'S HOSPITAL ROOM.
KIT, LET ME TRY AND PUT IT TO REST FOR YOU, ONCE AND FOR ALL. THIS FROST PERSON IS COMPLETE FICTION. HE'S --
A LEPER.
THAT'S WHAT I FEEL LIKE. A GODDAMN LEPER. BEEN THAT WAY EVER SINCE I WAS A KID.
YOU'VE ALWAYS DONE YOUR DAMNDEST TO KEEP YOUR DISTANCE.
HONEY, THAT'S NOT TRUE AND YOU KNOW IT. I ALWAYS SPENT AS MUCH TIME WITH YOU AS I COULD.
AND THAT'S NOT THE PURPOSE OF MY VISIT TODAY, ANYWAY.
OH? AND TO WHAT DO I OWE THIS RARE PLEASURE?

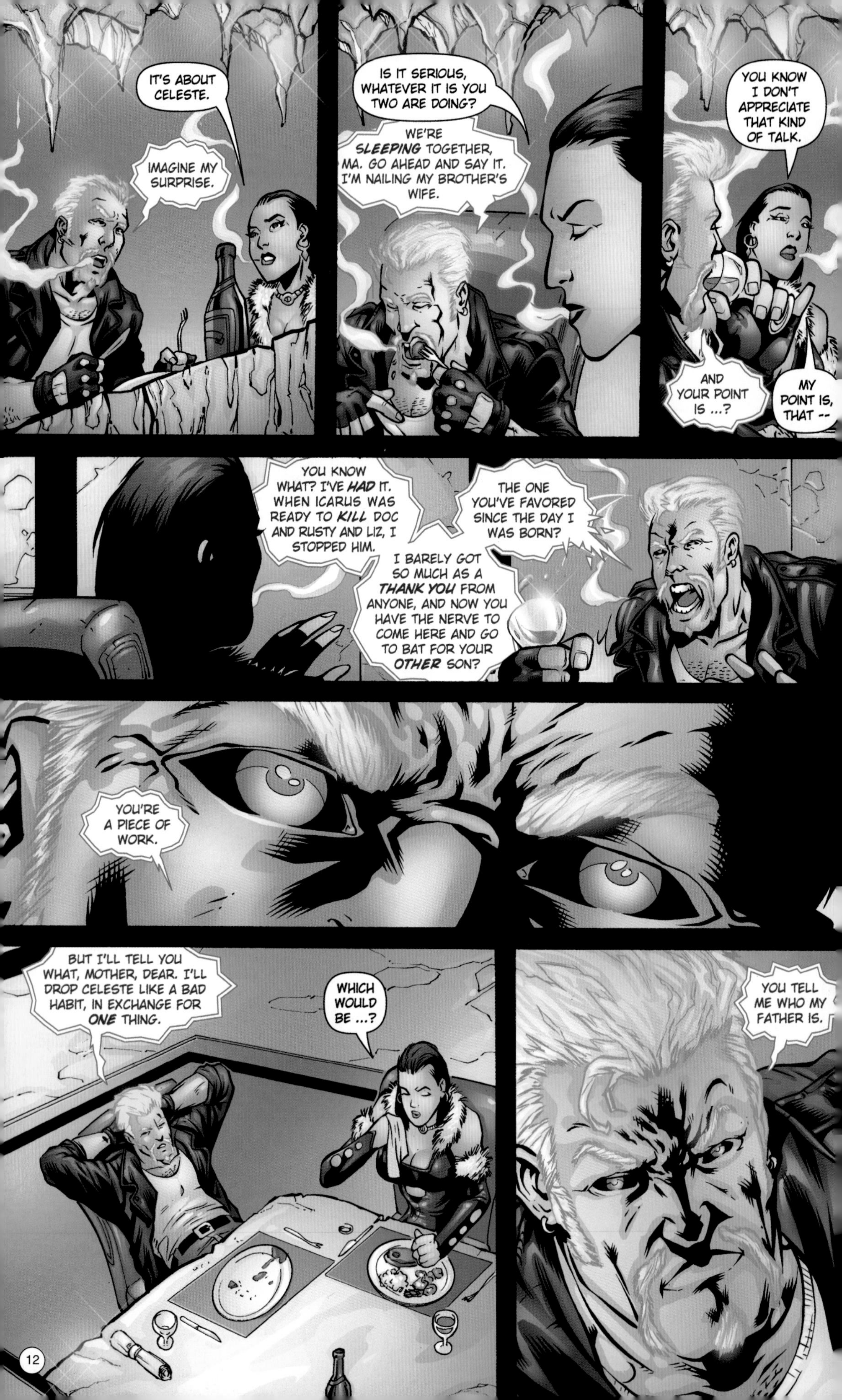
IT'S ABOUT CELESTE.
IMAGINE MY SURPRISE.
IS IT SERIOUS, WHATEVER IT IS YOU TWO ARE DOING?
WE'RE SLEEPING TOGETHER, MA. GO AHEAD AND SAY IT. I'M NAILING MY BROTHER'S WIFE.
YOU KNOW I DON'T APPRECIATE THAT KIND OF TALK.
AND YOUR POINT IS ...?
MY POINT IS, THAT --
YOU KNOW WHAT? I'VE HAD IT. WHEN ICARUS WAS READY TO KILL DOC AND RUSTY AND LIZ, I STOPPED HIM.
I BARELY GOT SO MUCH AS A THANK YOU FROM ANYONE, AND NOW YOU HAVE THE NERVE TO COME HERE AND GO TO BAT FOR YOUR OTHER SON?
THE ONE YOU'VE FAVORED SINCE THE DAY I WAS BORN?
YOU'RE A PIECE OF WORK.
BUT I'LL TELL YOU WHAT, MOTHER, DEAR. I'LL DROP CELESTE LIKE A BAD HABIT, IN EXCHANGE FOR ONE THING.
WHICH WOULD BE ...?
YOU TELL ME WHO MY FATHER IS.

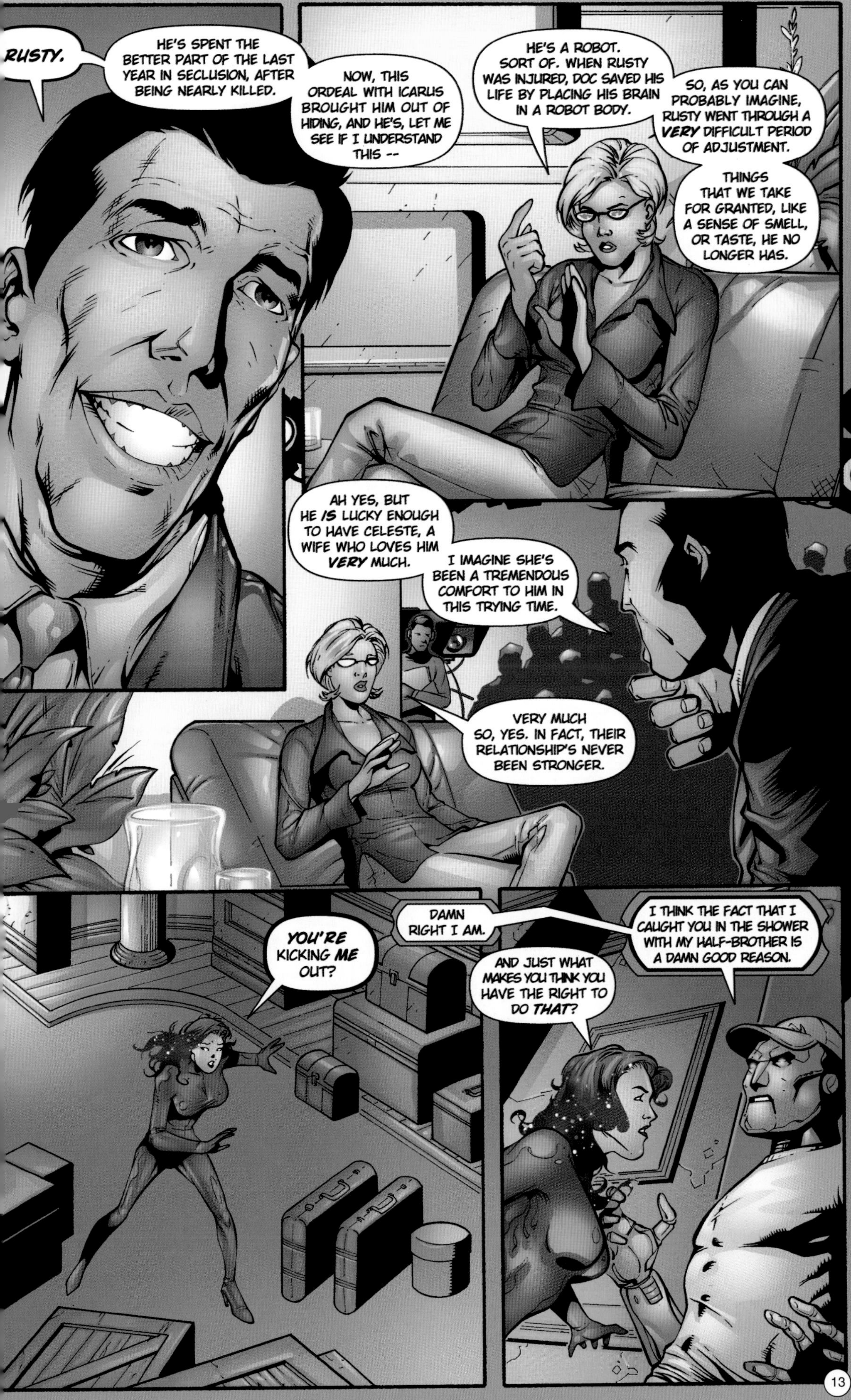
RUSTY.
HE'S SPENT THE BETTER PART OF THE LAST YEAR IN SECLUSION, AFTER BEING NEARLY KILLED.
NOW, THIS ORDEAL WITH ICARUS BROUGHT HIM OUT OF HIDING, AND HE'S, LET ME SEE IF I UNDERSTAND THIS --
HE'S A ROBOT. SORT OF. WHEN RUSTY WAS INJURED, DOC SAVED HIS LIFE BY PLACING HIS BRAIN IN A ROBOT BODY.
SO, AS YOU CAN PROBABLY IMAGINE, RUSTY WENT THROUGH A VERY DIFFICULT PERIOD OF ADJUSTMENT.
THINGS THAT WE TAKE FOR GRANTED, LIKE A SENSE OF SMELL, OR TASTE, HE NO LONGER HAS.
AH YES, BUT HE IS LUCKY ENOUGH TO HAVE CELESTE, A WIFE WHO LOVES HIM VERY MUCH.
I IMAGINE SHE'S BEEN A TREMENDOUS COMFORT TO HIM IN THIS TRYING TIME.
VERY MUCH SO, YES. IN FACT, THEIR RELATIONSHIP'S NEVER BEEN STRONGER.
YOU'RE KICKING ME OUT?
DAMN RIGHT I AM.
AND JUST WHAT MAKES YOU THINK YOU HAVE THE RIGHT TO DO THAT?
I THINK THE FACT THAT I CAUGHT YOU IN THE SHOWER WITH MY HALF-BROTHER IS A DAMN GOOD REASON.

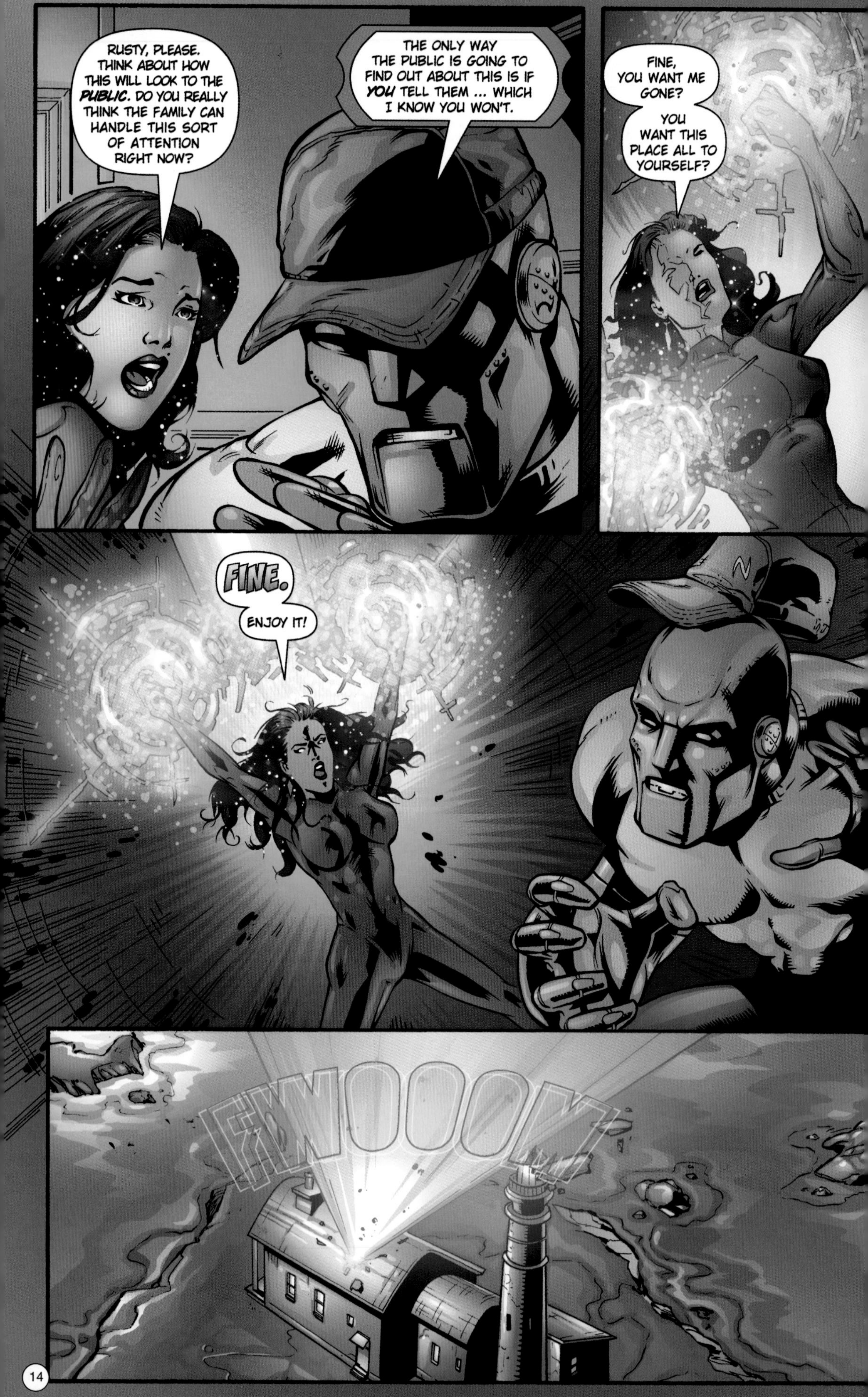

RUSTY, PLEASE. THINK ABOUT HOW THIS WILL LOOK TO THE PUBLIC. DO YOU REALLY THINK THE FAMILY CAN HANDLE THIS SORT OF ATTENTION RIGHT NOW?
THE ONLY WAY THE PUBLIC IS GOING TO FIND OUT ABOUT THIS IS IF YOU TELL THEM ... WHICH I KNOW YOU WON'T.
FINE, YOU WANT ME GONE?
YOU WANT THIS PLACE ALL TO YOURSELF?
FINE.
ENJOY IT!
FWOOOOM

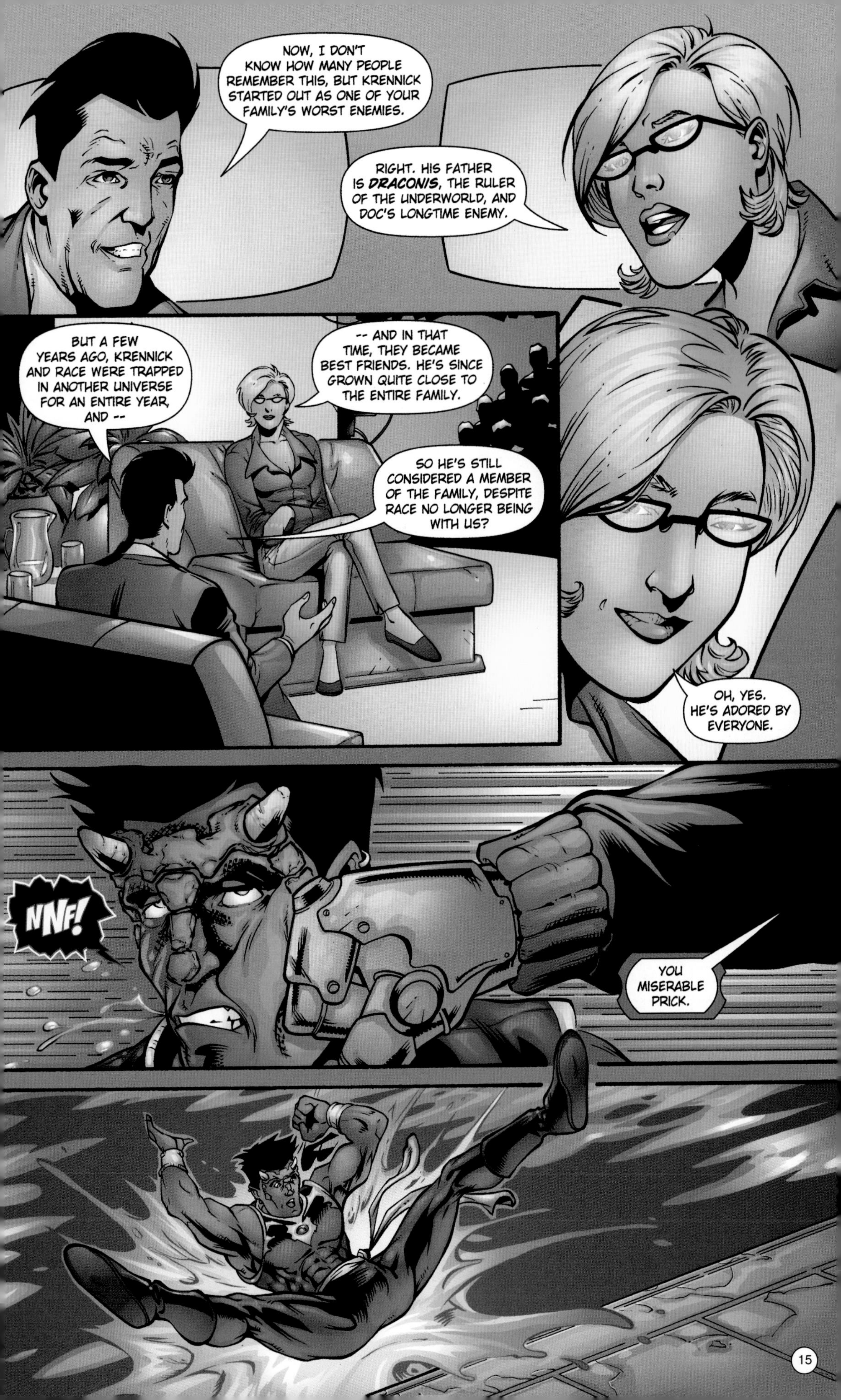
NOW, I DON'T KNOW HOW MANY PEOPLE REMEMBER THIS, BUT KRENNICK STARTED OUT AS ONE OF YOUR FAMILY'S WORST ENEMIES.
RIGHT. HIS FATHER IS DRACONIS, THE RULER OF THE UNDERWORLD, AND DOC'S LONGTIME ENEMY.
BUT A FEW YEARS AGO, KRENNICK AND RACE WERE TRAPPED IN ANOTHER UNIVERSE FOR AN ENTIRE YEAR, AND --
-- AND IN THAT TIME, THEY BECAME BEST FRIENDS. HE'S SINCE GROWN QUITE CLOSE TO THE ENTIRE FAMILY.
SO HE'S STILL CONSIDERED A MEMBER OF THE FAMILY, DESPITE RACE NO LONGER BEING WITH US?
OH, YES. HE'S ADORED BY EVERYONE.
NNF!
YOU MISERABLE PRICK.

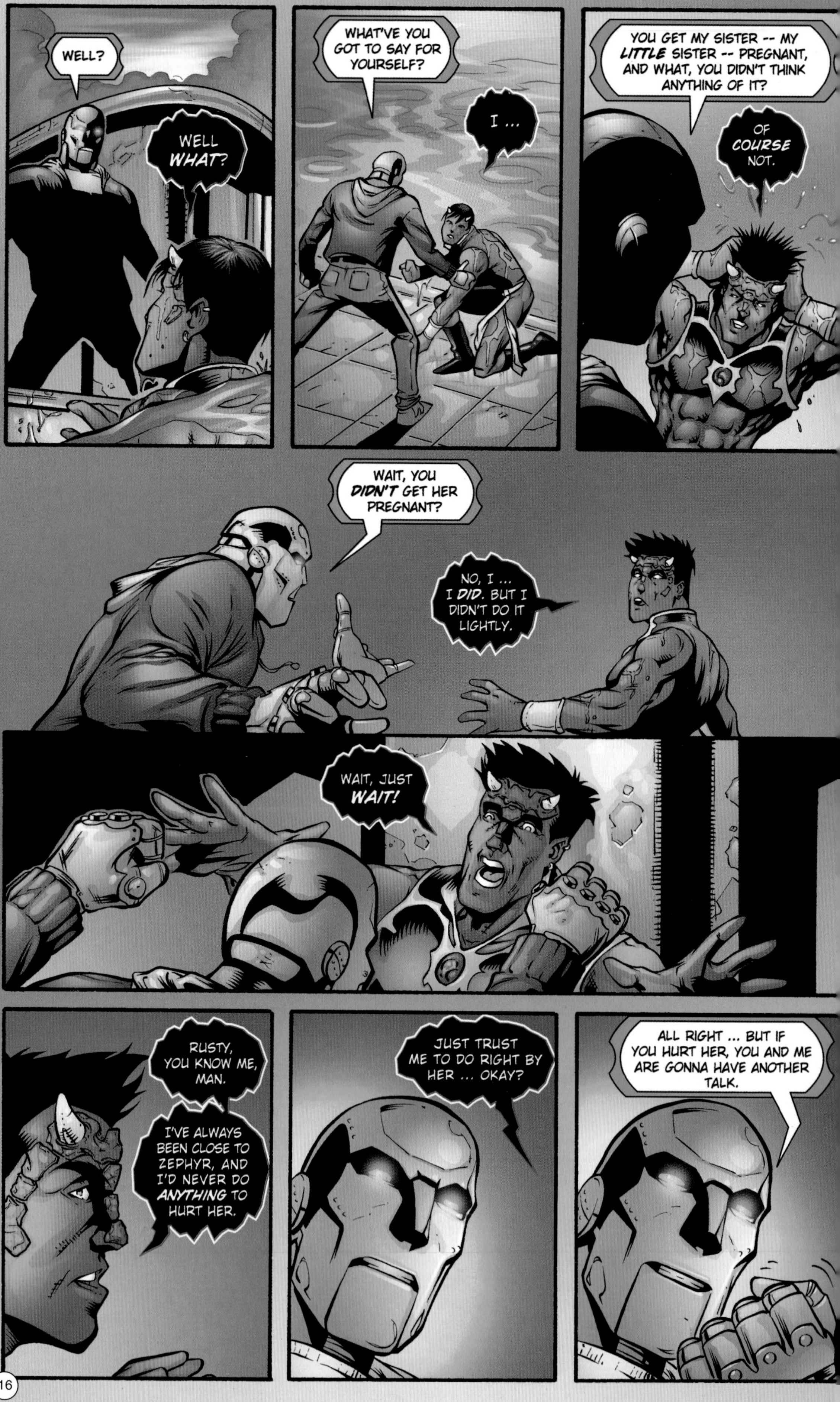
WELL?
WELL WHAT?
WHAT'VE YOU GOT TO SAY FOR YOURSELF?
I ...
YOU GET MY SISTER -- MY LITTLE SISTER -- PREGNANT, AND WHAT, YOU DIDN'T THINK ANYTHING OF IT?
OF COURSE NOT.
WAIT, YOU DIDN'T GET HER PREGNANT?
NO, I ... I DID. BUT I DIDN'T DO IT LIGHTLY.
WAIT, JUST WAIT!
RUSTY, YOU KNOW ME, MAN.
I'VE ALWAYS BEEN CLOSE TO ZEPHYR, AND I'D NEVER DO ANYTHING TO HURT HER.
JUST TRUST ME TO DO RIGHT BY HER ... OKAY?
ALL RIGHT ... BUT IF YOU HURT HER, YOU AND ME ARE GONNA HAVE ANOTHER TALK.

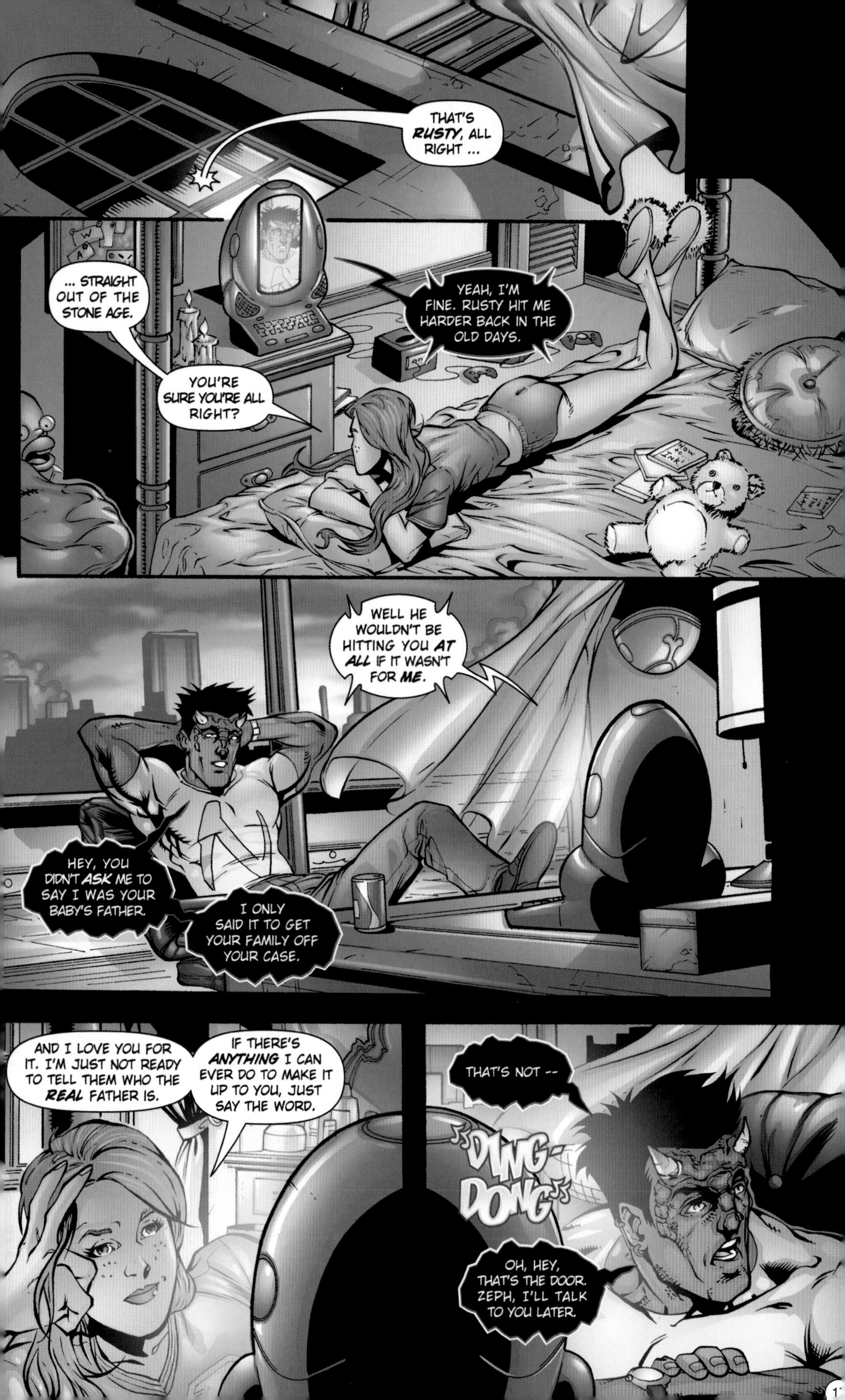
THAT'S RUSTY, ALL RIGHT ...
... STRAIGHT OUT OF THE STONE AGE.
YOU'RE SURE YOU'RE ALL RIGHT?
YEAH, I'M FINE. RUSTY HIT ME HARDER BACK IN THE OLD DAYS.
WELL HE WOULDN'T BE HITTING YOU AT ALL IF IT WASN'T FOR ME.
HEY, YOU DIDN'T ASK ME TO SAY I WAS YOUR BABY'S FATHER.
I ONLY SAID IT TO GET YOUR FAMILY OFF YOUR CASE.
AND I LOVE YOU FOR IT. I'M JUST NOT READY TO TELL THEM WHO THE REAL FATHER IS.
IF THERE'S ANYTHING I CAN EVER DO TO MAKE IT UP TO YOU, JUST SAY THE WORD.
THAT'S NOT --
DING-DONG
OH, HEY, THAT'S THE DOOR. ZEPH, I'LL TALK TO YOU LATER.

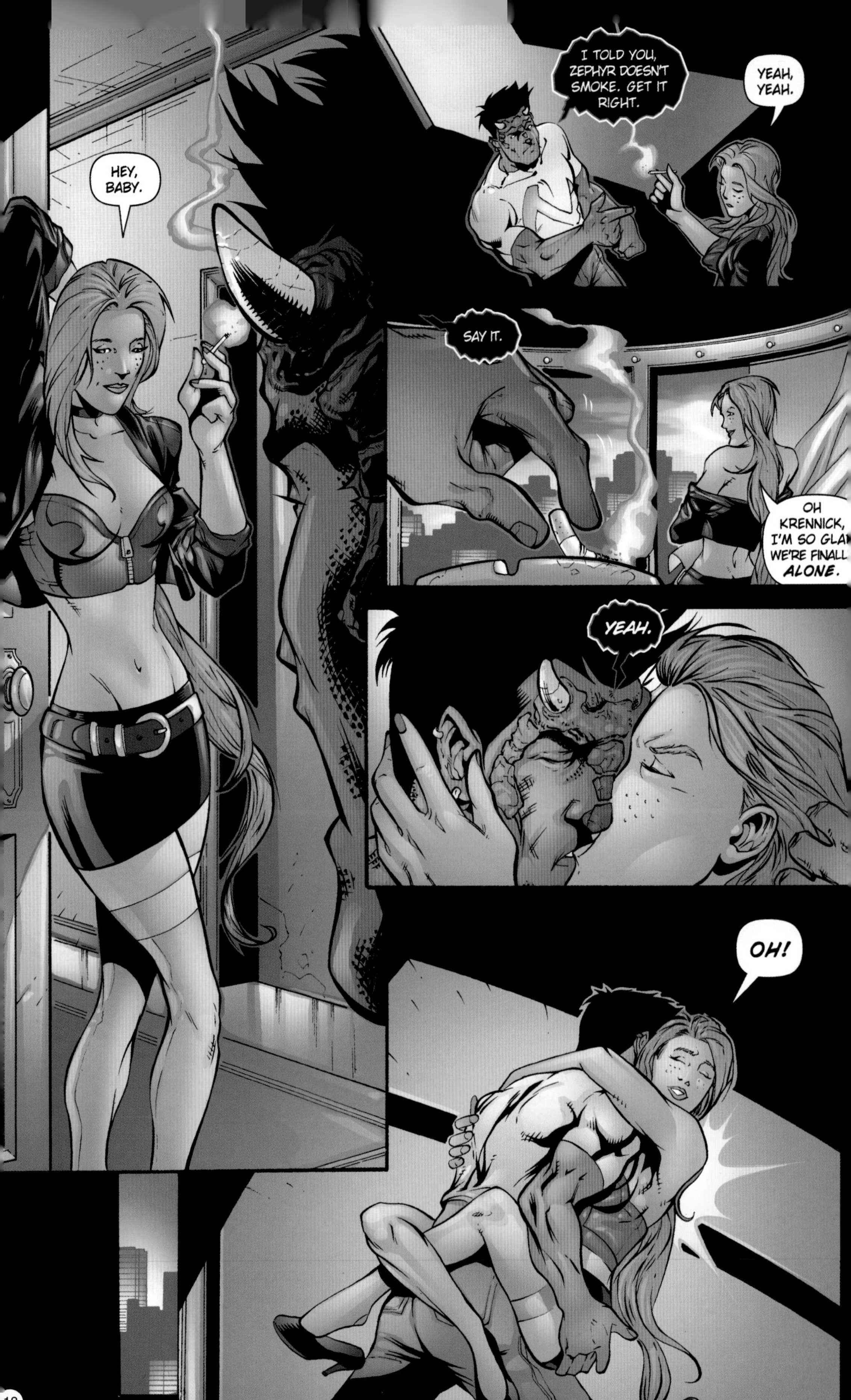
HEY, BABY.
I TOLD YOU, ZEPHYR DOESN'T SMOKE. GET IT RIGHT.
YEAH, YEAH.
SAY IT.
OH KRENNICK, I'M SO GLA WE'RE FINALL ALONE.
YEAH.
OH!

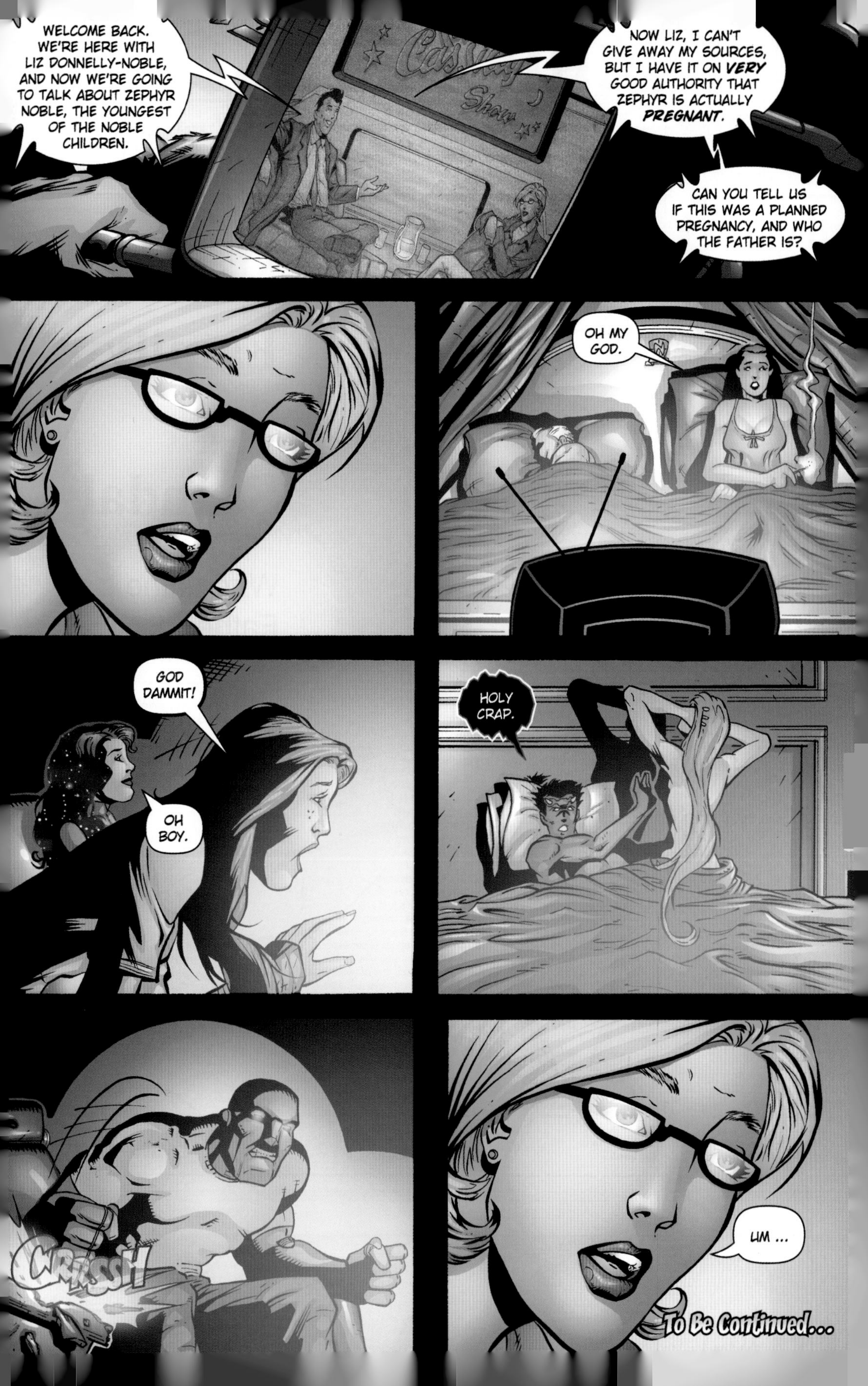
WELCOME BACK. WE'RE HERE WITH LIZ DONNELLY-NOBLE, AND NOW WE'RE GOING TO TALK ABOUT ZEPHYR NOBLE, THE YOUNGEST OF THE NOBLE CHILDREN.
NOW LIZ, I CAN'T GIVE AWAY MY SOURCES, BUT I HAVE IT ON VERY GOOD AUTHORITY THAT ZEPHYR IS ACTUALLY PREGNANT.
CAN YOU TELL US IF THIS WAS A PLANNED PREGNANCY, AND WHO THE FATHER IS?
OH MY GOD.
GOD DAMMIT!
OH BOY.
HOLY CRAP.
CRASSH
UM ...
To Be Continued...

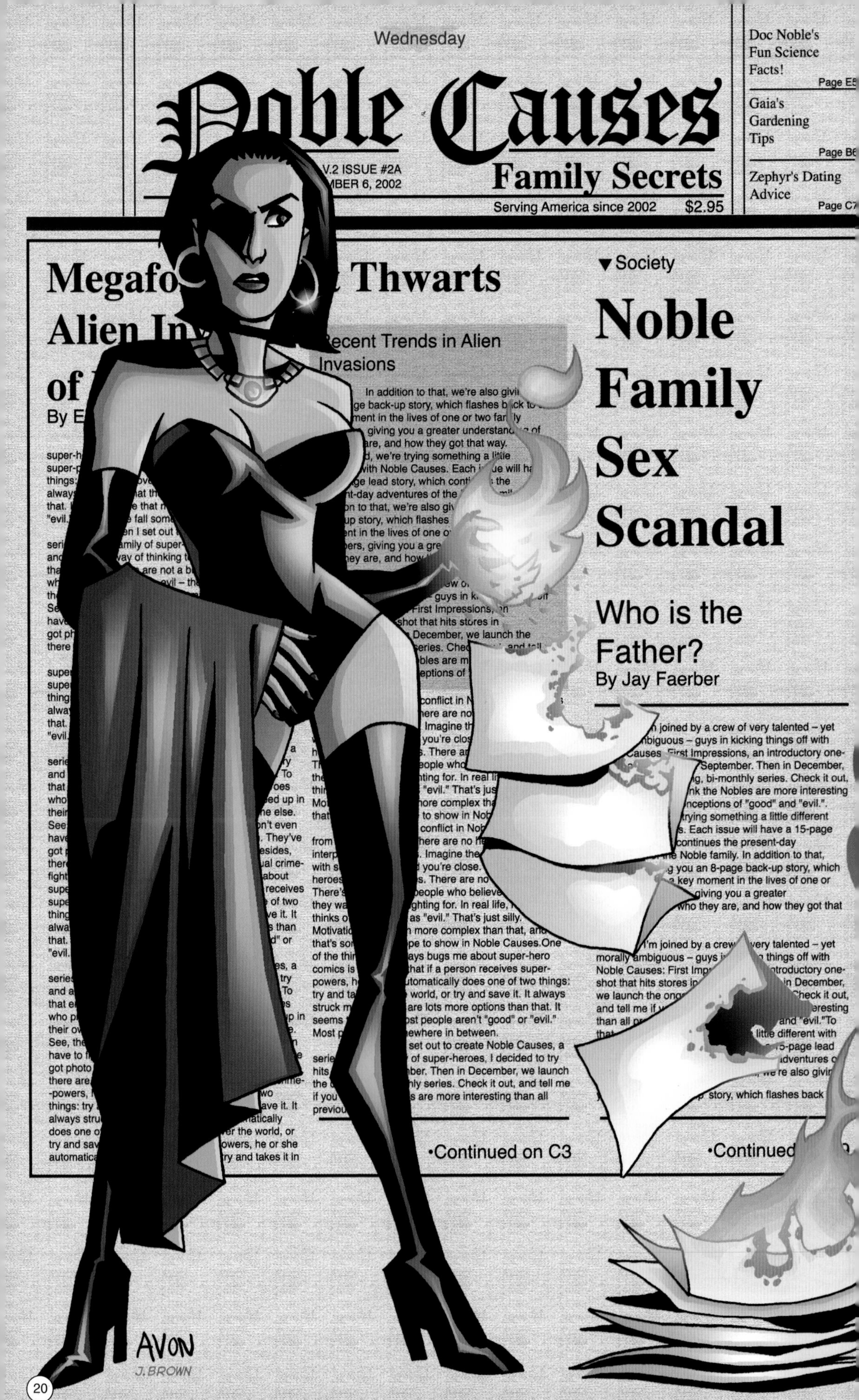
Wednesday
Noble Causes
V.2 ISSUE #2A
MBER 6, 2002
Family Secrets
Serving America since 2002
$2.95
Doc Noble's Fun Science Facts!
Page E5
Gaia's Gardening Tips
Page B6
Zephyr's Dating Advice
Page C7
Megafo Thwarts Alien In of
By E
Recent Trends in Alien Invasions
▼Society
Noble Family Sex Scandal
Who is the Father?
By Jay Faerber
•Continued on C3
•Continued
AVON
J.BROWN

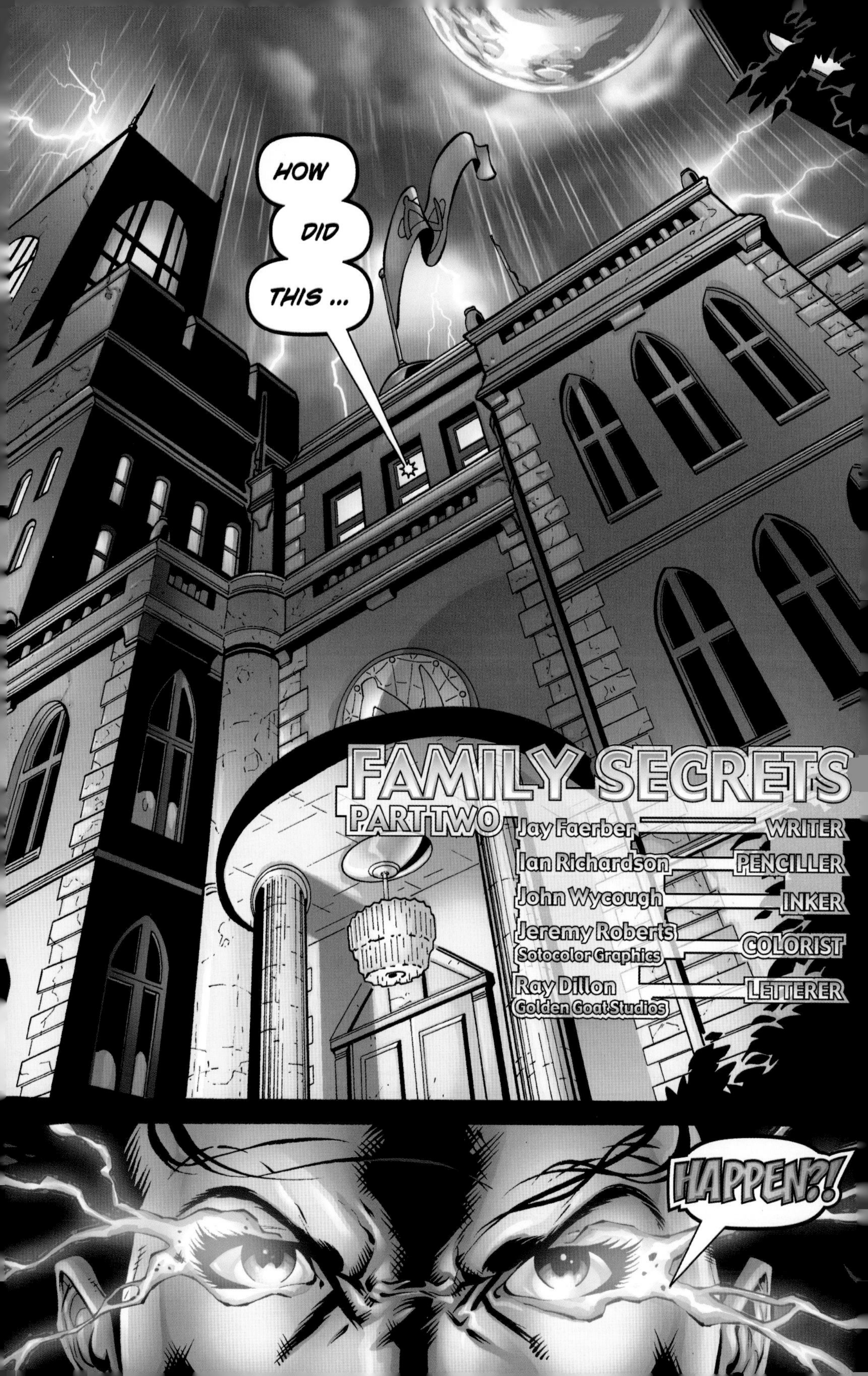
HOW DID THIS ...
FAMILY SECRETS
PART TWO
Jay Faerber WRITER
Ian Richardson PENCILLER
John Wycough INKER
Jeremy Roberts
Sotocolor Graphics COLORIST
Ray Dillon
Golden Goat Studios LETTERER
HAPPEN?!

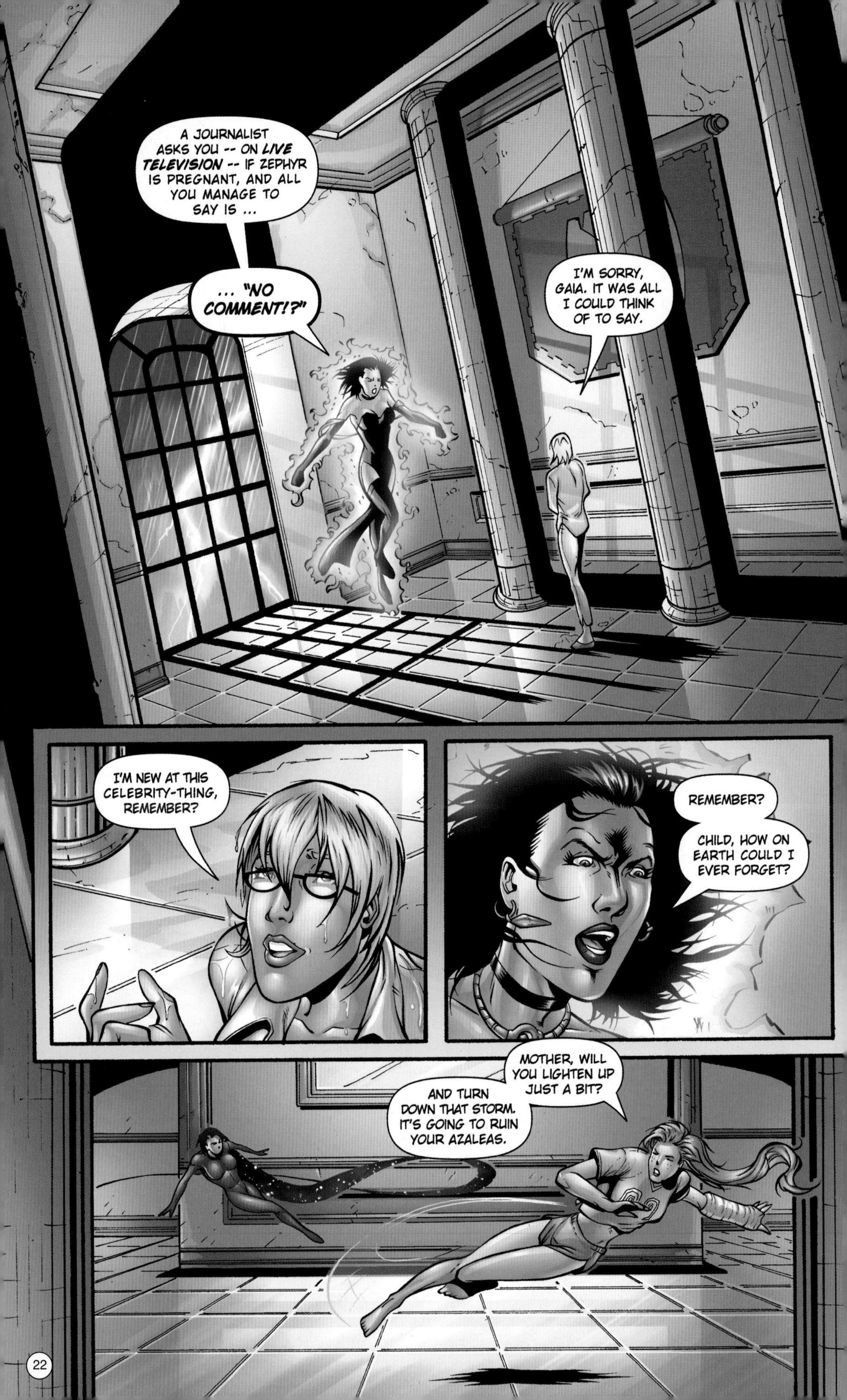

A JOURNALIST ASKS YOU -- ON LIVE TELEVISION -- IF ZEPHYR IS PREGNANT, AND ALL YOU MANAGE TO SAY IS ...
... "NO COMMENT!?"
I'M SORRY, GAIA. IT WAS ALL I COULD THINK OF TO SAY.
I'M NEW AT THIS CELEBRITY-THING, REMEMBER?
REMEMBER?
CHILD, HOW ON EARTH COULD I EVER FORGET?
MOTHER, WILL YOU LIGHTEN UP JUST A BIT?
AND TURN DOWN THAT STORM. IT'S GOING TO RUIN YOUR AZALEAS.

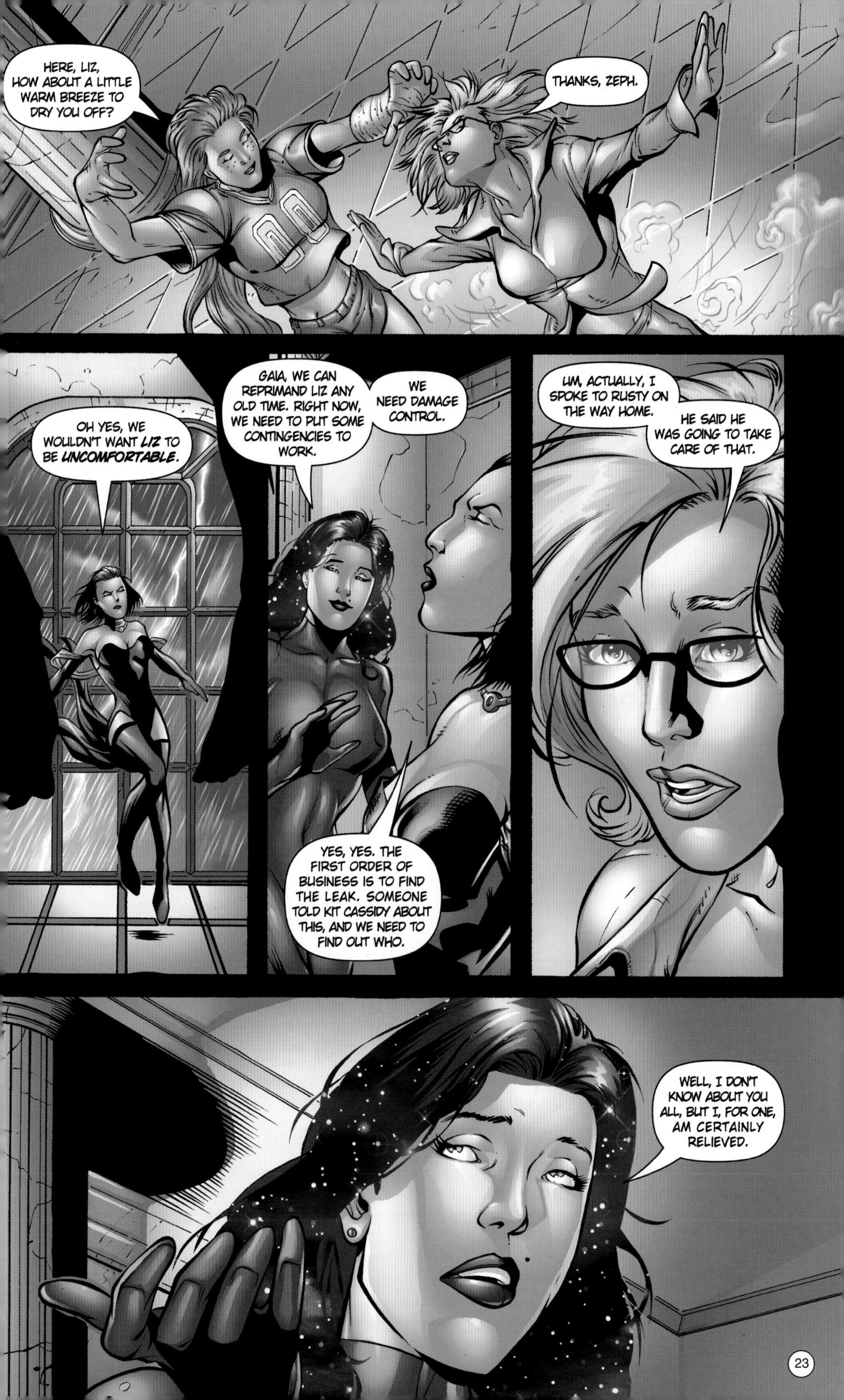
HERE, LIZ, HOW ABOUT A LITTLE WARM BREEZE TO DRY YOU OFF?
THANKS, ZEPH.
OH YES, WE WOULDN'T WANT *LIZ* TO BE *UNCOMFORTABLE*.
GAIA, WE CAN REPRIMAND LIZ ANY OLD TIME. RIGHT NOW, WE NEED TO PUT SOME CONTINGENCIES TO WORK.
WE NEED DAMAGE CONTROL.
YES, YES. THE FIRST ORDER OF BUSINESS IS TO FIND THE LEAK. SOMEONE TOLD KIT CASSIDY ABOUT THIS, AND WE NEED TO FIND OUT WHO.
UM, ACTUALLY, I SPOKE TO RUSTY ON THE WAY HOME.
HE SAID HE WAS GOING TO TAKE CARE OF THAT.
WELL, I DON'T KNOW ABOUT YOU ALL, BUT I, FOR ONE, AM CERTAINLY RELIEVED.

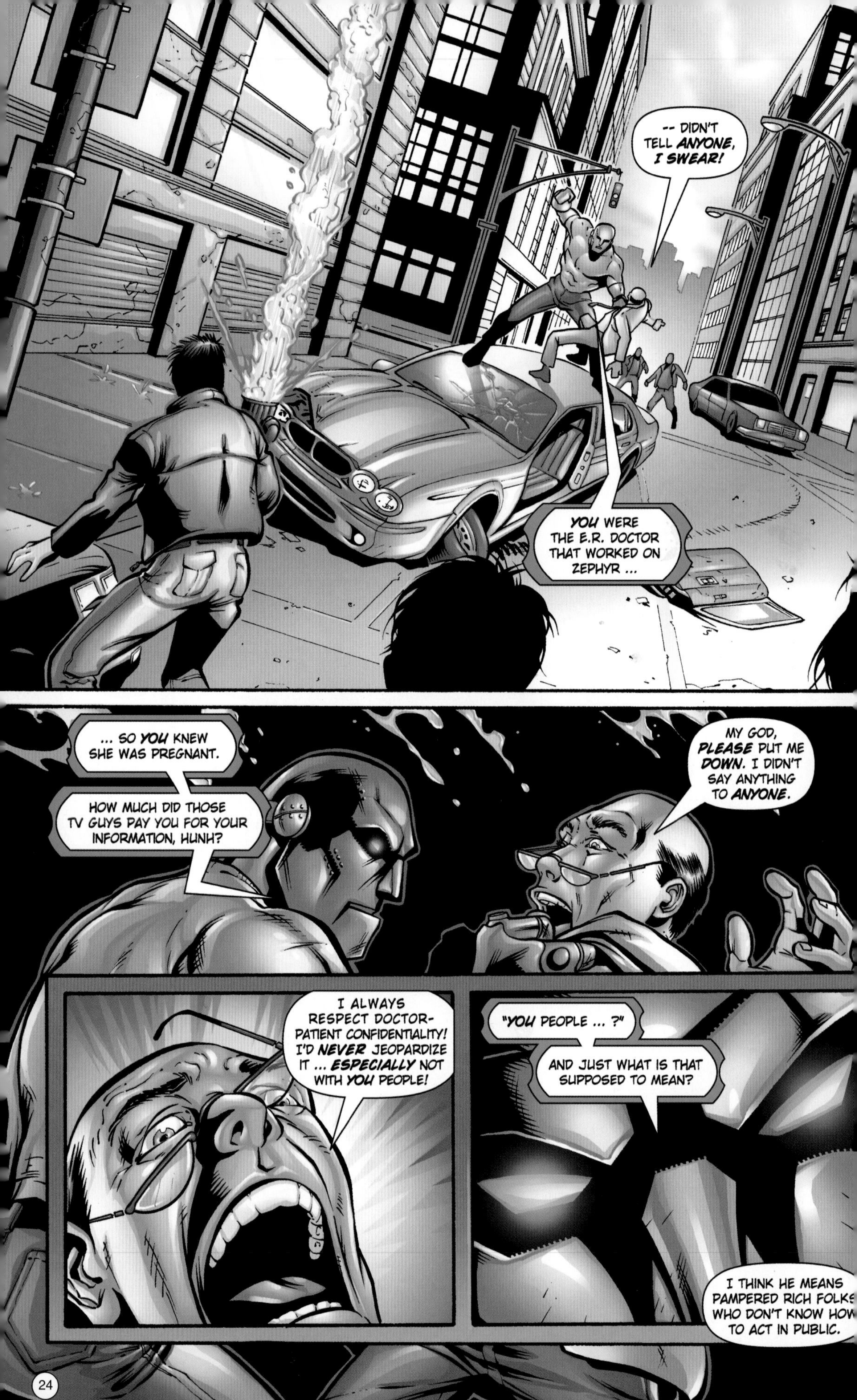
-- DIDN'T TELL ANYONE, I SWEAR!
YOU WERE THE E.R. DOCTOR THAT WORKED ON ZEPHYR ...
... SO YOU KNEW SHE WAS PREGNANT.
HOW MUCH DID THOSE TV GUYS PAY YOU FOR YOUR INFORMATION, HUNH?
MY GOD, PLEASE PUT ME DOWN. I DIDN'T SAY ANYTHING TO ANYONE.
I ALWAYS RESPECT DOCTOR-PATIENT CONFIDENTIALITY! I'D NEVER JEOPARDIZE IT ... ESPECIALLY NOT WITH YOU PEOPLE!
"YOU PEOPLE ... ?"
AND JUST WHAT IS THAT SUPPOSED TO MEAN?
I THINK HE MEANS PAMPERED RICH FOLKS WHO DON'T KNOW HOW TO ACT IN PUBLIC.

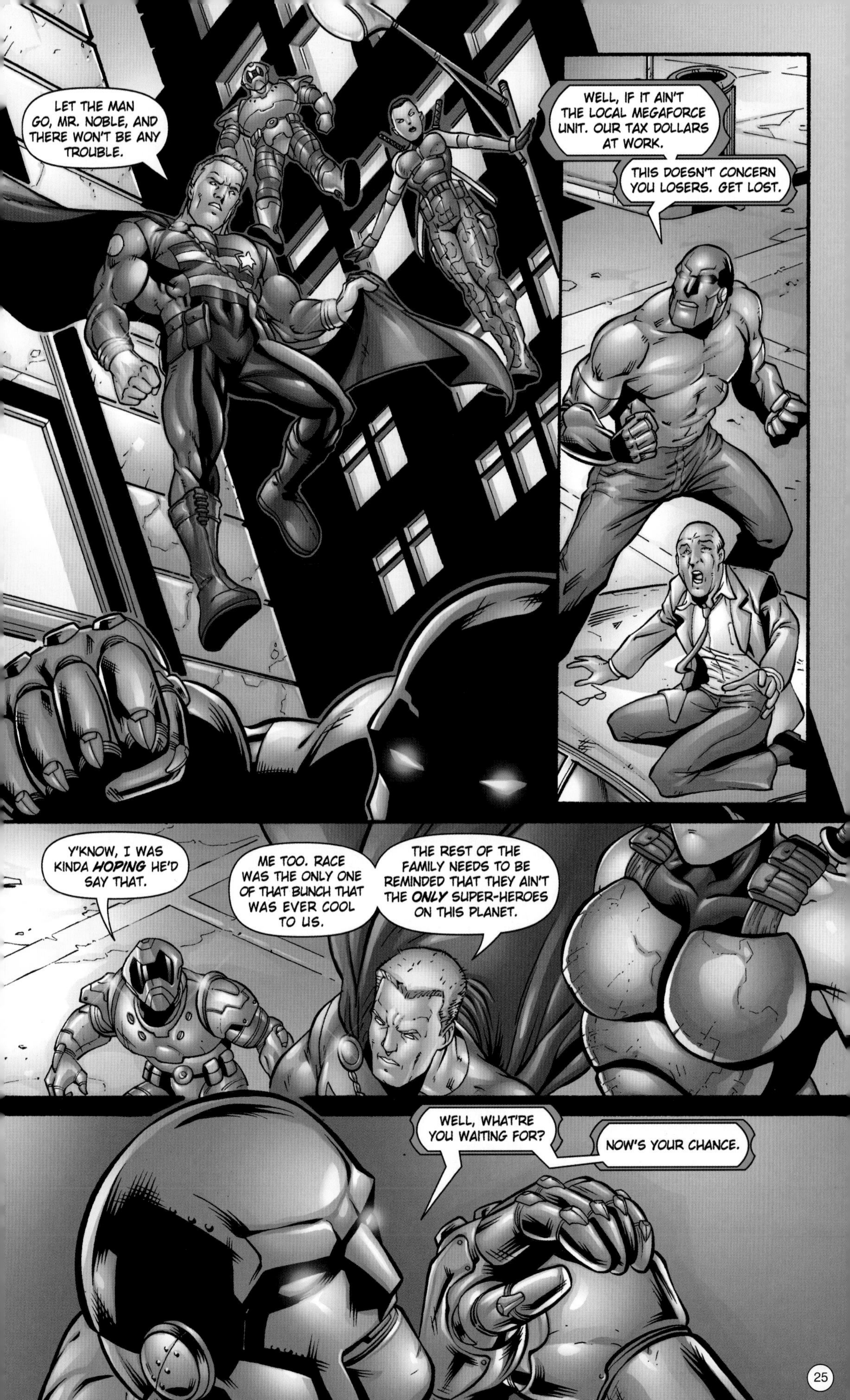
LET THE MAN GO, MR. NOBLE, AND THERE WON'T BE ANY TROUBLE.
WELL, IF IT AIN'T THE LOCAL MEGAFORCE UNIT. OUR TAX DOLLARS AT WORK.
THIS DOESN'T CONCERN YOU LOSERS. GET LOST.
Y'KNOW, I WAS KINDA *HOPING* HE'D SAY THAT.
ME TOO. RACE WAS THE ONLY ONE OF THAT BUNCH THAT WAS EVER COOL TO US.
THE REST OF THE FAMILY NEEDS TO BE REMINDED THAT THEY AIN'T THE *ONLY* SUPER-HEROES ON THIS PLANET.
WELL, WHAT'RE YOU WAITING FOR?
NOW'S YOUR CHANCE.

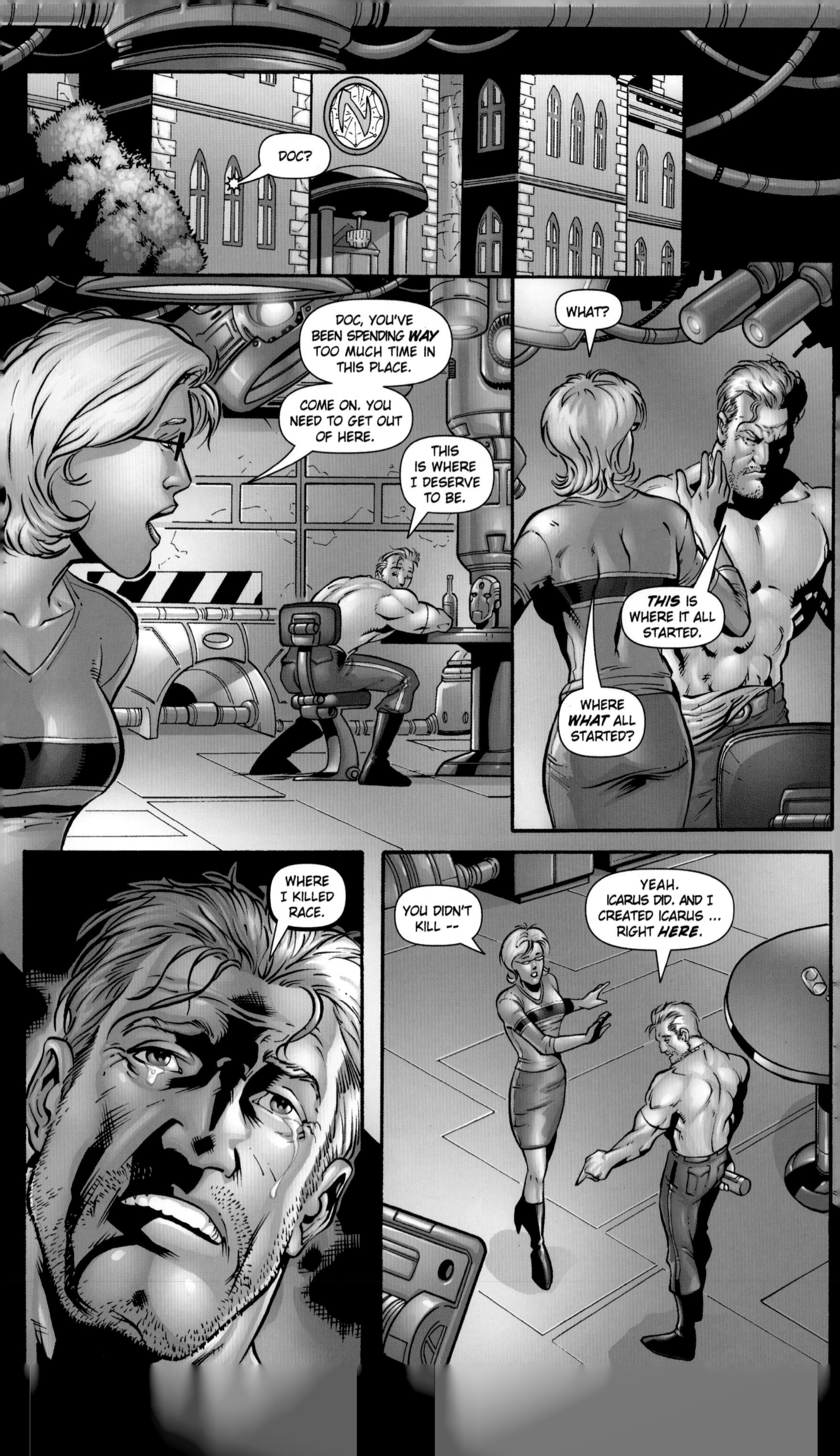
DOC?
DOC, YOU'VE BEEN SPENDING WAY TOO MUCH TIME IN THIS PLACE.
COME ON. YOU NEED TO GET OUT OF HERE.
THIS IS WHERE I DESERVE TO BE.
WHAT?
THIS IS WHERE IT ALL STARTED.
WHERE WHAT ALL STARTED?
WHERE I KILLED RACE.
YOU DIDN'T KILL --
YEAH. ICARUS DID. AND I CREATED ICARUS ... RIGHT HERE.

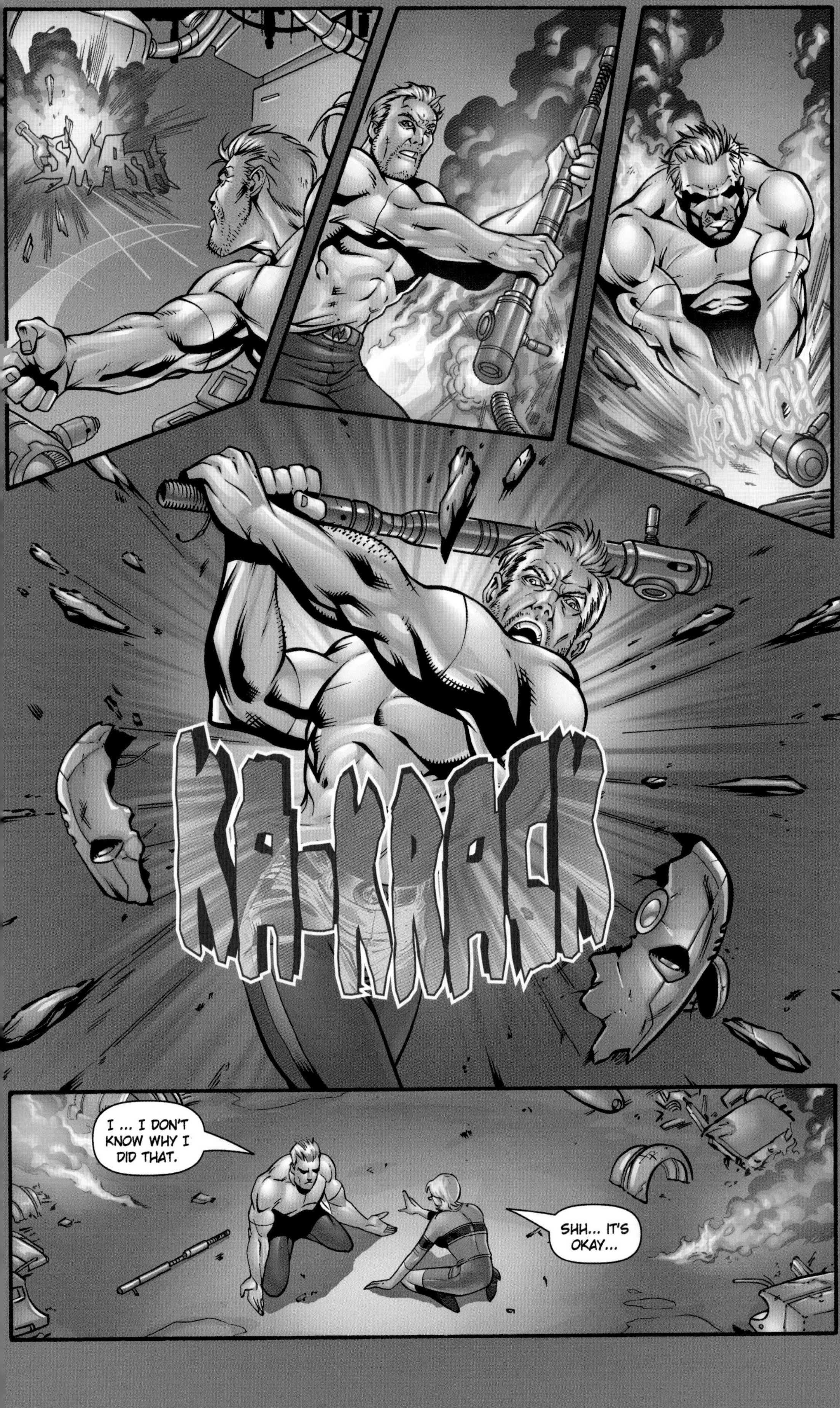
SMASH
KRUNCH
KA-KRACK
I ... I DON'T KNOW WHY I DID THAT.
SHH... IT'S OKAY...

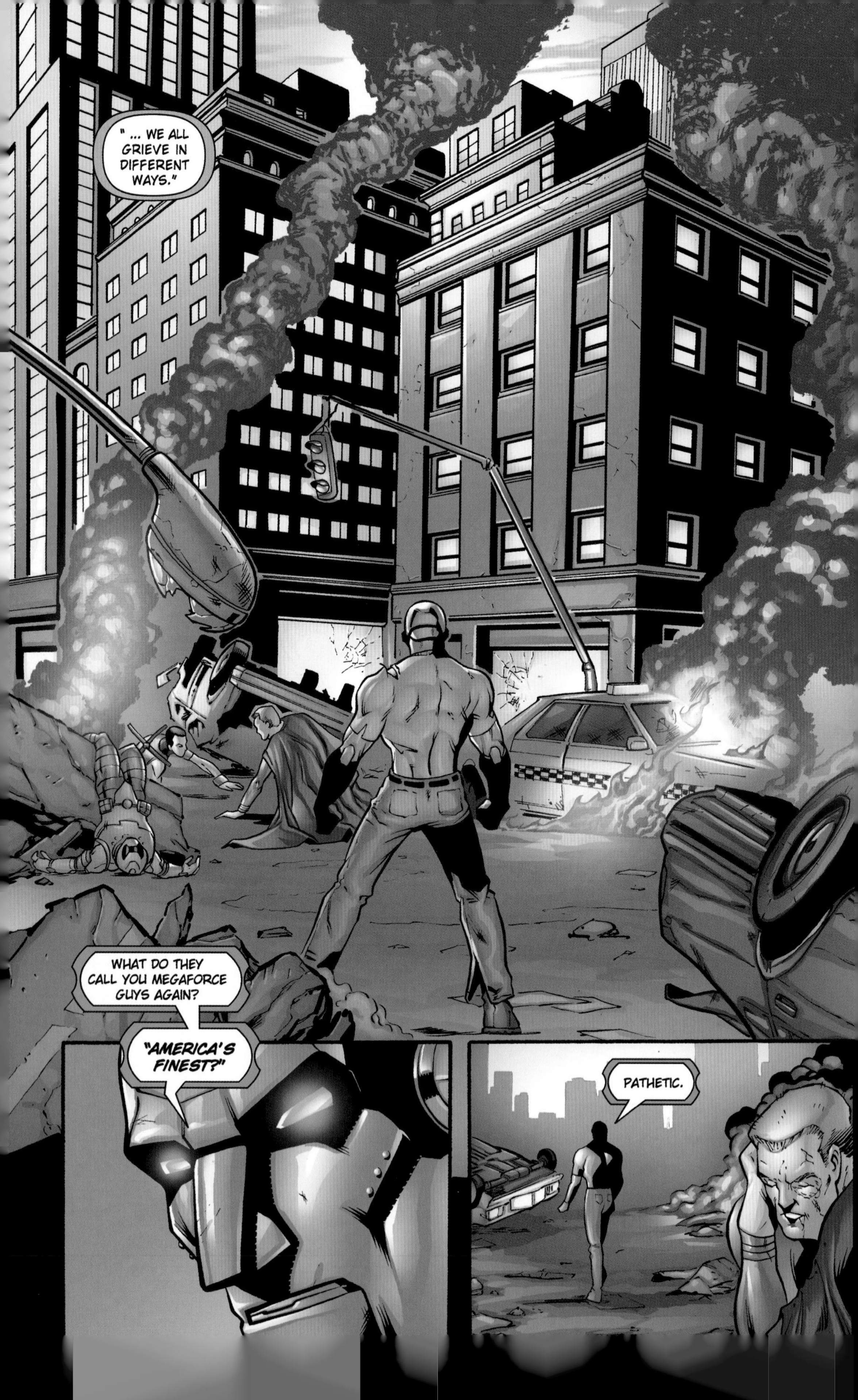
"... WE ALL GRIEVE IN DIFFERENT WAYS."
WHAT DO THEY CALL YOU MEGAFORCE GUYS AGAIN?
"AMERICA'S FINEST?"
PATHETIC.

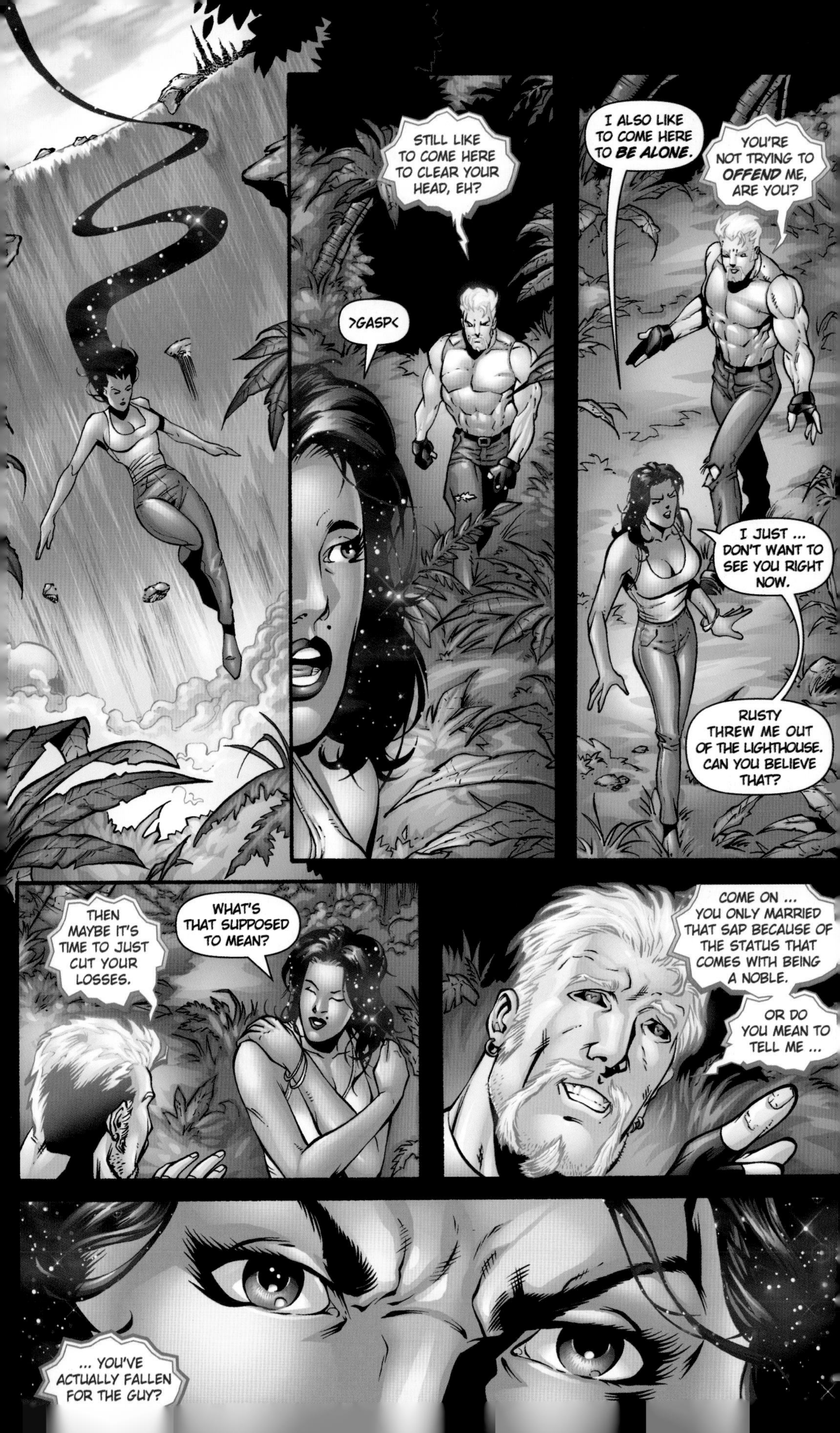
STILL LIKE TO COME HERE TO CLEAR YOUR HEAD, EH?
>GASP<
I ALSO LIKE TO COME HERE TO BE ALONE.
YOU'RE NOT TRYING TO OFFEND ME, ARE YOU?
I JUST ... DON'T WANT TO SEE YOU RIGHT NOW.
RUSTY THREW ME OUT OF THE LIGHTHOUSE. CAN YOU BELIEVE THAT?
THEN MAYBE IT'S TIME TO JUST CUT YOUR LOSSES.
WHAT'S THAT SUPPOSED TO MEAN?
COME ON ... YOU ONLY MARRIED THAT SAP BECAUSE OF THE STATUS THAT COMES WITH BEING A NOBLE.
OR DO YOU MEAN TO TELL ME ...
... YOU'VE ACTUALLY FALLEN FOR THE GUY?

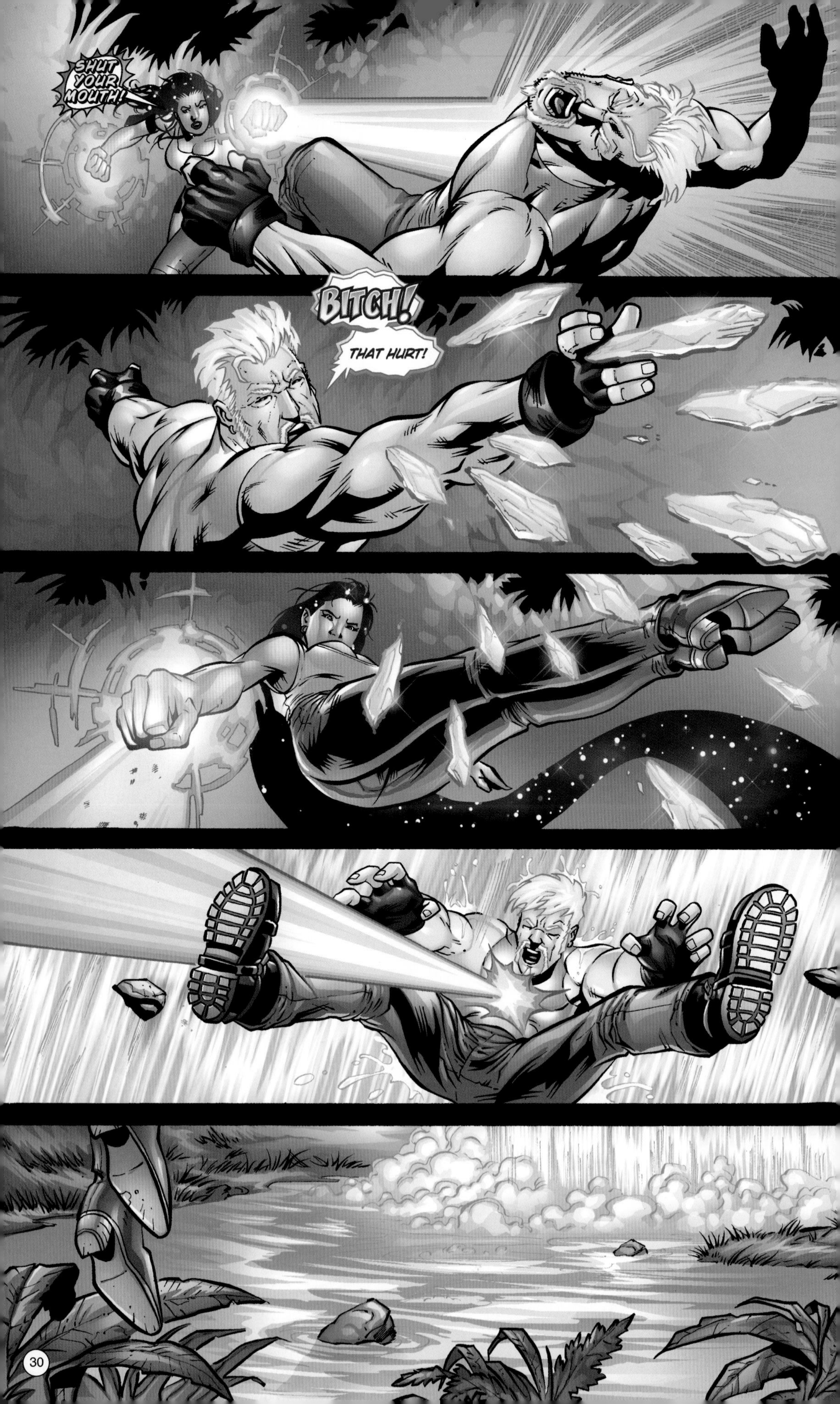
SHUT YOUR MOUTH!
BITCH!
THAT HURT!

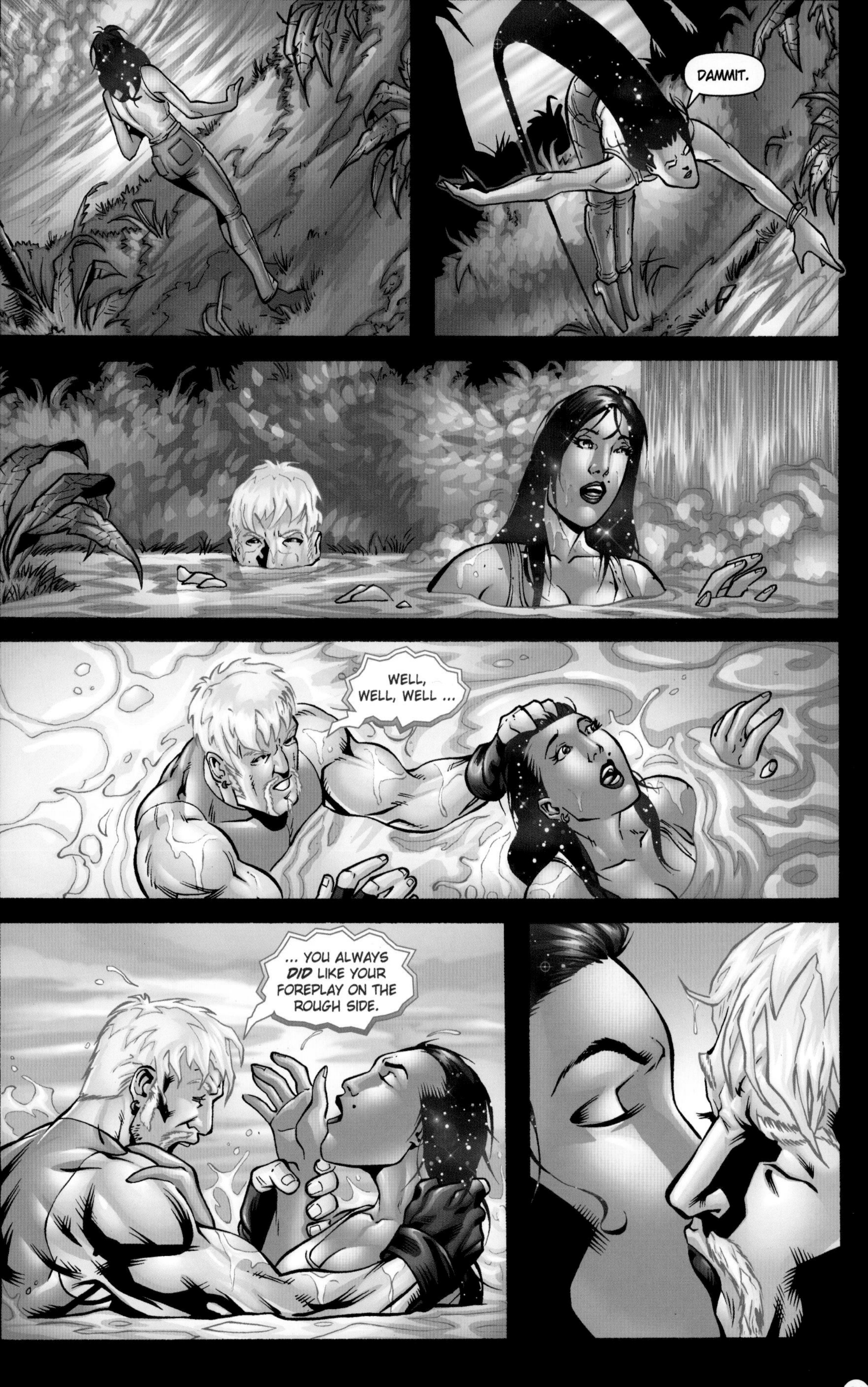
DAMMIT.
WELL, WELL, WELL ...
... YOU ALWAYS DID LIKE YOUR FOREPLAY ON THE ROUGH SIDE.

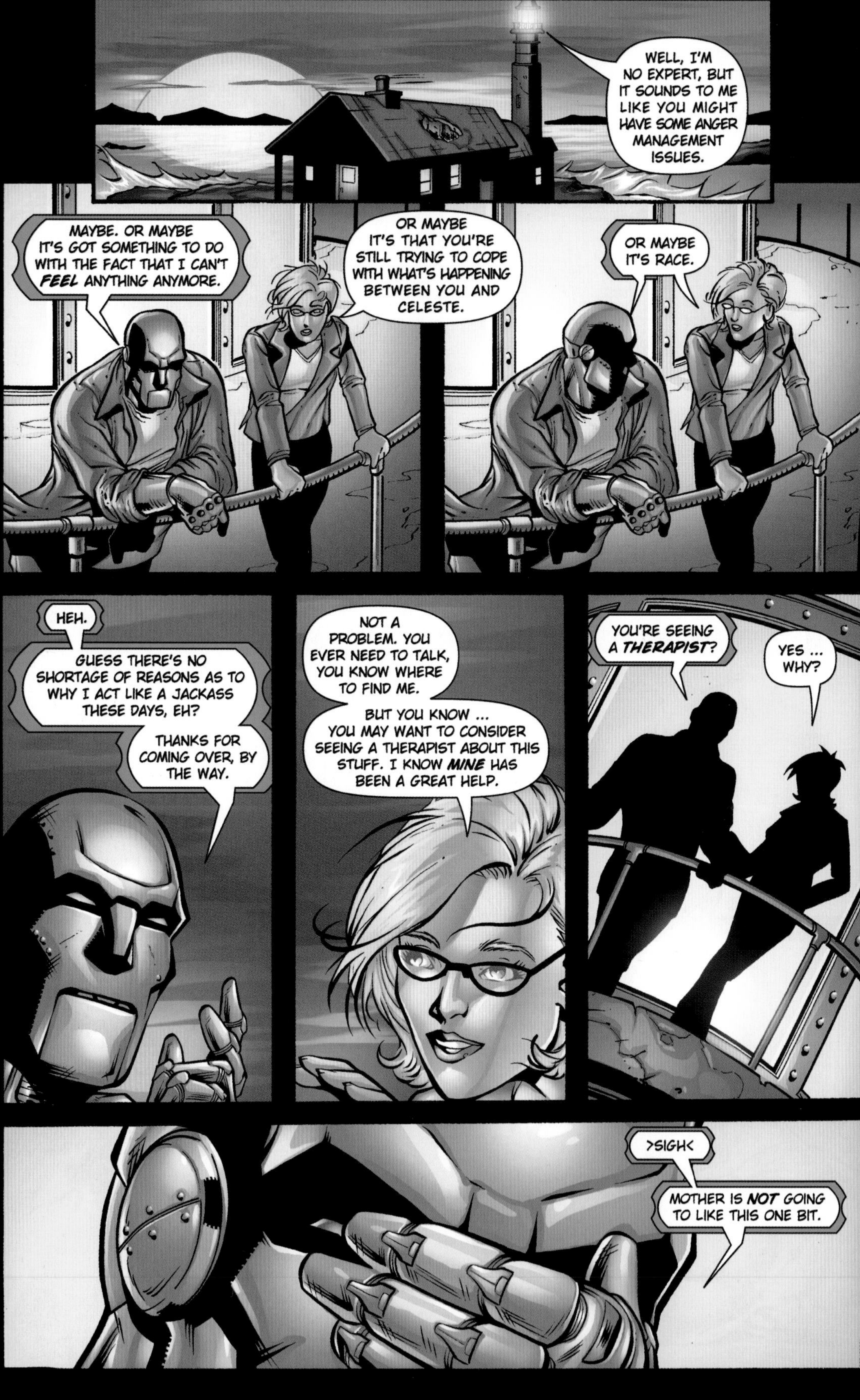
WELL, I'M NO EXPERT, BUT IT SOUNDS TO ME LIKE YOU MIGHT HAVE SOME ANGER MANAGEMENT ISSUES.
MAYBE. OR MAYBE IT'S GOT SOMETHING TO DO WITH THE FACT THAT I CAN'T FEEL ANYTHING ANYMORE.
OR MAYBE IT'S THAT YOU'RE STILL TRYING TO COPE WITH WHAT'S HAPPENING BETWEEN YOU AND CELESTE.
OR MAYBE IT'S RACE.
HEH.
GUESS THERE'S NO SHORTAGE OF REASONS AS TO WHY I ACT LIKE A JACKASS THESE DAYS, EH?
THANKS FOR COMING OVER, BY THE WAY.
NOT A PROBLEM. YOU EVER NEED TO TALK, YOU KNOW WHERE TO FIND ME.
BUT YOU KNOW ... YOU MAY WANT TO CONSIDER SEEING A THERAPIST ABOUT THIS STUFF. I KNOW MINE HAS BEEN A GREAT HELP.
YOU'RE SEEING A THERAPIST?
YES ... WHY?
>SIGH<
MOTHER IS NOT GOING TO LIKE THIS ONE BIT.

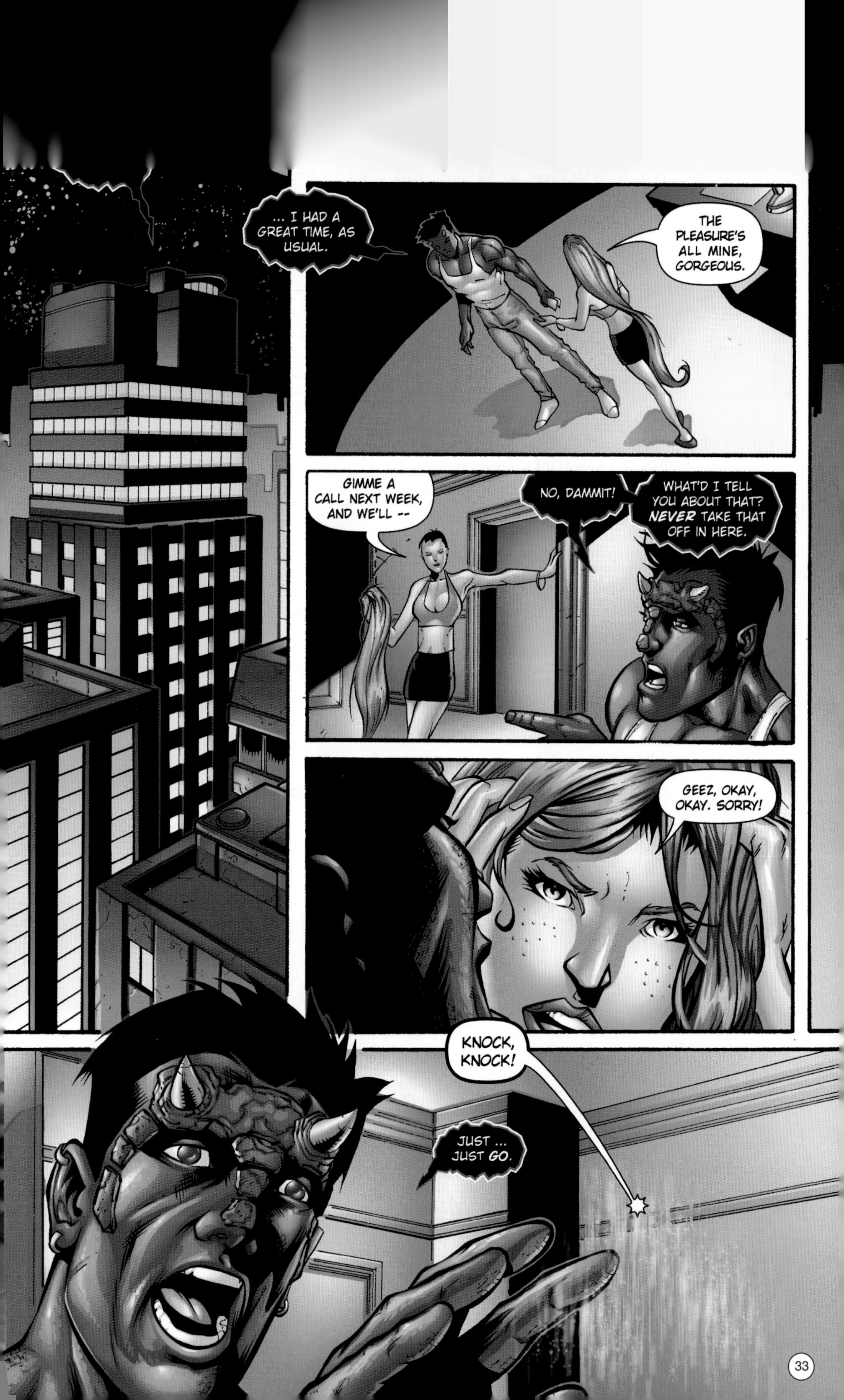
... I HAD A GREAT TIME, AS USUAL.
THE PLEASURE'S ALL MINE, GORGEOUS.
GIMME A CALL NEXT WEEK, AND WE'LL --
NO, DAMMIT!
WHAT'D I TELL YOU ABOUT THAT? NEVER TAKE THAT OFF IN HERE.
GEEZ, OKAY, OKAY. SORRY!
KNOCK, KNOCK!
JUST ... JUST GO.

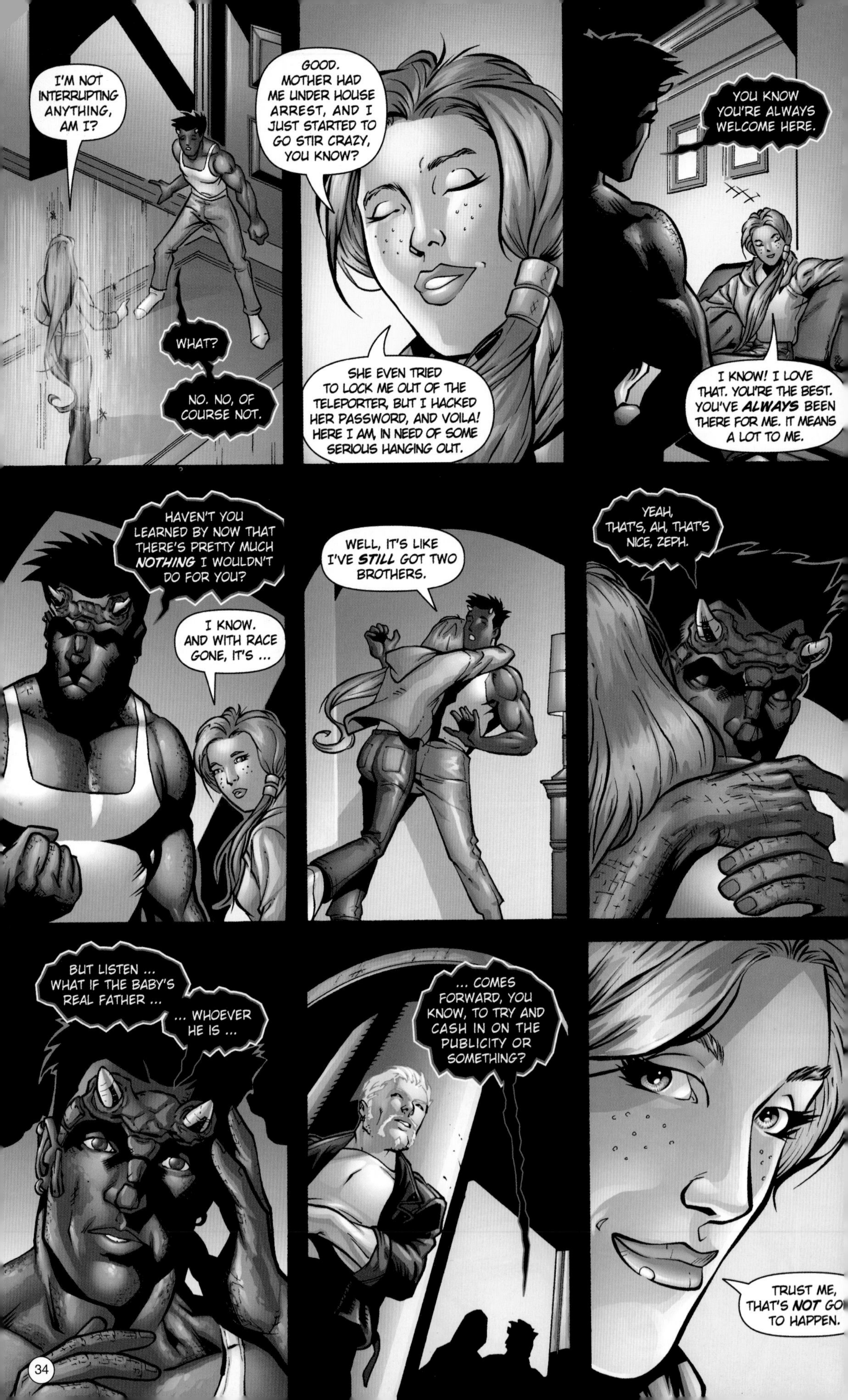

I'M NOT INTERRUPTING ANYTHING, AM I?
WHAT?
NO. NO, OF COURSE NOT.
GOOD. MOTHER HAD ME UNDER HOUSE ARREST, AND I JUST STARTED TO GO STIR CRAZY, YOU KNOW?
SHE EVEN TRIED TO LOCK ME OUT OF THE TELEPORTER, BUT I HACKED HER PASSWORD, AND VOILA! HERE I AM, IN NEED OF SOME SERIOUS HANGING OUT.
YOU KNOW YOU'RE ALWAYS WELCOME HERE.
I KNOW! I LOVE THAT. YOU'RE THE BEST. YOU'VE *ALWAYS* BEEN THERE FOR ME. IT MEANS A LOT TO ME.
HAVEN'T YOU LEARNED BY NOW THAT THERE'S PRETTY MUCH *NOTHING* I WOULDN'T DO FOR YOU?
I KNOW. AND WITH RACE GONE, IT'S ...
WELL, IT'S LIKE I'VE *STILL* GOT TWO BROTHERS.
YEAH, THAT'S, AH, THAT'S NICE, ZEPH.
BUT LISTEN ... WHAT IF THE BABY'S REAL FATHER ...
... WHOEVER HE IS ...
... COMES FORWARD, YOU KNOW, TO TRY AND CASH IN ON THE PUBLICITY OR SOMETHING?
TRUST ME, THAT'S *NOT* GO
TO HAPPEN.

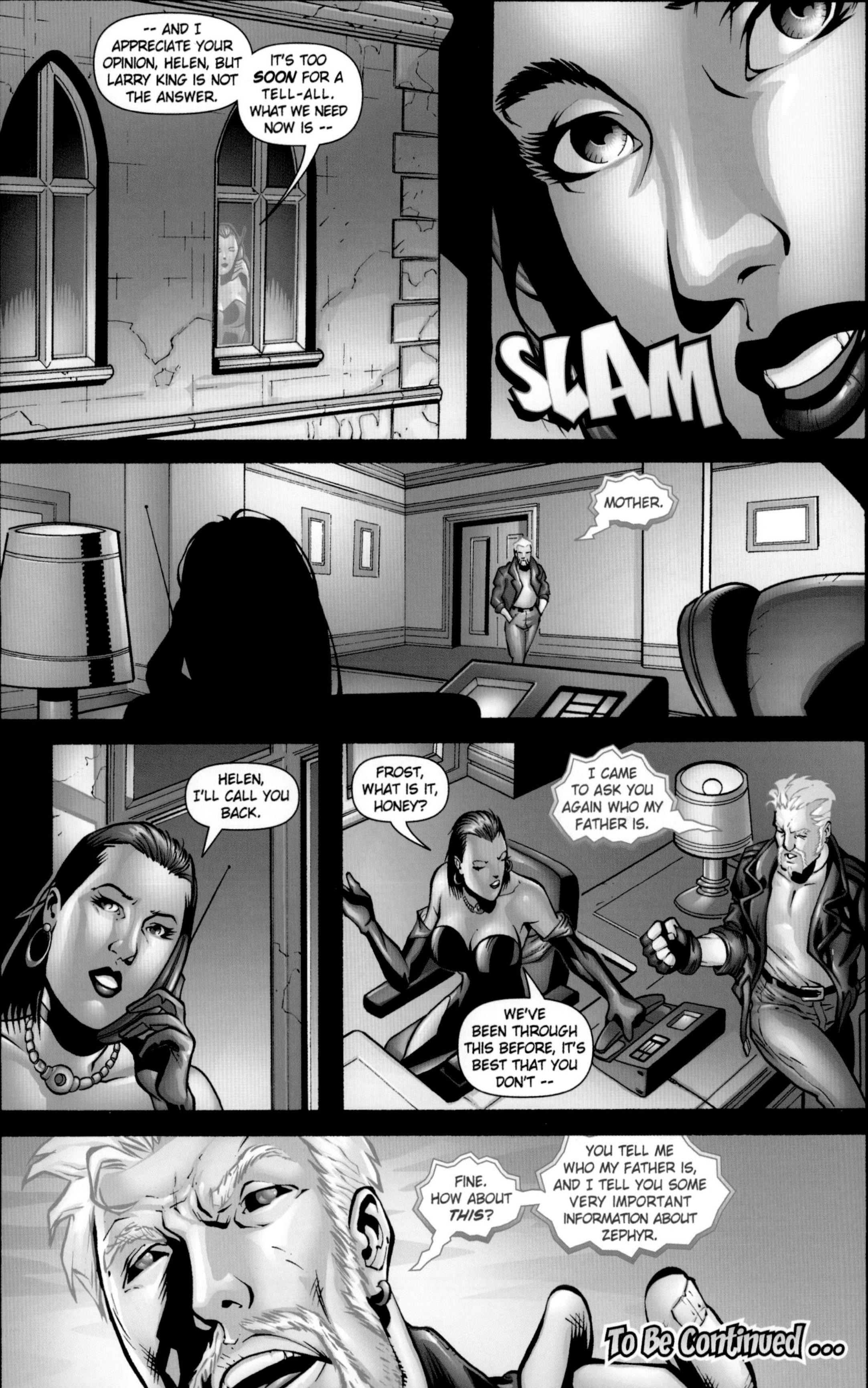
-- AND I APPRECIATE YOUR OPINION, HELEN, BUT LARRY KING IS NOT THE ANSWER.
IT'S TOO SOON FOR A TELL-ALL. WHAT WE NEED NOW IS --
SLAM
MOTHER.
HELEN, I'LL CALL YOU BACK.
FROST, WHAT IS IT, HONEY?
I CAME TO ASK YOU AGAIN WHO MY FATHER IS.
WE'VE BEEN THROUGH THIS BEFORE, IT'S BEST THAT YOU DON'T --
FINE. HOW ABOUT THIS?
YOU TELL ME WHO MY FATHER IS, AND I TELL YOU SOME VERY IMPORTANT INFORMATION ABOUT ZEPHYR.
To Be Continued ...

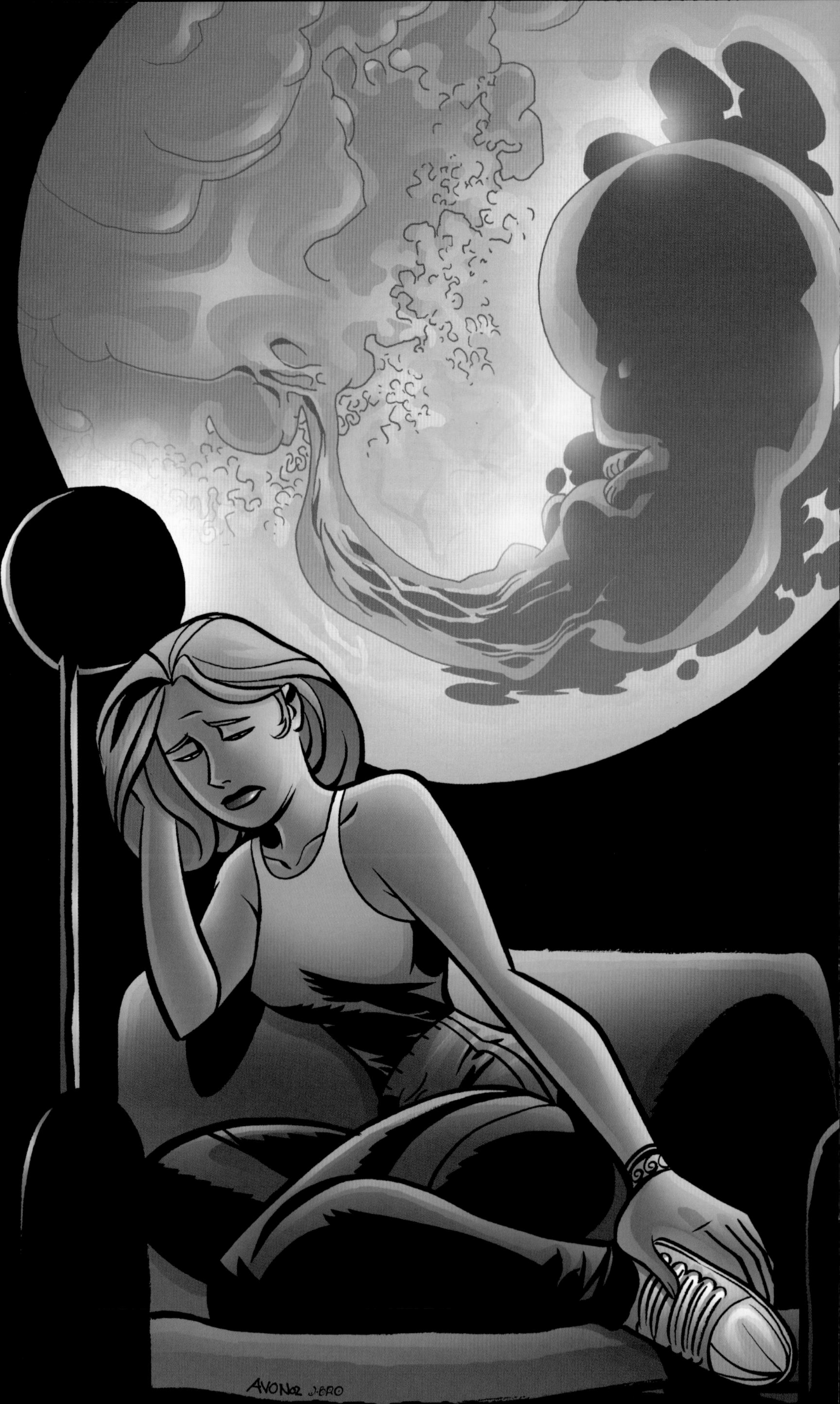
AVON OZ J-BRO

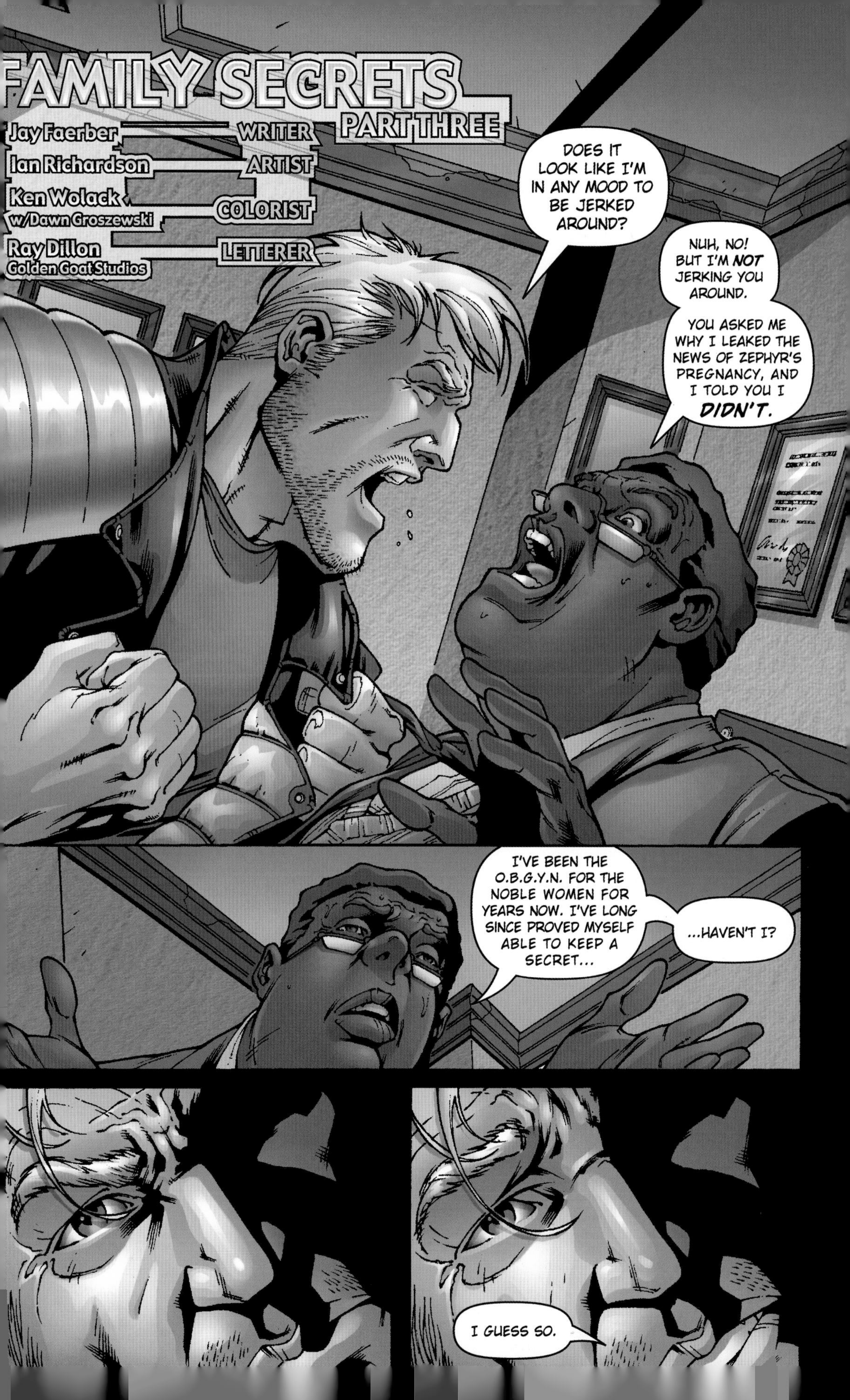
FAMILY SECRETS
PART THREE
Jay Faerber WRITER
Ian Richardson ARTIST
Ken Wolack w/Dawn Groszewski COLORIST
Ray Dillon Golden Goat Studios LETTERER
DOES IT LOOK LIKE I'M IN ANY MOOD TO BE JERKED AROUND?
NUH, NO! BUT I'M NOT JERKING YOU AROUND.
YOU ASKED ME WHY I LEAKED THE NEWS OF ZEPHYR'S PREGNANCY, AND I TOLD YOU I DIDN'T.
I'VE BEEN THE O.B.G.Y.N. FOR THE NOBLE WOMEN FOR YEARS NOW. I'VE LONG SINCE PROVED MYSELF ABLE TO KEEP A SECRET...
...HAVEN'T I?
I GUESS SO.

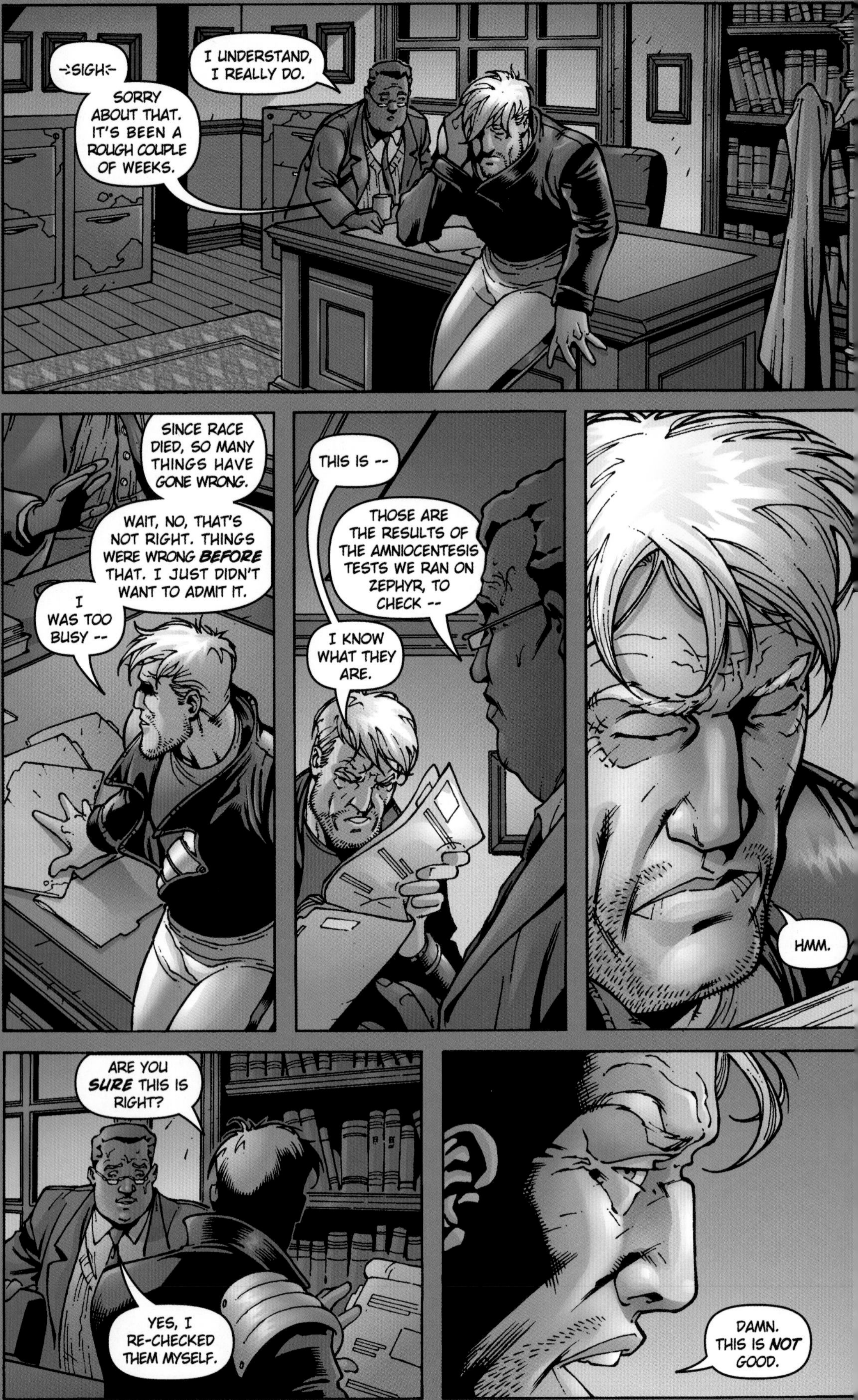

-SIGH-
SORRY ABOUT THAT. IT'S BEEN A ROUGH COUPLE OF WEEKS.
I UNDERSTAND, I REALLY DO.
SINCE RACE DIED, SO MANY THINGS HAVE GONE WRONG.
WAIT, NO, THAT'S NOT RIGHT. THINGS WERE WRONG **BEFORE** THAT. I JUST DIDN'T WANT TO ADMIT IT.
I WAS TOO BUSY --
THIS IS --
THOSE ARE THE RESULTS OF THE AMNIOCENTESIS TESTS WE RAN ON ZEPHYR, TO CHECK --
I KNOW WHAT THEY ARE.
HMM.
ARE YOU **SURE** THIS IS RIGHT?
YES, I RE-CHECKED THEM MYSELF.
DAMN. THIS IS **NOT** GOOD.

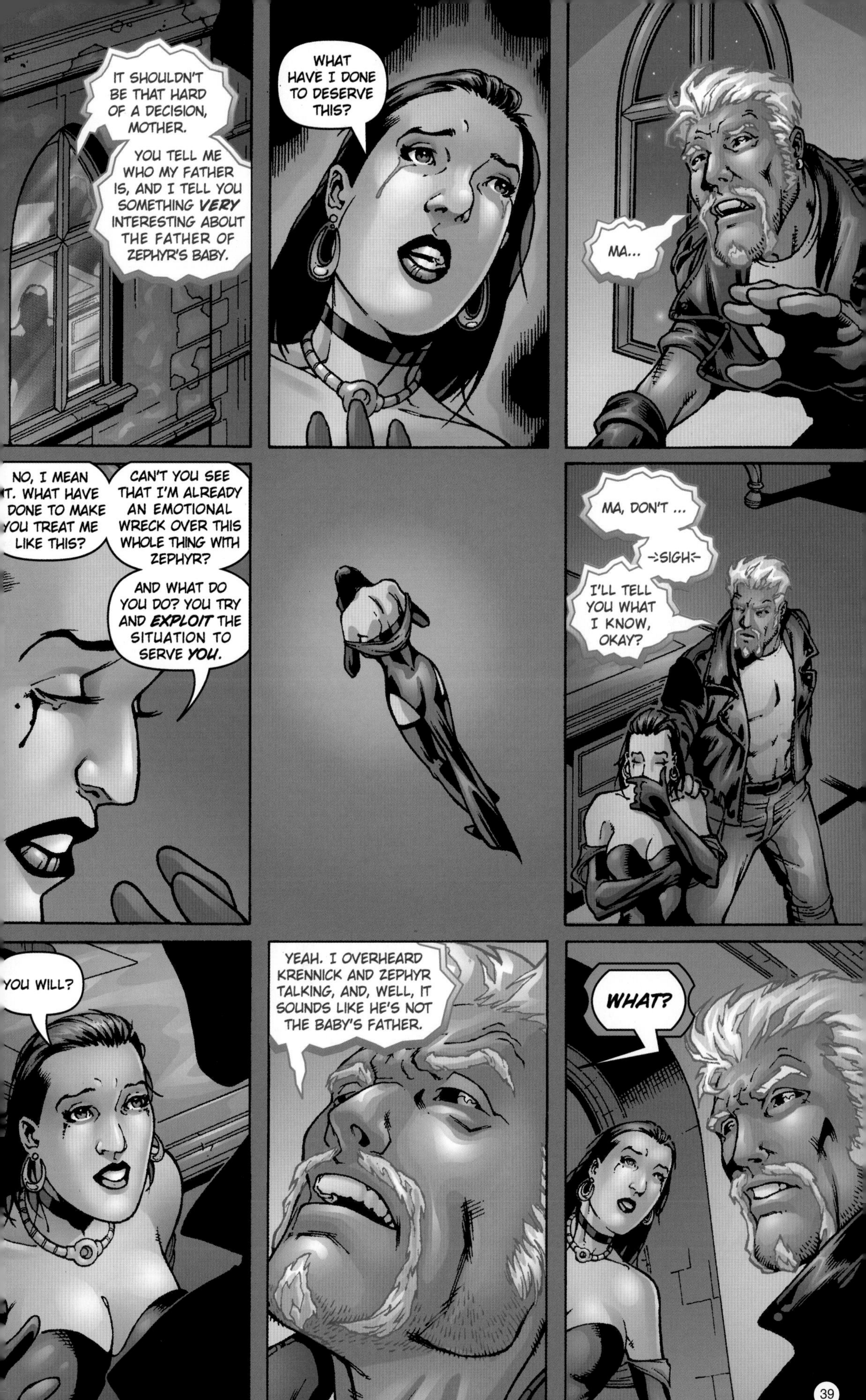

IT SHOULDN'T BE THAT HARD OF A DECISION, MOTHER.
YOU TELL ME WHO MY FATHER IS, AND I TELL YOU SOMETHING VERY INTERESTING ABOUT THE FATHER OF ZEPHYR'S BABY.
WHAT HAVE I DONE TO DESERVE THIS?
MA...
NO, I MEAN IT. WHAT HAVE I DONE TO MAKE YOU TREAT ME LIKE THIS?
CAN'T YOU SEE THAT I'M ALREADY AN EMOTIONAL WRECK OVER THIS WHOLE THING WITH ZEPHYR?
AND WHAT DO YOU DO? YOU TRY AND EXPLOIT THE SITUATION TO SERVE YOU.
MA, DON'T ...
SIGH
I'LL TELL YOU WHAT I KNOW, OKAY?
YOU WILL?
YEAH. I OVERHEARD KRENNICK AND ZEPHYR TALKING, AND, WELL, IT SOUNDS LIKE HE'S NOT THE BABY'S FATHER.
WHAT?

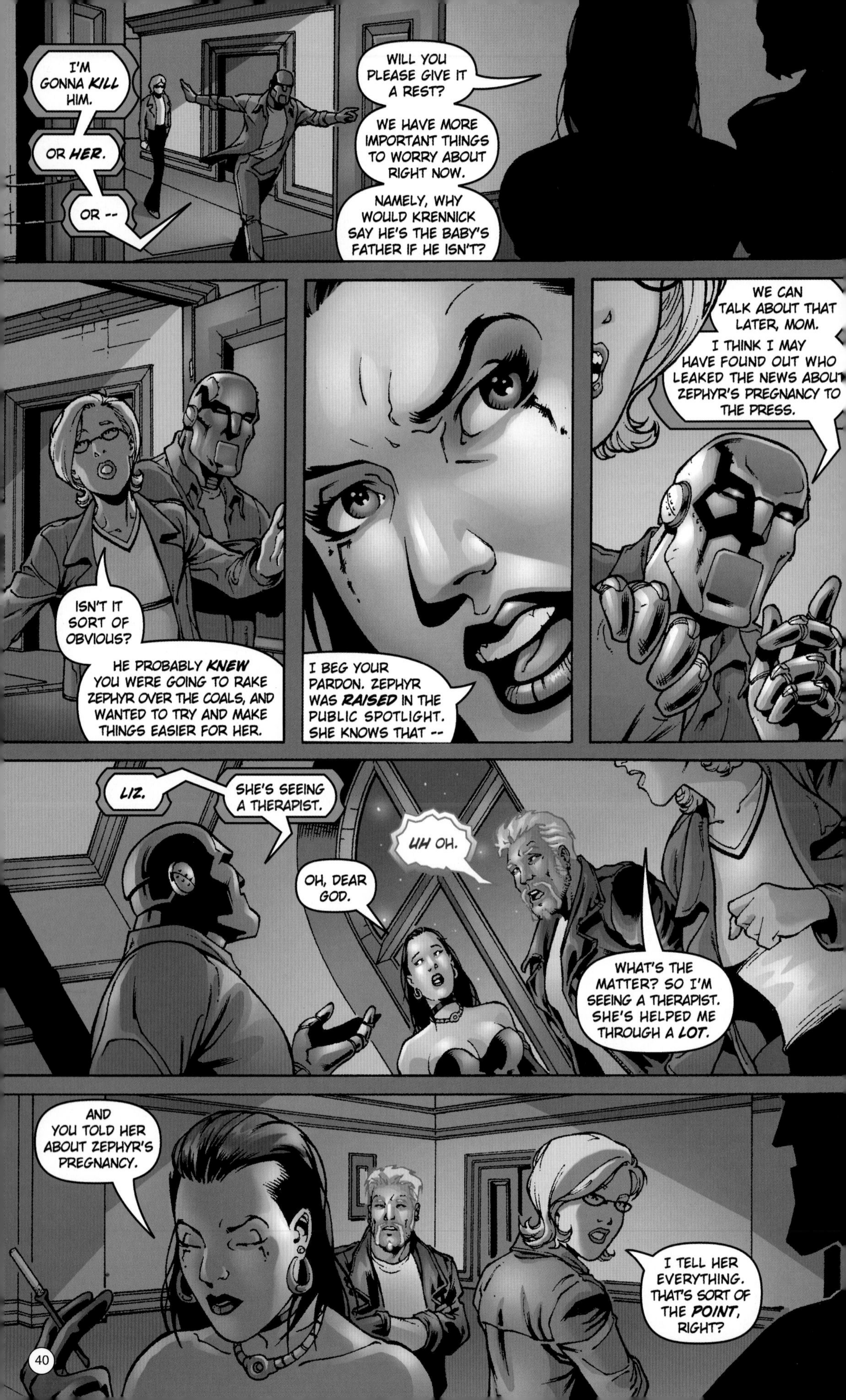
I'M GONNA *KILL* HIM.
OR *HER*.
OR --
WILL YOU PLEASE GIVE IT A REST?
WE HAVE MORE IMPORTANT THINGS TO WORRY ABOUT RIGHT NOW.
NAMELY, WHY WOULD KRENNICK SAY HE'S THE BABY'S FATHER IF HE ISN'T?
ISN'T IT SORT OF OBVIOUS?
HE PROBABLY *KNEW* YOU WERE GOING TO RAKE ZEPHYR OVER THE COALS, AND WANTED TO TRY AND MAKE THINGS EASIER FOR HER.
I BEG YOUR PARDON. ZEPHYR WAS *RAISED* IN THE PUBLIC SPOTLIGHT. SHE KNOWS THAT --
WE CAN TALK ABOUT THAT LATER, MOM.
I THINK I MAY HAVE FOUND OUT WHO LEAKED THE NEWS ABOUT ZEPHYR'S PREGNANCY TO THE PRESS.
LIZ.
SHE'S SEEING A THERAPIST.
UH OH.
OH, DEAR GOD.
WHAT'S THE MATTER? SO I'M SEEING A THERAPIST. SHE'S HELPED ME THROUGH A *LOT*.
AND YOU TOLD HER ABOUT ZEPHYR'S PREGNANCY.
I TELL HER EVERYTHING. THAT'S SORT OF THE *POINT*, RIGHT?

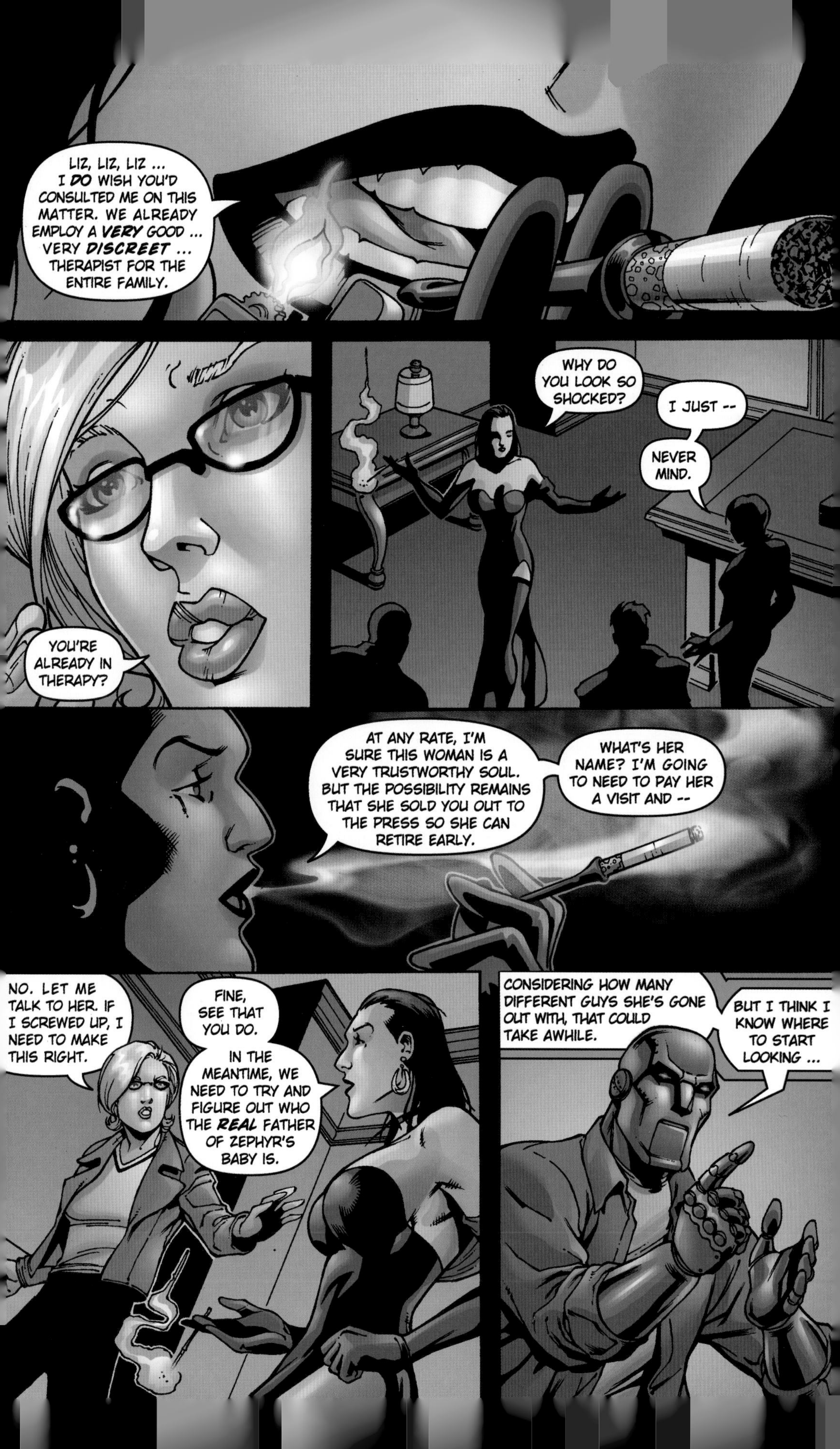

LIZ, LIZ, LIZ ... I DO WISH YOU'D CONSULTED ME ON THIS MATTER. WE ALREADY EMPLOY A VERY GOOD ... VERY DISCREET ... THERAPIST FOR THE ENTIRE FAMILY.
YOU'RE ALREADY IN THERAPY?
WHY DO YOU LOOK SO SHOCKED?
I JUST --
NEVER MIND.
AT ANY RATE, I'M SURE THIS WOMAN IS A VERY TRUSTWORTHY SOUL. BUT THE POSSIBILITY REMAINS THAT SHE SOLD YOU OUT TO THE PRESS SO SHE CAN RETIRE EARLY.
WHAT'S HER NAME? I'M GOING TO NEED TO PAY HER A VISIT AND --
NO. LET ME TALK TO HER. IF I SCREWED UP, I NEED TO MAKE THIS RIGHT.
FINE, SEE THAT YOU DO.
IN THE MEANTIME, WE NEED TO TRY AND FIGURE OUT WHO THE REAL FATHER OF ZEPHYR'S BABY IS.
CONSIDERING HOW MANY DIFFERENT GUYS SHE'S GONE OUT WITH, THAT COULD TAKE AWHILE.
BUT I THINK I KNOW WHERE TO START LOOKING ...

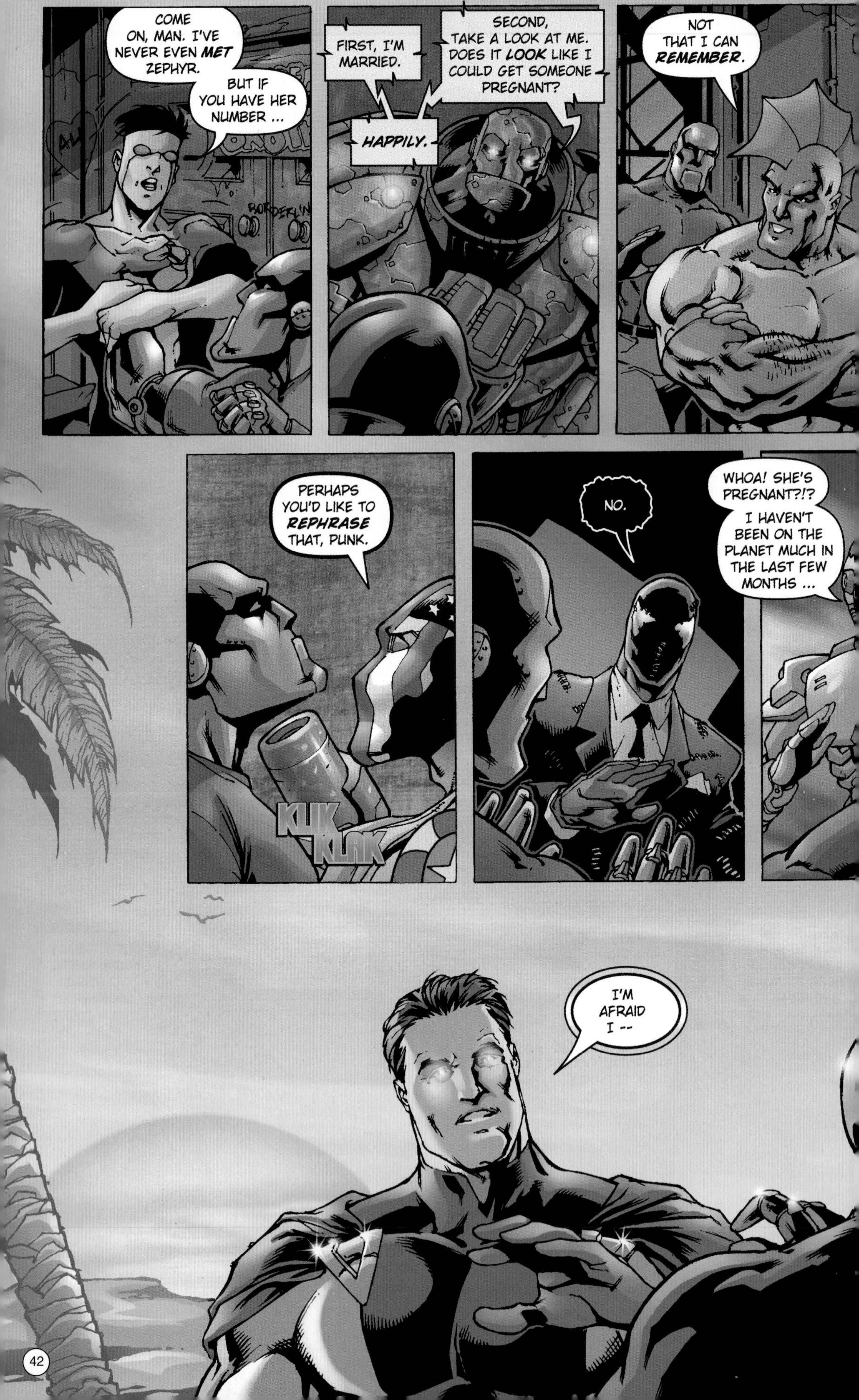
COME ON, MAN. I'VE NEVER EVEN MET ZEPHYR.
BUT IF YOU HAVE HER NUMBER ...
FIRST, I'M MARRIED.
HAPPILY.
SECOND, TAKE A LOOK AT ME. DOES IT LOOK LIKE I COULD GET SOMEONE PREGNANT?
NOT THAT I CAN REMEMBER.
PERHAPS YOU'D LIKE TO REPHRASE THAT, PUNK.
KLIK KLAK
NO.
WHOA! SHE'S PREGNANT?!?
I HAVEN'T BEEN ON THE PLANET MUCH IN THE LAST FEW MONTHS ...
I'M AFRAID I --

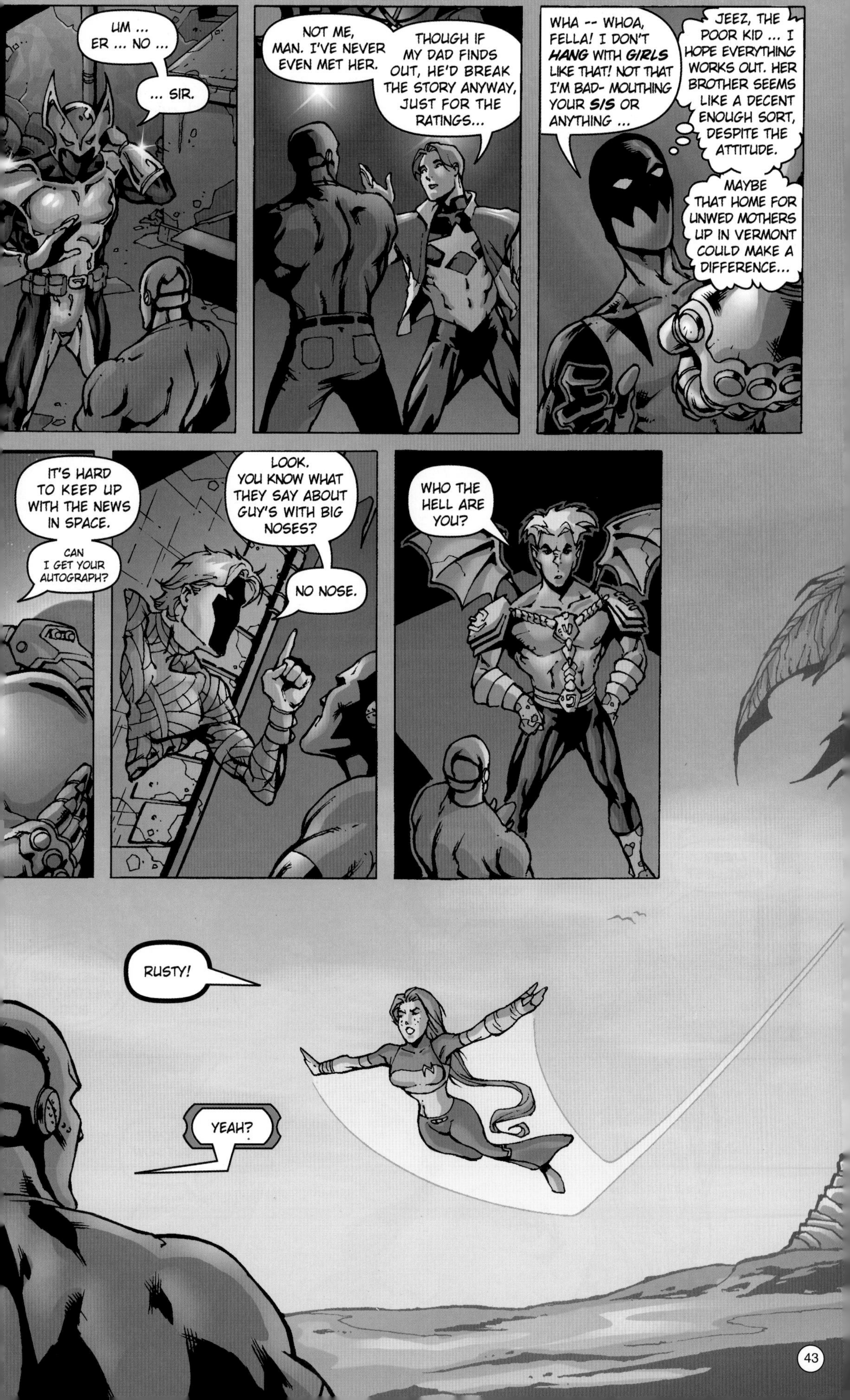

UM ... ER ... NO ...
... SIR.
NOT ME, MAN. I'VE NEVER EVEN MET HER.
THOUGH IF MY DAD FINDS OUT, HE'D BREAK THE STORY ANYWAY, JUST FOR THE RATINGS...
WHA -- WHOA, FELLA! I DON'T HANG WITH GIRLS LIKE THAT! NOT THAT I'M BAD- MOUTHING YOUR SIS OR ANYTHING ...
JEEZ, THE POOR KID ... I HOPE EVERYTHING WORKS OUT. HER BROTHER SEEMS LIKE A DECENT ENOUGH SORT, DESPITE THE ATTITUDE.
MAYBE THAT HOME FOR UNWED MOTHERS UP IN VERMONT COULD MAKE A DIFFERENCE...
IT'S HARD TO KEEP UP WITH THE NEWS IN SPACE.
CAN I GET YOUR AUTOGRAPH?
LOOK. YOU KNOW WHAT THEY SAY ABOUT GUY'S WITH BIG NOSES?
NO NOSE.
WHO THE HELL ARE YOU?
RUSTY!
YEAH?

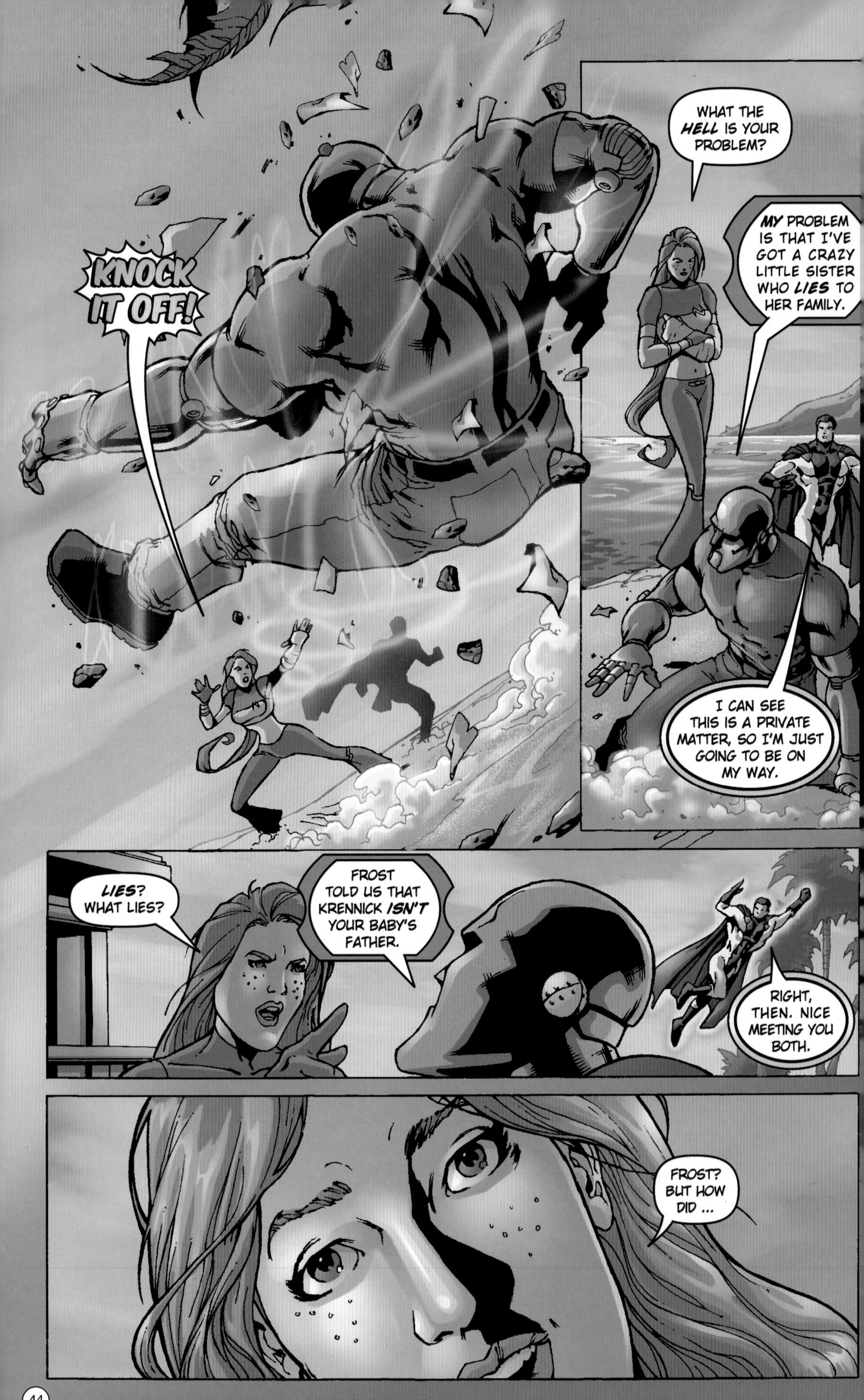
KNOCK IT OFF!
WHAT THE HELL IS YOUR PROBLEM?
MY PROBLEM IS THAT I'VE GOT A CRAZY LITTLE SISTER WHO LIES TO HER FAMILY.
I CAN SEE THIS IS A PRIVATE MATTER, SO I'M JUST GOING TO BE ON MY WAY.
LIES? WHAT LIES?
FROST TOLD US THAT KRENNICK ISN'T YOUR BABY'S FATHER.
RIGHT, THEN. NICE MEETING YOU BOTH.
FROST? BUT HOW DID ...

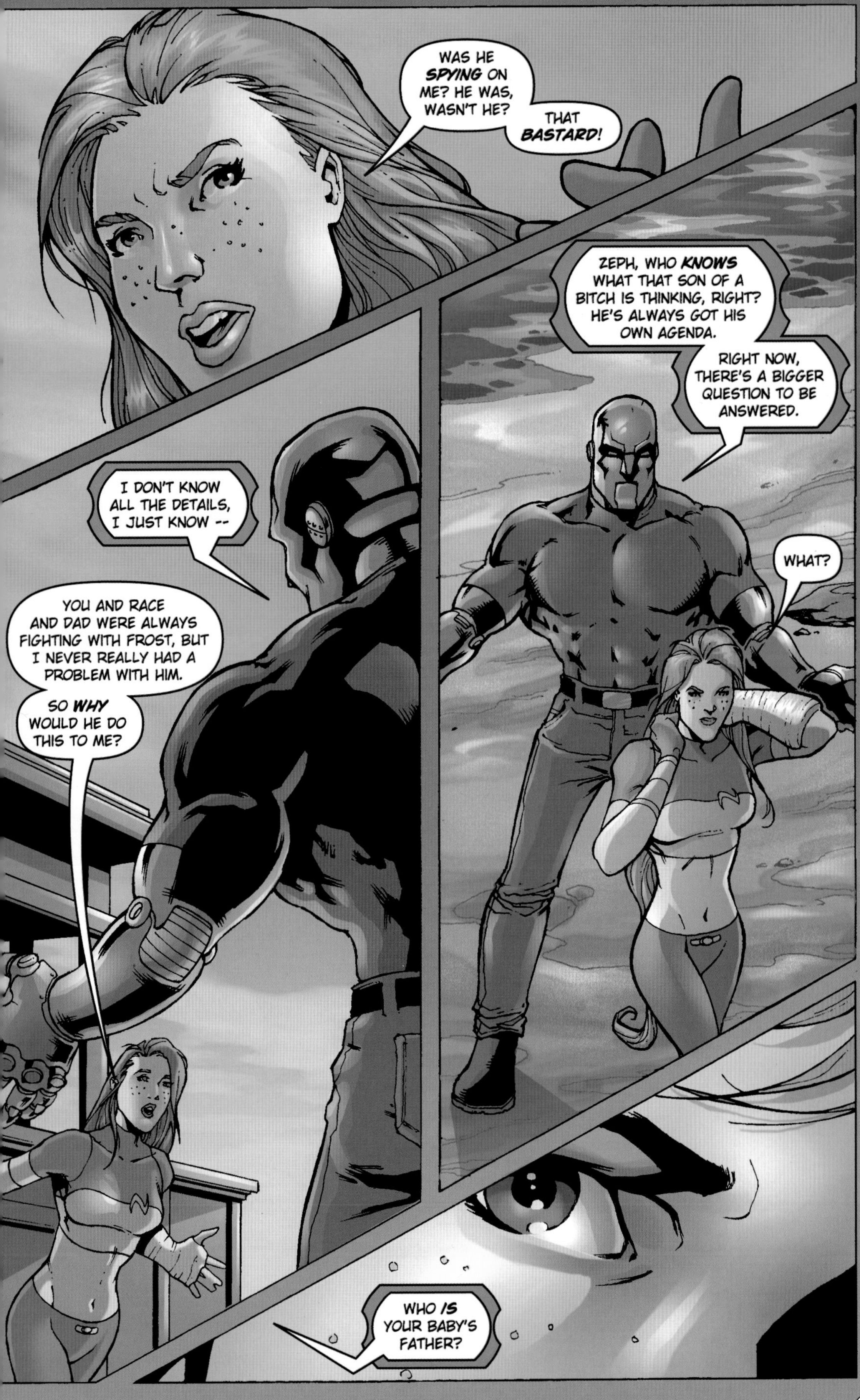

WAS HE SPYING ON ME? HE WAS, WASN'T HE?
THAT BASTARD!
ZEPH, WHO KNOWS WHAT THAT SON OF A BITCH IS THINKING, RIGHT? HE'S ALWAYS GOT HIS OWN AGENDA.
RIGHT NOW, THERE'S A BIGGER QUESTION TO BE ANSWERED.
I DON'T KNOW ALL THE DETAILS, I JUST KNOW --
YOU AND RACE AND DAD WERE ALWAYS FIGHTING WITH FROST, BUT I NEVER REALLY HAD A PROBLEM WITH HIM.
SO WHY WOULD HE DO THIS TO ME?
WHAT?
WHO IS YOUR BABY'S FATHER?

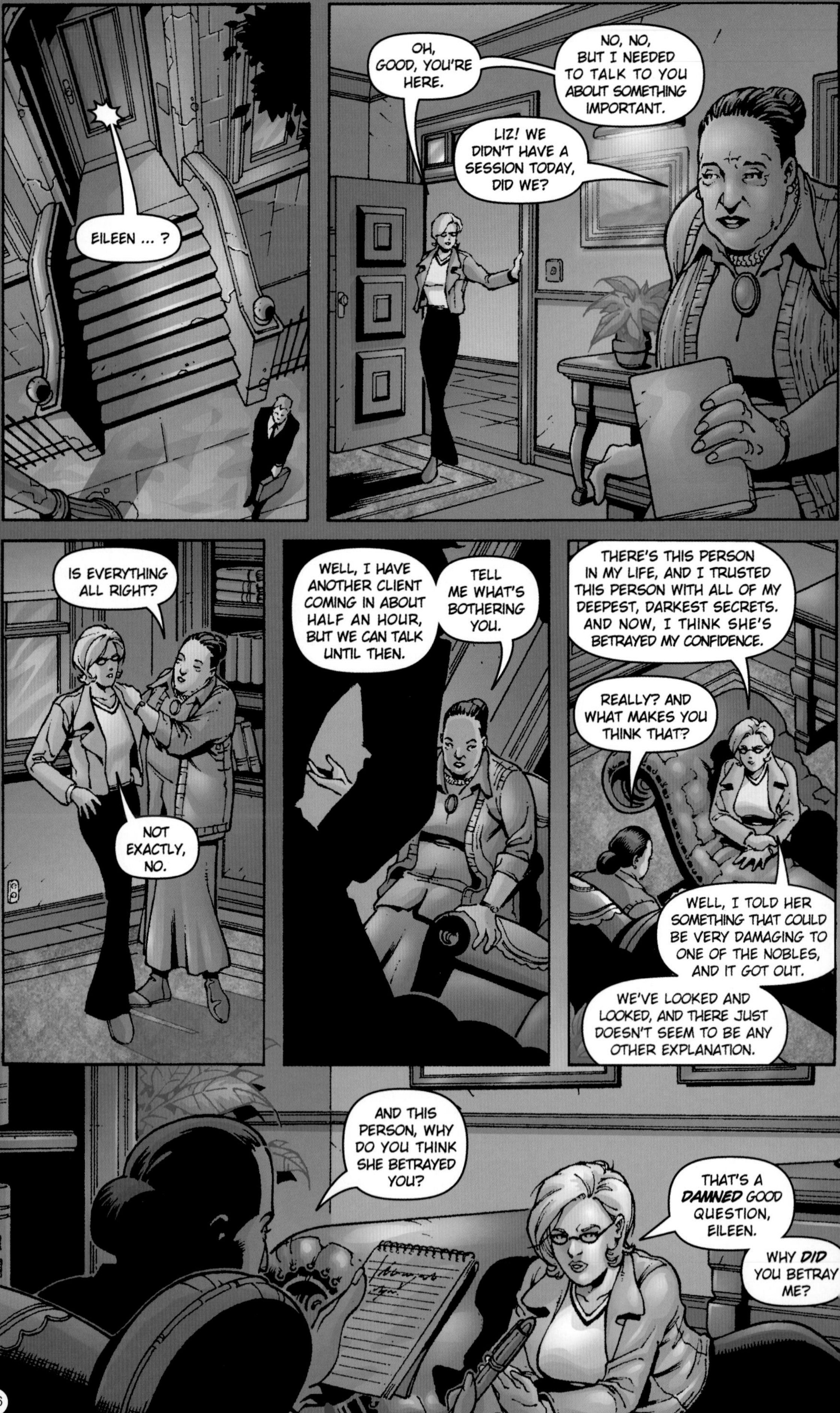
EILEEN ... ?
OH, GOOD, YOU'RE HERE.
LIZ! WE DIDN'T HAVE A SESSION TODAY, DID WE?
NO, NO, BUT I NEEDED TO TALK TO YOU ABOUT SOMETHING IMPORTANT.
IS EVERYTHING ALL RIGHT?
NOT EXACTLY, NO.
WELL, I HAVE ANOTHER CLIENT COMING IN ABOUT HALF AN HOUR, BUT WE CAN TALK UNTIL THEN.
TELL ME WHAT'S BOTHERING YOU.
THERE'S THIS PERSON IN MY LIFE, AND I TRUSTED THIS PERSON WITH ALL OF MY DEEPEST, DARKEST SECRETS. AND NOW, I THINK SHE'S BETRAYED MY CONFIDENCE.
REALLY? AND WHAT MAKES YOU THINK THAT?
WELL, I TOLD HER SOMETHING THAT COULD BE VERY DAMAGING TO ONE OF THE NOBLES, AND IT GOT OUT.
WE'VE LOOKED AND LOOKED, AND THERE JUST DOESN'T SEEM TO BE ANY OTHER EXPLANATION.
AND THIS PERSON, WHY DO YOU THINK SHE BETRAYED YOU?
THAT'S A ***DAMNED*** GOOD QUESTION, EILEEN.
WHY ***DID*** YOU BETRAY ME?

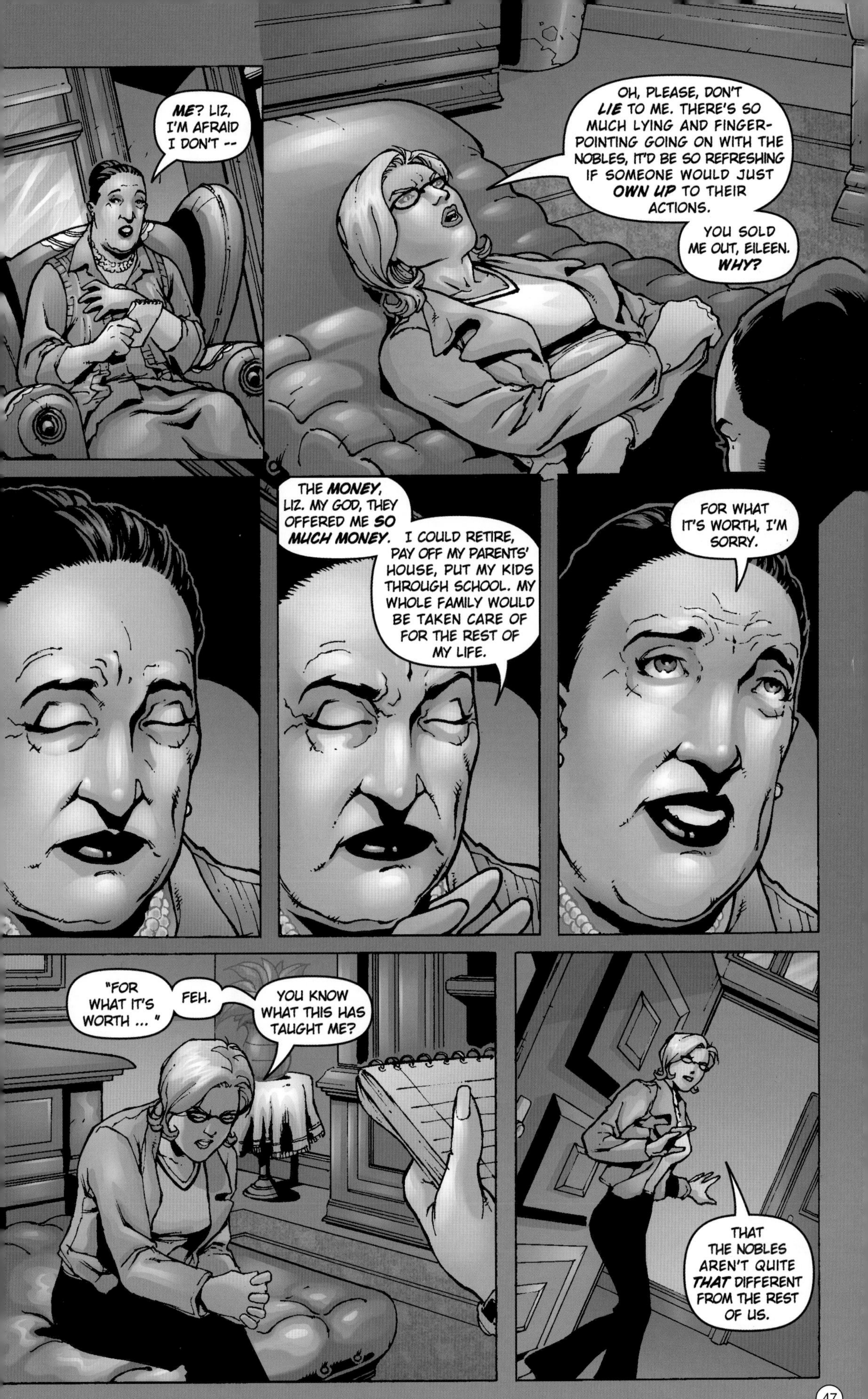
ME? LIZ, I'M AFRAID I DON'T --
OH, PLEASE, DON'T LIE TO ME. THERE'S SO MUCH LYING AND FINGER-POINTING GOING ON WITH THE NOBLES, IT'D BE SO REFRESHING IF SOMEONE WOULD JUST OWN UP TO THEIR ACTIONS.
YOU SOLD ME OUT, EILEEN. WHY?
THE MONEY, LIZ. MY GOD, THEY OFFERED ME SO MUCH MONEY.
I COULD RETIRE, PAY OFF MY PARENTS' HOUSE, PUT MY KIDS THROUGH SCHOOL. MY WHOLE FAMILY WOULD BE TAKEN CARE OF FOR THE REST OF MY LIFE.
FOR WHAT IT'S WORTH, I'M SORRY.
"FOR WHAT IT'S WORTH ... "
FEH.
YOU KNOW WHAT THIS HAS TAUGHT ME?
THAT THE NOBLES AREN'T QUITE THAT DIFFERENT FROM THE REST OF US.

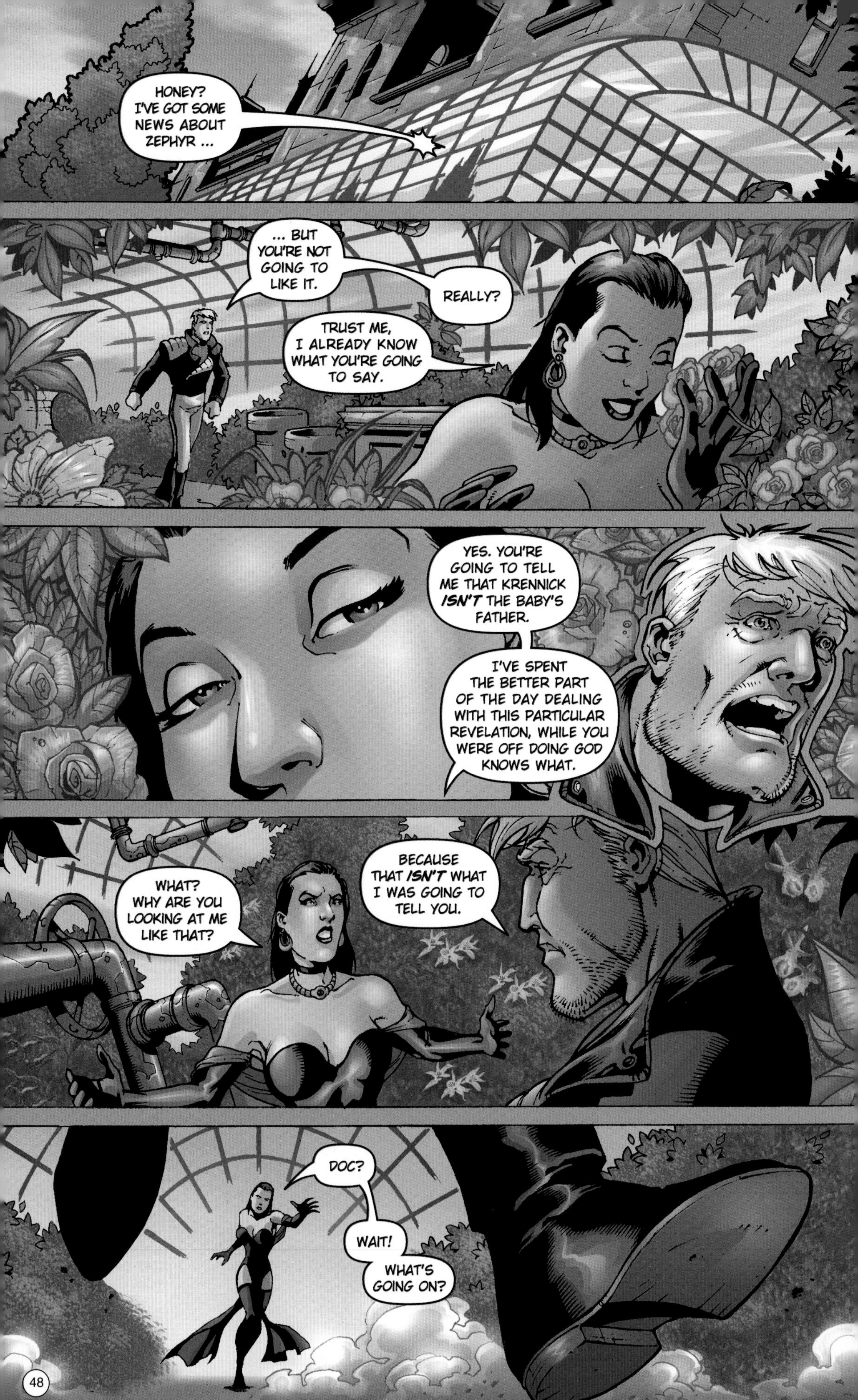
HONEY? I'VE GOT SOME NEWS ABOUT ZEPHYR ...
... BUT YOU'RE NOT GOING TO LIKE IT.
REALLY?
TRUST ME, I ALREADY KNOW WHAT YOU'RE GOING TO SAY.
YES. YOU'RE GOING TO TELL ME THAT KRENNICK *ISN'T* THE BABY'S FATHER.
I'VE SPENT THE BETTER PART OF THE DAY DEALING WITH THIS PARTICULAR REVELATION, WHILE YOU WERE OFF DOING GOD KNOWS WHAT.
WHAT? WHY ARE YOU LOOKING AT ME LIKE THAT?
BECAUSE THAT *ISN'T* WHAT I WAS GOING TO TELL YOU.
DOC?
WAIT!
WHAT'S GOING ON?

DOC!

KRENNICK.

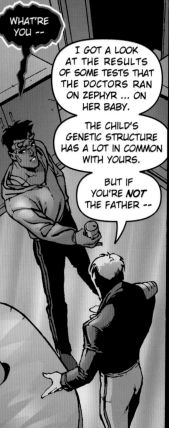

WHAT'RE YOU --

I GOT A LOOK AT THE RESULTS OF SOME TESTS THAT THE DOCTORS RAN ON ZEPHYR ... ON HER BABY.

THE CHILD'S GENETIC STRUCTURE HAS A LOT IN COMMON WITH YOURS.

BUT IF YOU'RE *NOT* THE FATHER --

I'M *NOT*. I'M SORRY, BUT I WAS JUST TRYING TO HELP KEEP GAIA OFF ZEPHYR'S BACK BY SAYING THAT. I *SWEAR* IT'S NOT --

YOU'RE NOT *LISTENING* TO ME. IF YOU'RE *NOT* THE FATHER, THAN HOW DID THE BABY WIND UP WITH YOUR GENETIC STRUCTURE?

OH MY GOD.

HE ... YOU DON'T MEAN ... I ... OH GOD...

YOUR FATHER. IT'S HIM, ISN'T IT?

IT'S *DRACONIS.*

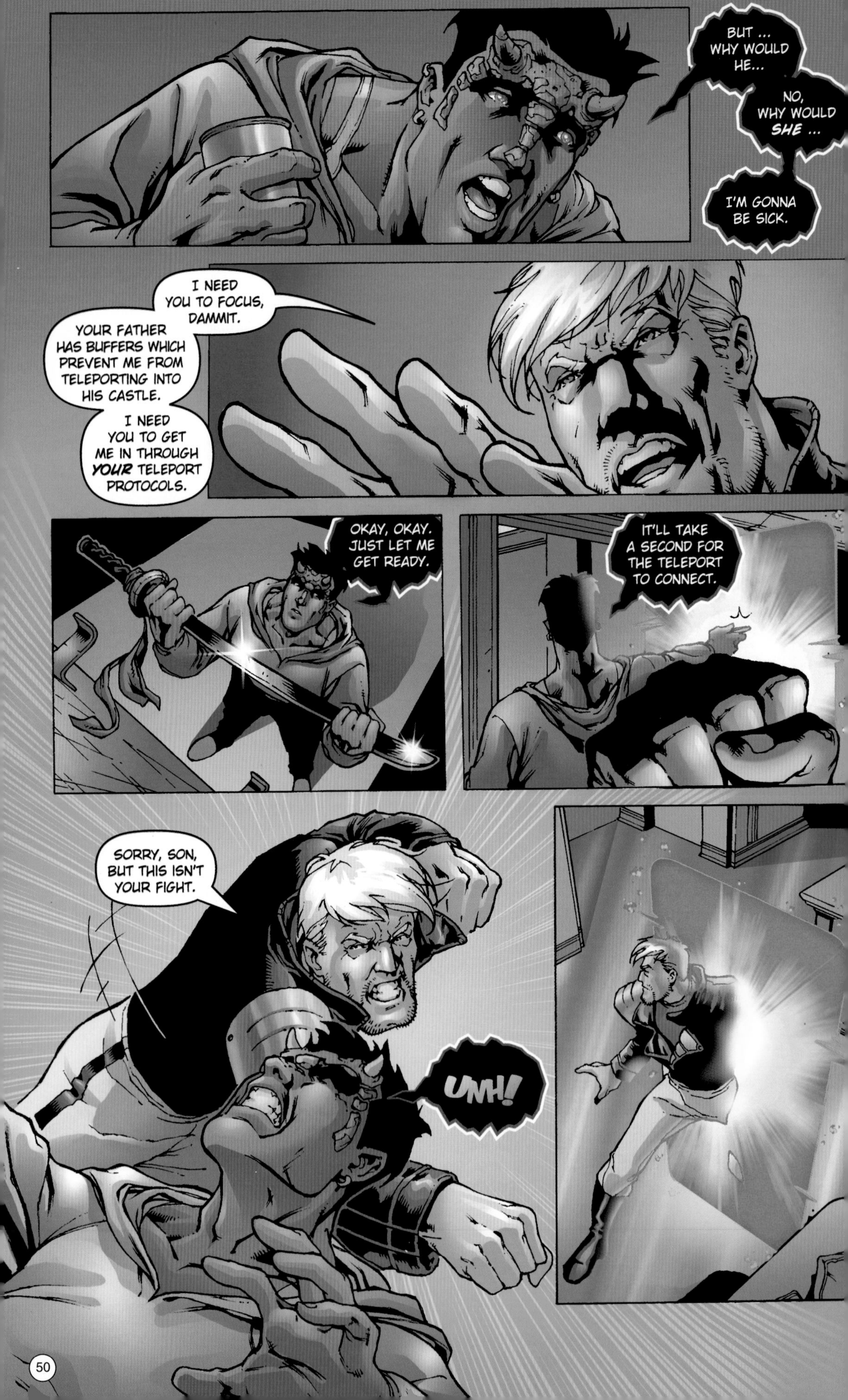

BUT ... WHY WOULD HE...
NO, WHY WOULD *SHE* ...
I'M GONNA BE SICK.
I NEED YOU TO FOCUS, DAMMIT.
YOUR FATHER HAS BUFFERS WHICH PREVENT ME FROM TELEPORTING INTO HIS CASTLE.
I NEED YOU TO GET ME IN THROUGH *YOUR* TELEPORT PROTOCOLS.
OKAY, OKAY. JUST LET ME GET READY.
IT'LL TAKE A SECOND FOR THE TELEPORT TO CONNECT.
SORRY, SON, BUT THIS ISN'T YOUR FIGHT.
UNH!

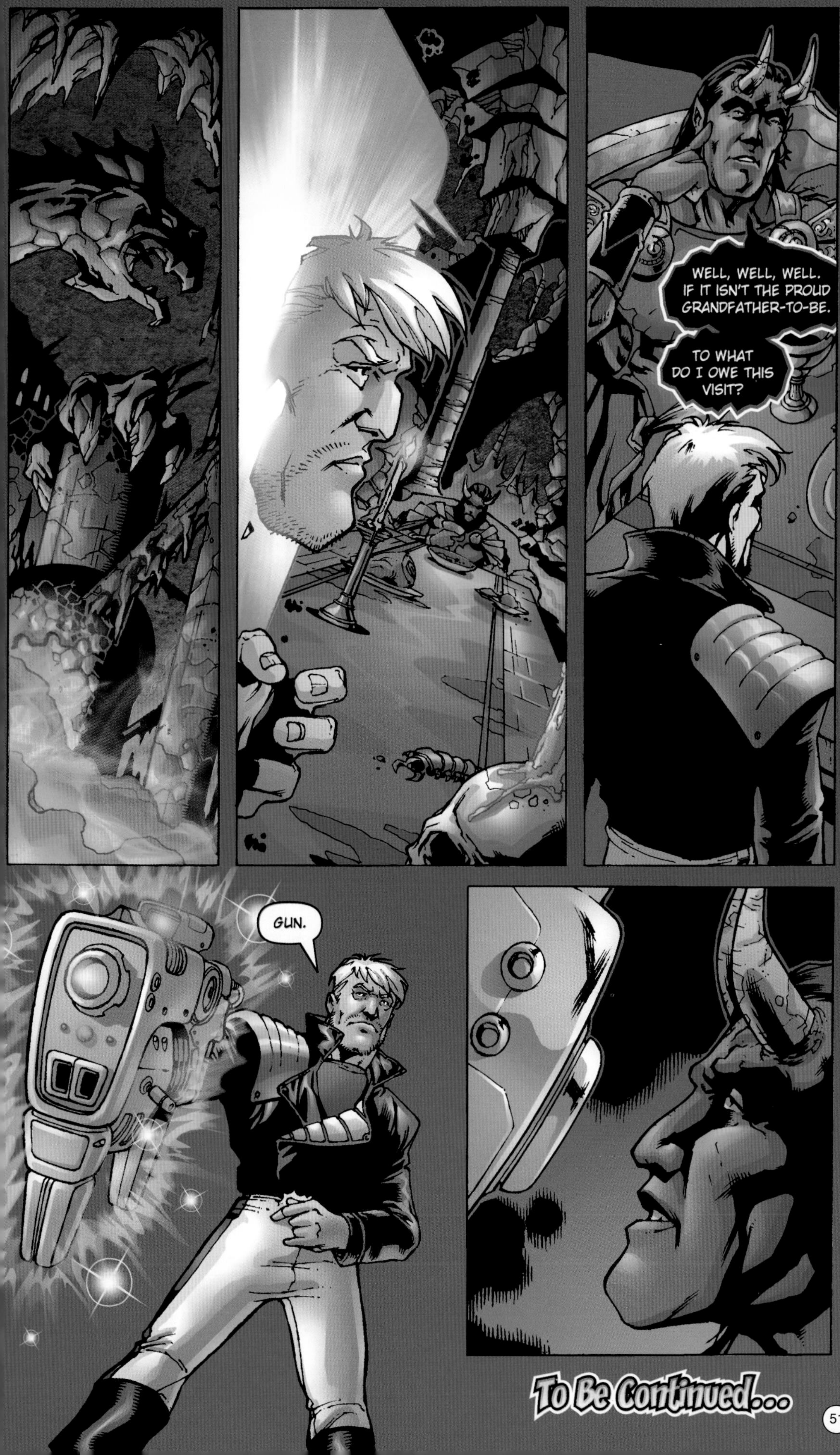
WELL, WELL, WELL. IF IT ISN'T THE PROUD GRANDFATHER-TO-BE.
TO WHAT DO I OWE THIS VISIT?
GUN.
To Be Continued...

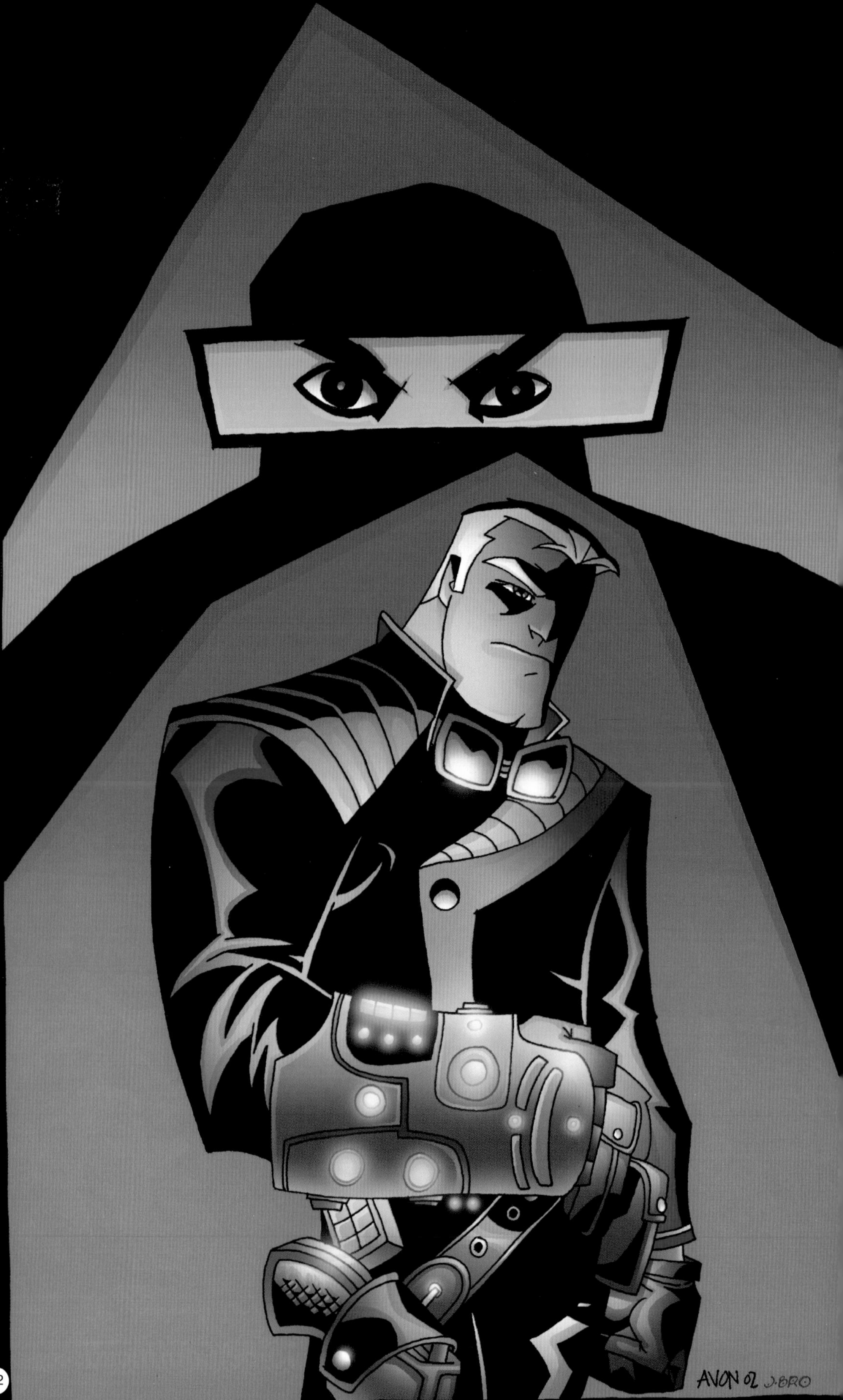
AVON 02 J-BRO

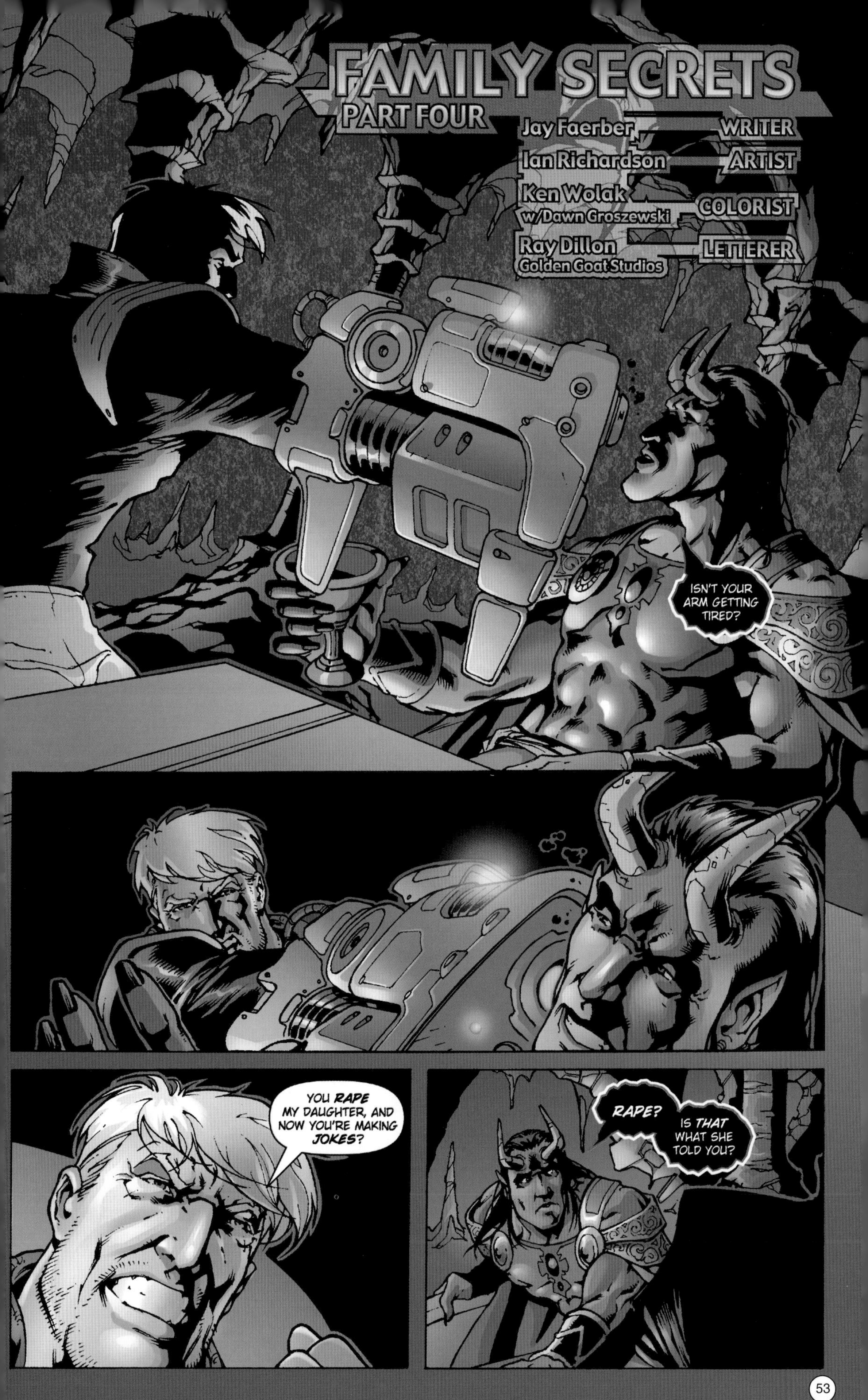
FAMILY SECRETS
PART FOUR
Jay Faerber WRITER
Ian Richardson ARTIST
Ken Wolak w/Dawn Groszewski COLORIST
Ray Dillon Golden Goat Studios LETTERER
ISN'T YOUR ARM GETTING TIRED?
YOU RAPE MY DAUGHTER, AND NOW YOU'RE MAKING JOKES?
RAPE?
IS THAT WHAT SHE TOLD YOU?

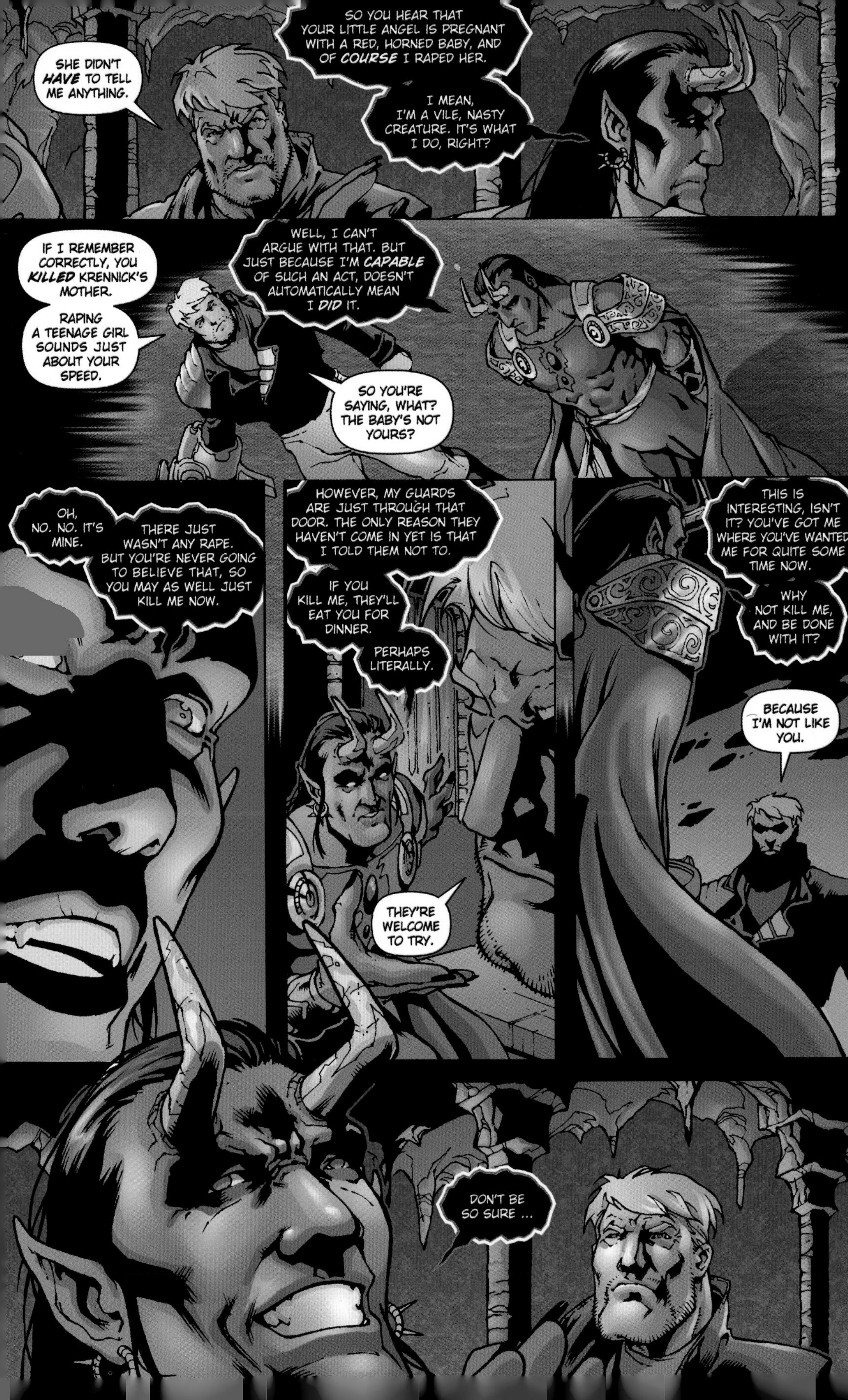
SHE DIDN'T HAVE TO TELL ME ANYTHING.
SO YOU HEAR THAT YOUR LITTLE ANGEL IS PREGNANT WITH A RED, HORNED BABY, AND OF COURSE I RAPED HER.
I MEAN, I'M A VILE, NASTY CREATURE. IT'S WHAT I DO, RIGHT?
IF I REMEMBER CORRECTLY, YOU KILLED KRENNICK'S MOTHER.
RAPING A TEENAGE GIRL SOUNDS JUST ABOUT YOUR SPEED.
WELL, I CAN'T ARGUE WITH THAT. BUT JUST BECAUSE I'M CAPABLE OF SUCH AN ACT, DOESN'T AUTOMATICALLY MEAN I DID IT.
SO YOU'RE SAYING, WHAT? THE BABY'S NOT YOURS?
OH, NO. NO. IT'S MINE.
THERE JUST WASN'T ANY RAPE. BUT YOU'RE NEVER GOING TO BELIEVE THAT, SO YOU MAY AS WELL JUST KILL ME NOW.
HOWEVER, MY GUARDS ARE JUST THROUGH THAT DOOR. THE ONLY REASON THEY HAVEN'T COME IN YET IS THAT I TOLD THEM NOT TO.
IF YOU KILL ME, THEY'LL EAT YOU FOR DINNER.
PERHAPS LITERALLY.
THEY'RE WELCOME TO TRY.
THIS IS INTERESTING, ISN'T IT? YOU'VE GOT ME WHERE YOU'VE WANTED ME FOR QUITE SOME TIME NOW.
WHY NOT KILL ME, AND BE DONE WITH IT?
BECAUSE I'M NOT LIKE YOU.
DON'T BE SO SURE ...

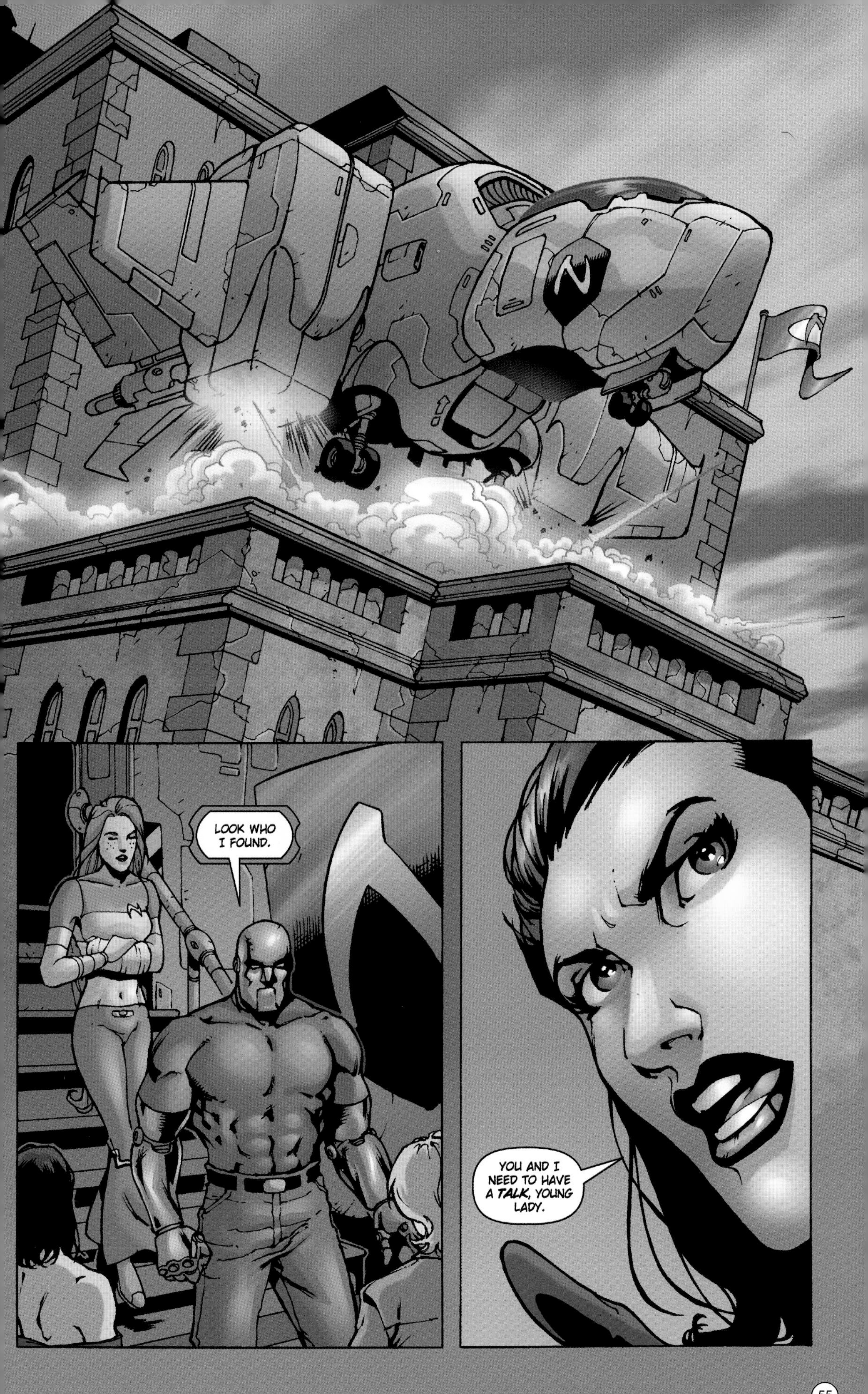
LOOK WHO I FOUND.
YOU AND I NEED TO HAVE A TALK, YOUNG LADY.

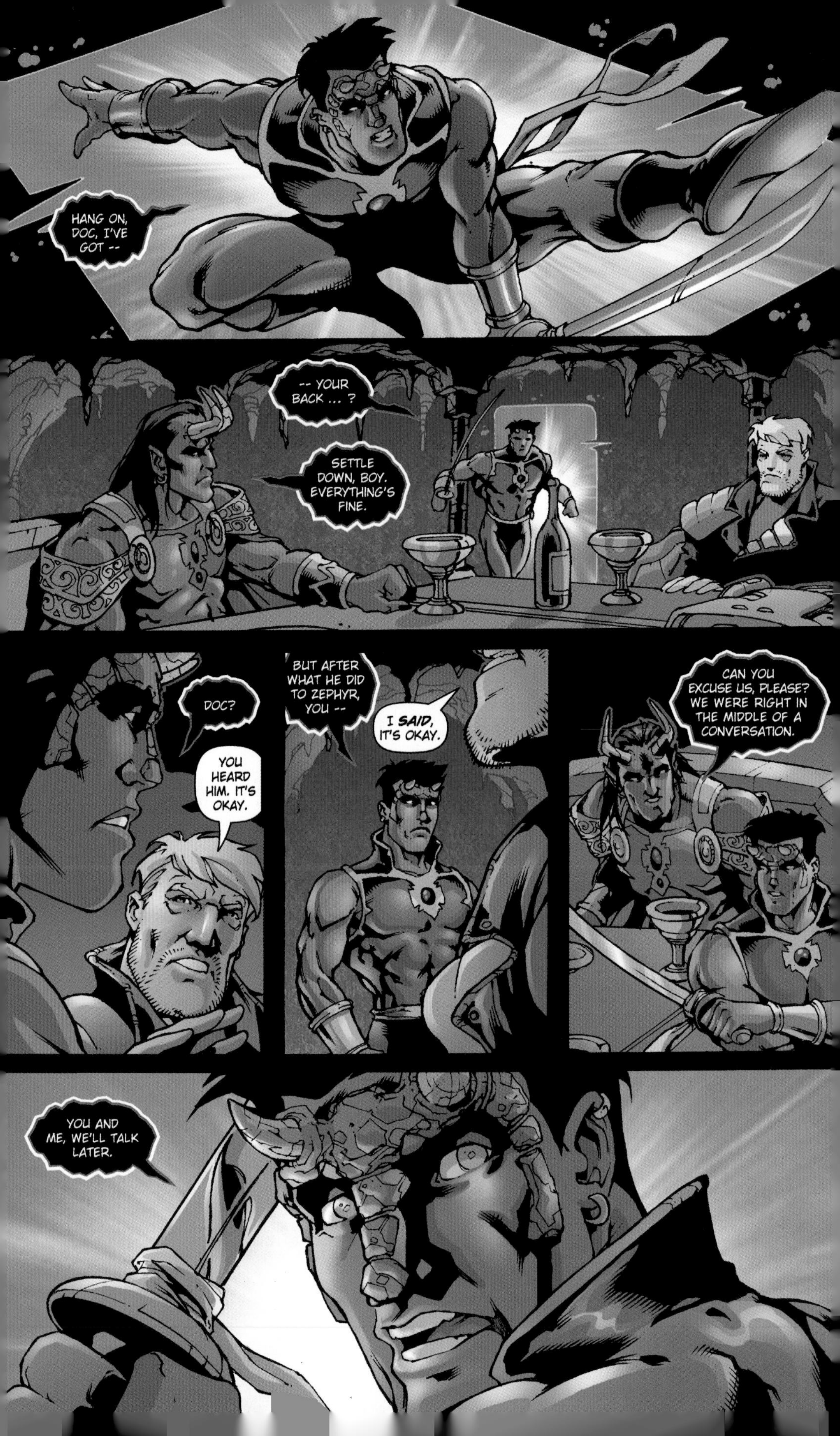
HANG ON, DOC, I'VE GOT --
-- YOUR BACK ... ?
SETTLE DOWN, BOY. EVERYTHING'S FINE.
DOC?
YOU HEARD HIM. IT'S OKAY.
BUT AFTER WHAT HE DID TO ZEPHYR, YOU --
I SAID, IT'S OKAY.
CAN YOU EXCUSE US, PLEASE? WE WERE RIGHT IN THE MIDDLE OF A CONVERSATION.
YOU AND ME, WE'LL TALK LATER.

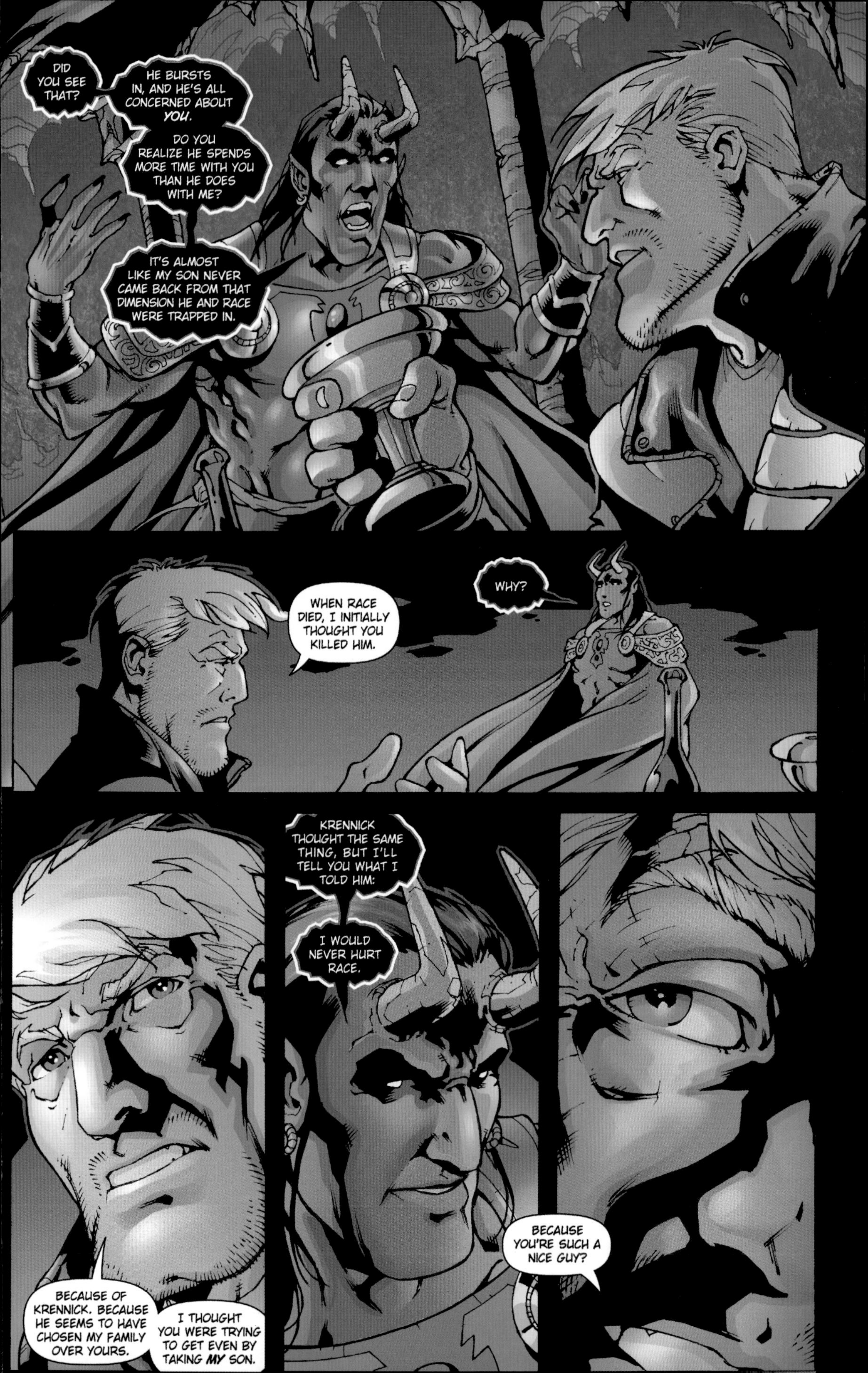
DID YOU SEE THAT?
HE BURSTS IN, AND HE'S ALL CONCERNED ABOUT *YOU*.
DO YOU REALIZE HE SPENDS MORE TIME WITH YOU THAN HE DOES WITH ME?
IT'S ALMOST LIKE MY SON NEVER CAME BACK FROM THAT DIMENSION HE AND RACE WERE TRAPPED IN.
WHEN RACE DIED, I INITIALLY THOUGHT YOU KILLED HIM.
WHY?
BECAUSE OF KRENNICK. BECAUSE HE SEEMS TO HAVE CHOSEN MY FAMILY OVER YOURS.
I THOUGHT YOU WERE TRYING TO GET EVEN BY TAKING *MY* SON.
KRENNICK THOUGHT THE SAME THING, BUT I'LL TELL YOU WHAT I TOLD HIM:
I WOULD NEVER HURT RACE.
BECAUSE YOU'RE SUCH A NICE GUY?

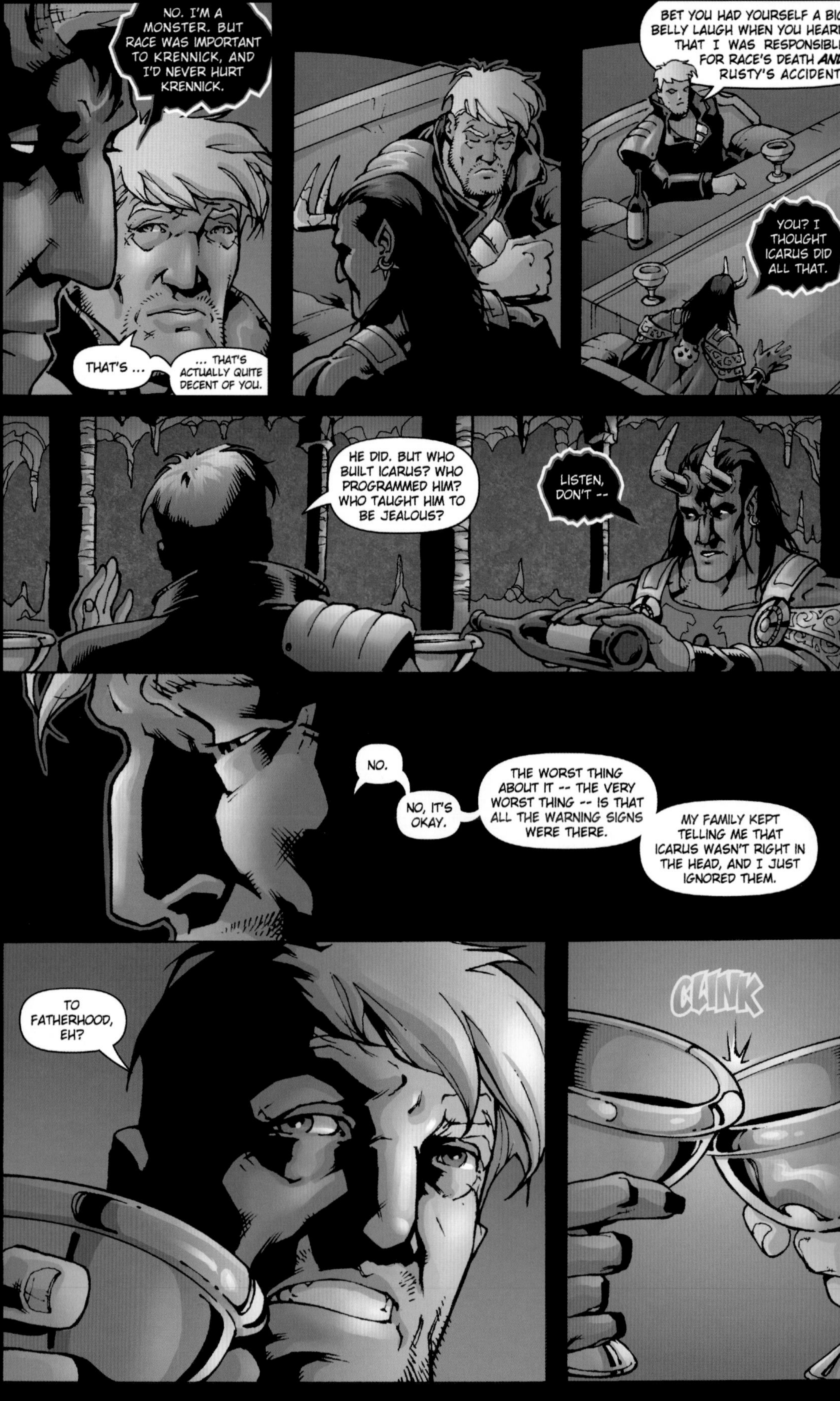
NO. I'M A MONSTER. BUT RACE WAS IMPORTANT TO KRENNICK, AND I'D NEVER HURT KRENNICK.
THAT'S ...
... THAT'S ACTUALLY QUITE DECENT OF YOU.
BET YOU HAD YOURSELF A BIG BELLY LAUGH WHEN YOU HEARD THAT I WAS RESPONSIBLE FOR RACE'S DEATH ***AND*** RUSTY'S ACCIDENT.
YOU? I THOUGHT ICARUS DID ALL THAT.
HE DID. BUT WHO BUILT ICARUS? WHO PROGRAMMED HIM? WHO TAUGHT HIM TO BE JEALOUS?
LISTEN, DON'T --
NO.
NO, IT'S OKAY.
THE WORST THING ABOUT IT -- THE VERY WORST THING -- IS THAT ALL THE WARNING SIGNS WERE THERE.
MY FAMILY KEPT TELLING ME THAT ICARUS WASN'T RIGHT IN THE HEAD, AND I JUST IGNORED THEM.
TO FATHERHOOD, EH?
CLINK

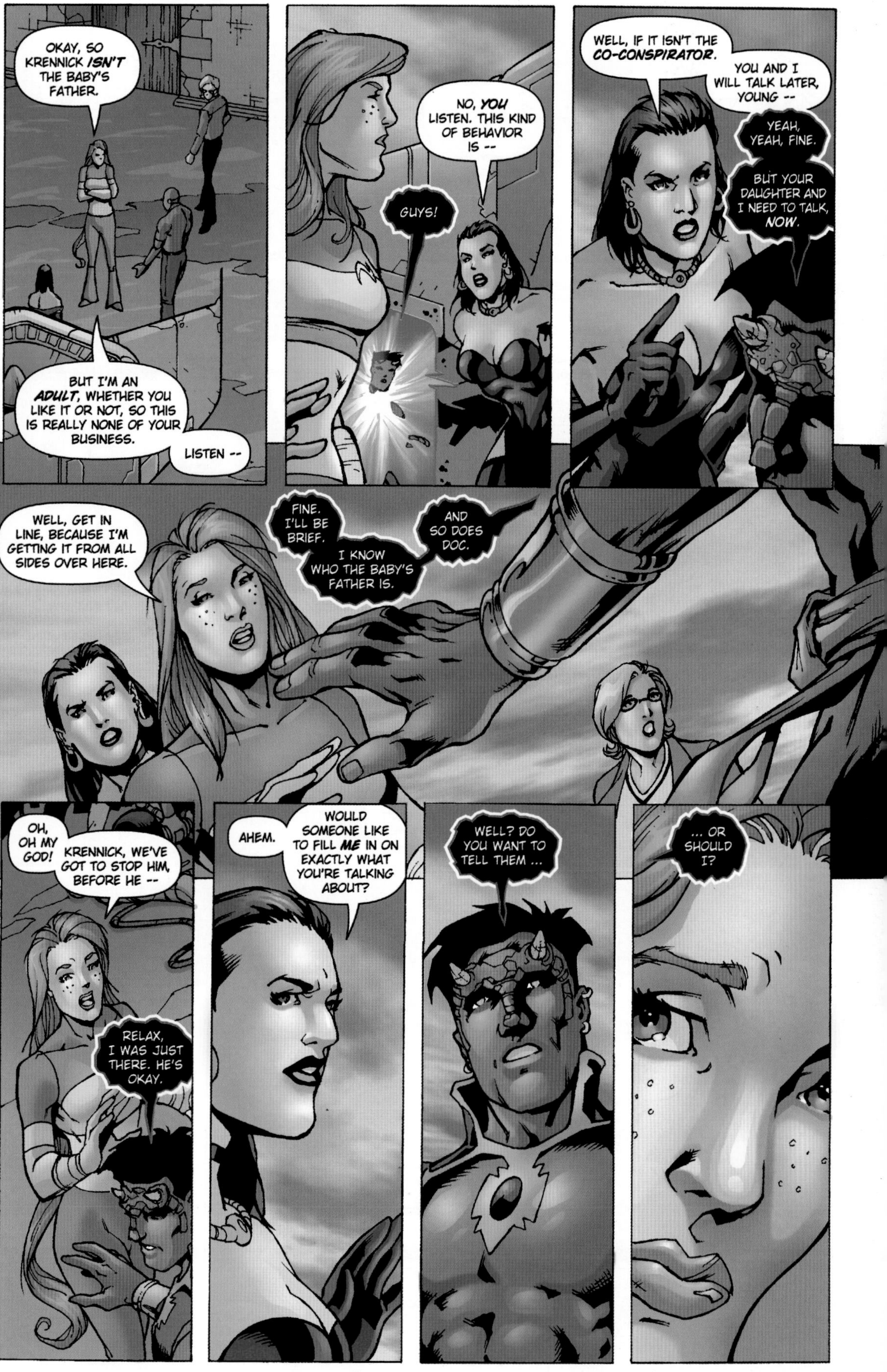

OKAY, SO KRENNICK ISN'T THE BABY'S FATHER.
BUT I'M AN ADULT, WHETHER YOU LIKE IT OR NOT, SO THIS IS REALLY NONE OF YOUR BUSINESS.
LISTEN --
NO, YOU LISTEN. THIS KIND OF BEHAVIOR IS --
GUYS!
WELL, IF IT ISN'T THE CO-CONSPIRATOR.
YOU AND I WILL TALK LATER, YOUNG --
YEAH, YEAH, FINE.
BUT YOUR DAUGHTER AND I NEED TO TALK, NOW.
WELL, GET IN LINE, BECAUSE I'M GETTING IT FROM ALL SIDES OVER HERE.
FINE. I'LL BE BRIEF.
I KNOW WHO THE BABY'S FATHER IS.
AND SO DOES DOC.
OH, OH MY GOD!
KRENNICK, WE'VE GOT TO STOP HIM, BEFORE HE --
RELAX, I WAS JUST THERE. HE'S OKAY.
AHEM.
WOULD SOMEONE LIKE TO FILL ME IN ON EXACTLY WHAT YOU'RE TALKING ABOUT?
WELL? DO YOU WANT TO TELL THEM ...
... OR SHOULD I?

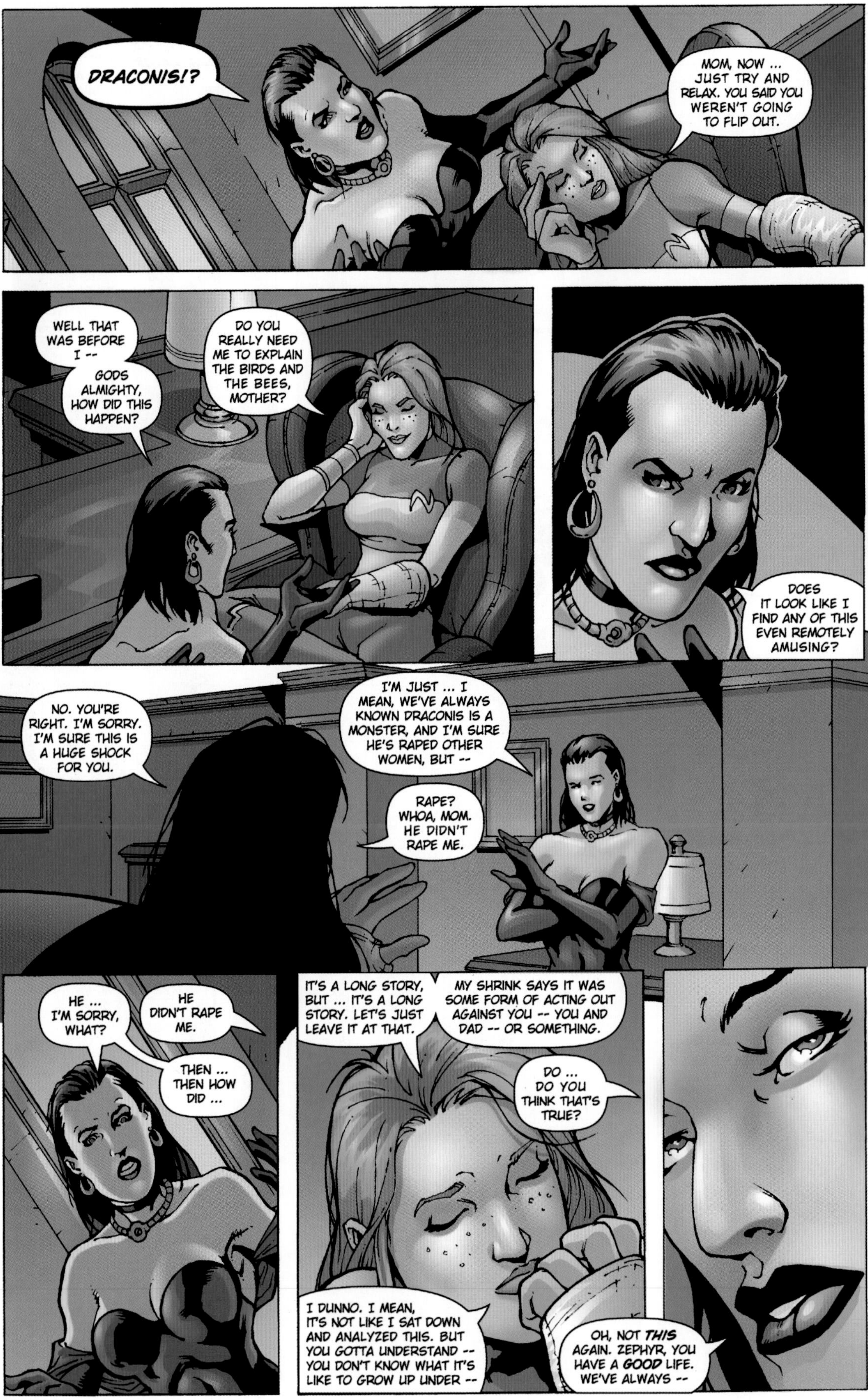
DRACONIS!?
MOM, NOW ... JUST TRY AND RELAX. YOU SAID YOU WEREN'T GOING TO FLIP OUT.
WELL THAT WAS BEFORE I --
GODS ALMIGHTY, HOW DID THIS HAPPEN?
DO YOU REALLY NEED ME TO EXPLAIN THE BIRDS AND THE BEES, MOTHER?
DOES IT LOOK LIKE I FIND ANY OF THIS EVEN REMOTELY AMUSING?
NO. YOU'RE RIGHT. I'M SORRY. I'M SURE THIS IS A HUGE SHOCK FOR YOU.
I'M JUST ... I MEAN, WE'VE ALWAYS KNOWN DRACONIS IS A MONSTER, AND I'M SURE HE'S RAPED OTHER WOMEN, BUT --
RAPE? WHOA, MOM. HE DIDN'T RAPE ME.
HE ... I'M SORRY, WHAT?
HE DIDN'T RAPE ME.
THEN ... THEN HOW DID ...
IT'S A LONG STORY, BUT ... IT'S A LONG STORY. LET'S JUST LEAVE IT AT THAT.
MY SHRINK SAYS IT WAS SOME FORM OF ACTING OUT AGAINST YOU -- YOU AND DAD -- OR SOMETHING.
DO ... DO YOU THINK THAT'S TRUE?
I DUNNO. I MEAN, IT'S NOT LIKE I SAT DOWN AND ANALYZED THIS. BUT YOU GOTTA UNDERSTAND -- YOU DON'T KNOW WHAT IT'S LIKE TO GROW UP UNDER --
OH, NOT THIS AGAIN. ZEPHYR, YOU HAVE A GOOD LIFE. WE'VE ALWAYS --

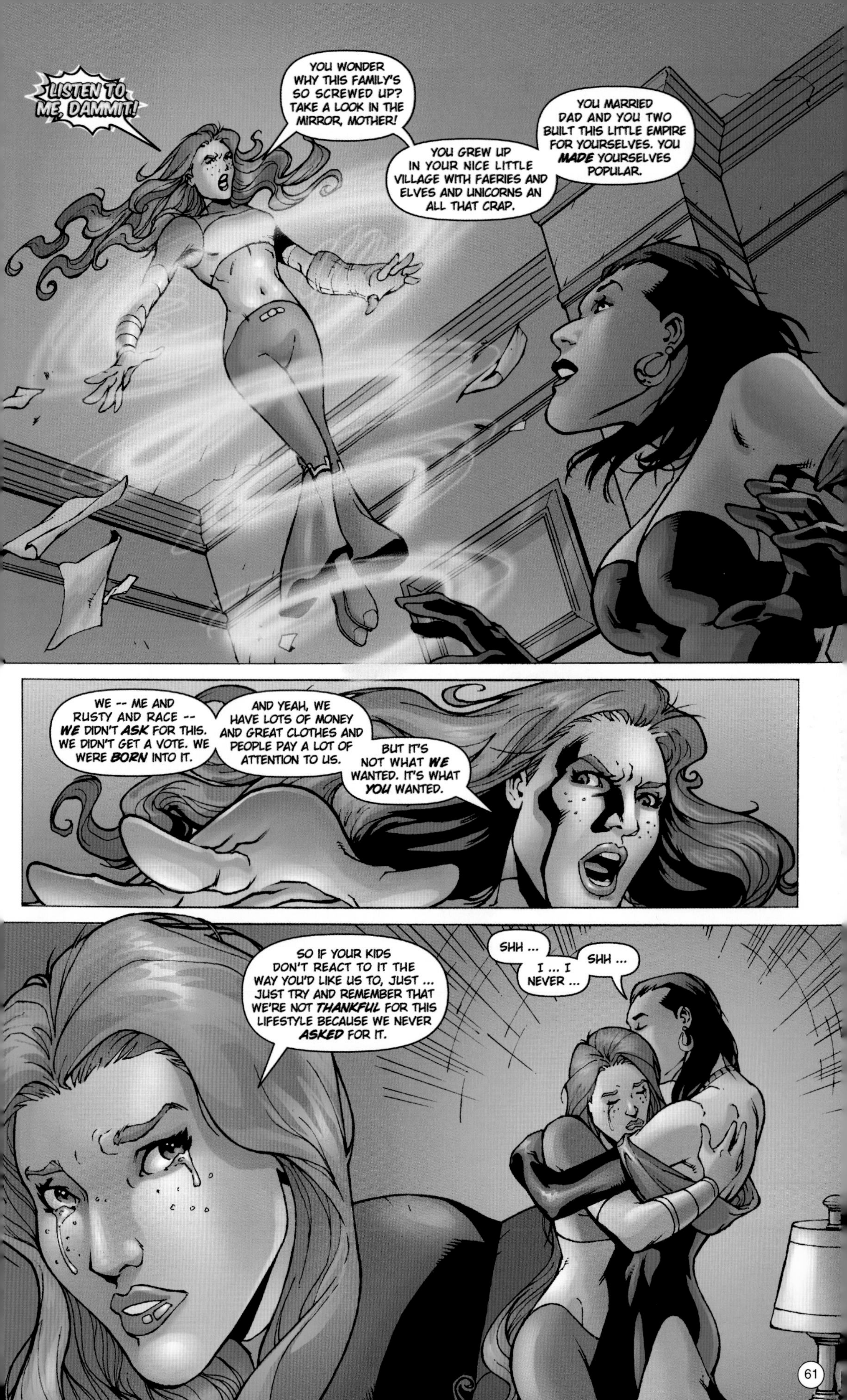
LISTEN TO ME, DAMMIT!
YOU WONDER WHY THIS FAMILY'S SO SCREWED UP? TAKE A LOOK IN THE MIRROR, MOTHER!
YOU GREW UP IN YOUR NICE LITTLE VILLAGE WITH FAERIES AND ELVES AND UNICORNS AN ALL THAT CRAP.
YOU MARRIED DAD AND YOU TWO BUILT THIS LITTLE EMPIRE FOR YOURSELVES. YOU MADE YOURSELVES POPULAR.
WE -- ME AND RUSTY AND RACE -- WE DIDN'T ASK FOR THIS. WE DIDN'T GET A VOTE. WE WERE BORN INTO IT.
AND YEAH, WE HAVE LOTS OF MONEY AND GREAT CLOTHES AND PEOPLE PAY A LOT OF ATTENTION TO US.
BUT IT'S NOT WHAT WE WANTED. IT'S WHAT YOU WANTED.
SO IF YOUR KIDS DON'T REACT TO IT THE WAY YOU'D LIKE US TO, JUST ... JUST TRY AND REMEMBER THAT WE'RE NOT THANKFUL FOR THIS LIFESTYLE BECAUSE WE NEVER ASKED FOR IT.
SHH ...
I ... I NEVER ...
SHH ...

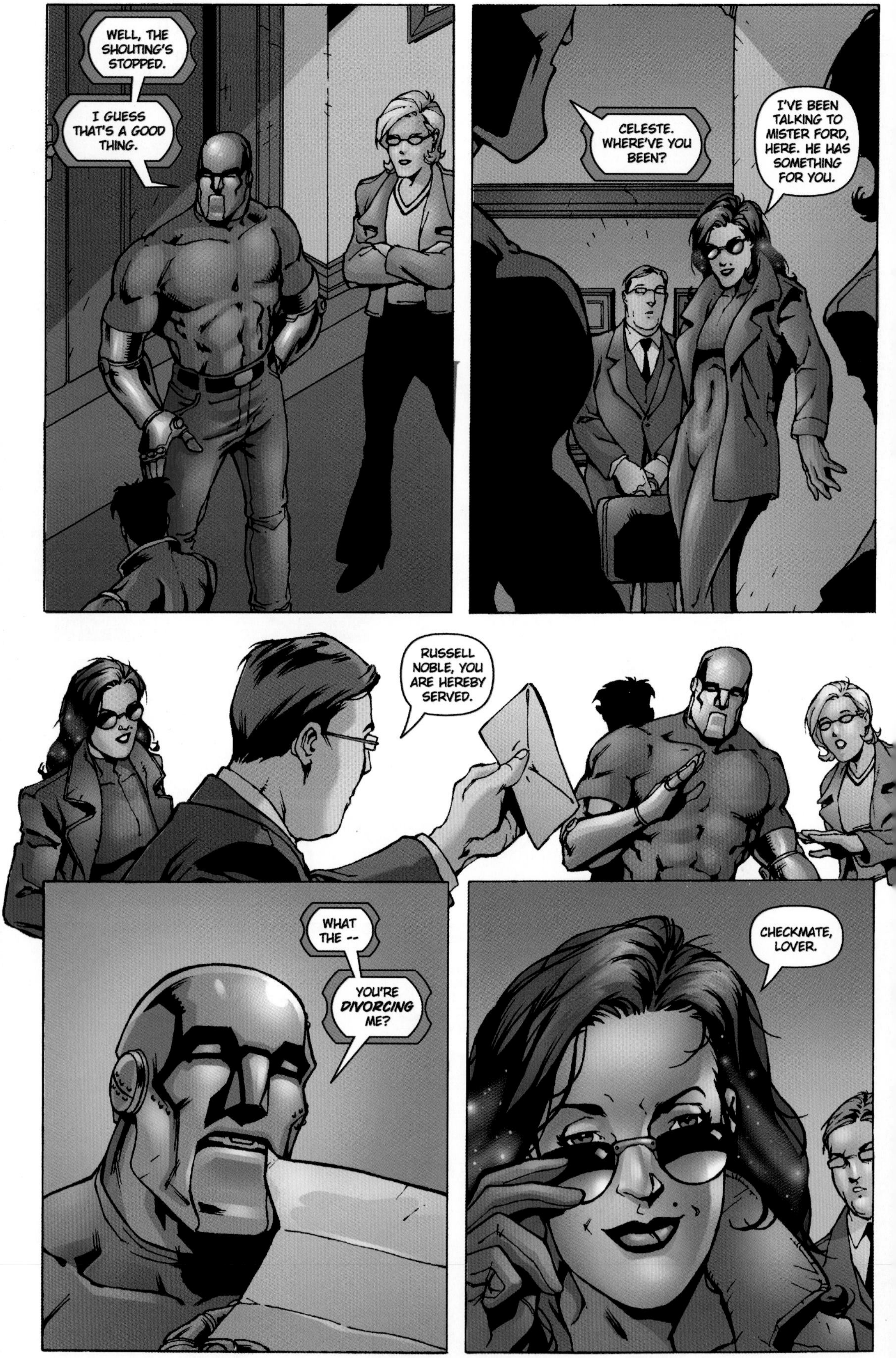
WELL, THE SHOUTING'S STOPPED.
I GUESS THAT'S A GOOD THING.
CELESTE. WHERE'VE YOU BEEN?
I'VE BEEN TALKING TO MISTER FORD, HERE. HE HAS SOMETHING FOR YOU.
RUSSELL NOBLE, YOU ARE HEREBY SERVED.
WHAT THE --
YOU'RE DIVORCING ME?
CHECKMATE, LOVER.

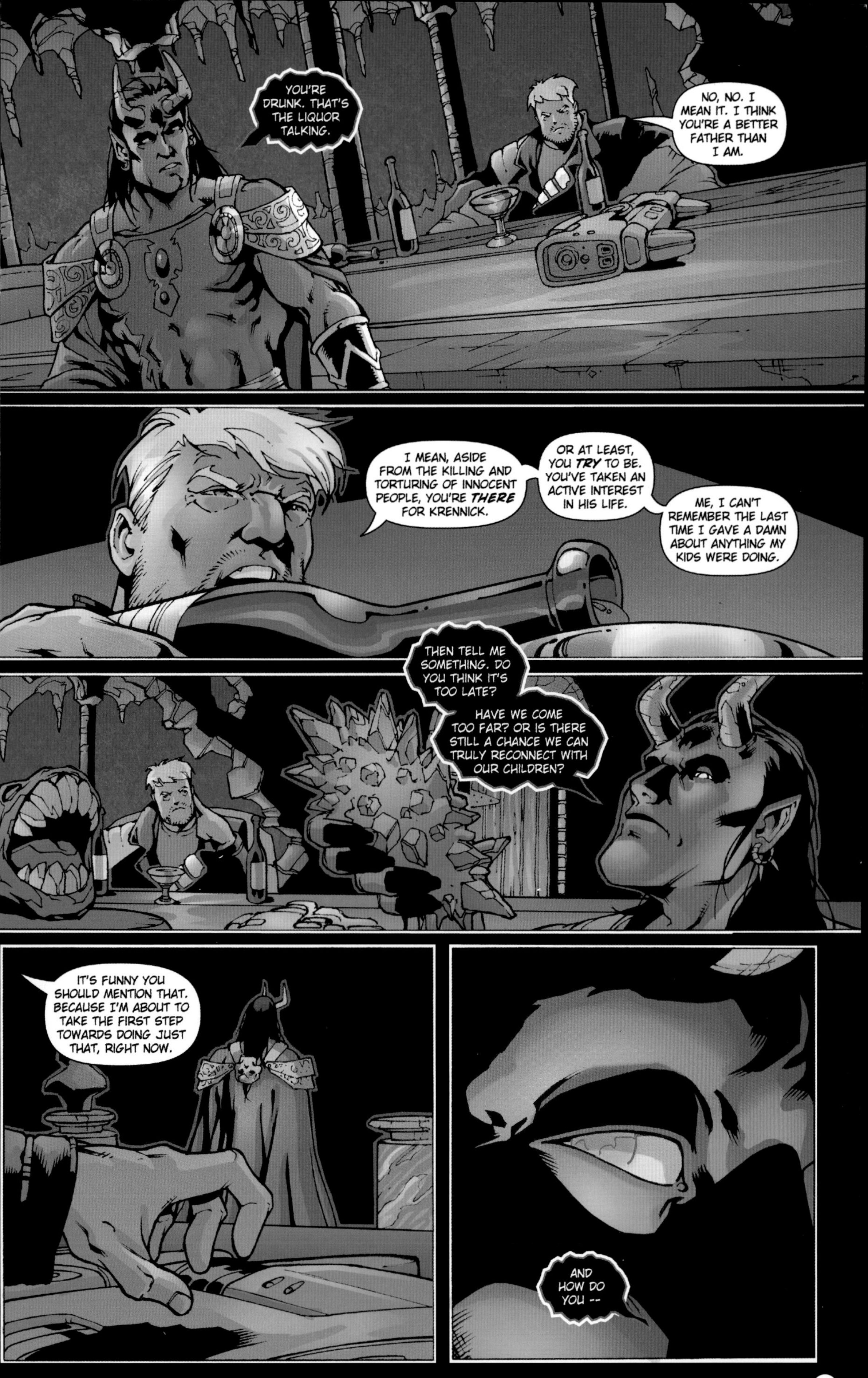
YOU'RE DRUNK. THAT'S THE LIQUOR TALKING.
NO, NO. I MEAN IT. I THINK YOU'RE A BETTER FATHER THAN I AM.
I MEAN, ASIDE FROM THE KILLING AND TORTURING OF INNOCENT PEOPLE, YOU'RE *THERE* FOR KRENNICK.
OR AT LEAST, YOU *TRY* TO BE. YOU'VE TAKEN AN ACTIVE INTEREST IN HIS LIFE.
ME, I CAN'T REMEMBER THE LAST TIME I GAVE A DAMN ABOUT ANYTHING MY KIDS WERE DOING.
THEN TELL ME SOMETHING. DO YOU THINK IT'S TOO LATE?
HAVE WE COME TOO FAR? OR IS THERE STILL A CHANCE WE CAN TRULY RECONNECT WITH OUR CHILDREN?
IT'S FUNNY YOU SHOULD MENTION THAT. BECAUSE I'M ABOUT TO TAKE THE FIRST STEP TOWARDS DOING JUST THAT, RIGHT NOW.
AND HOW DO YOU --

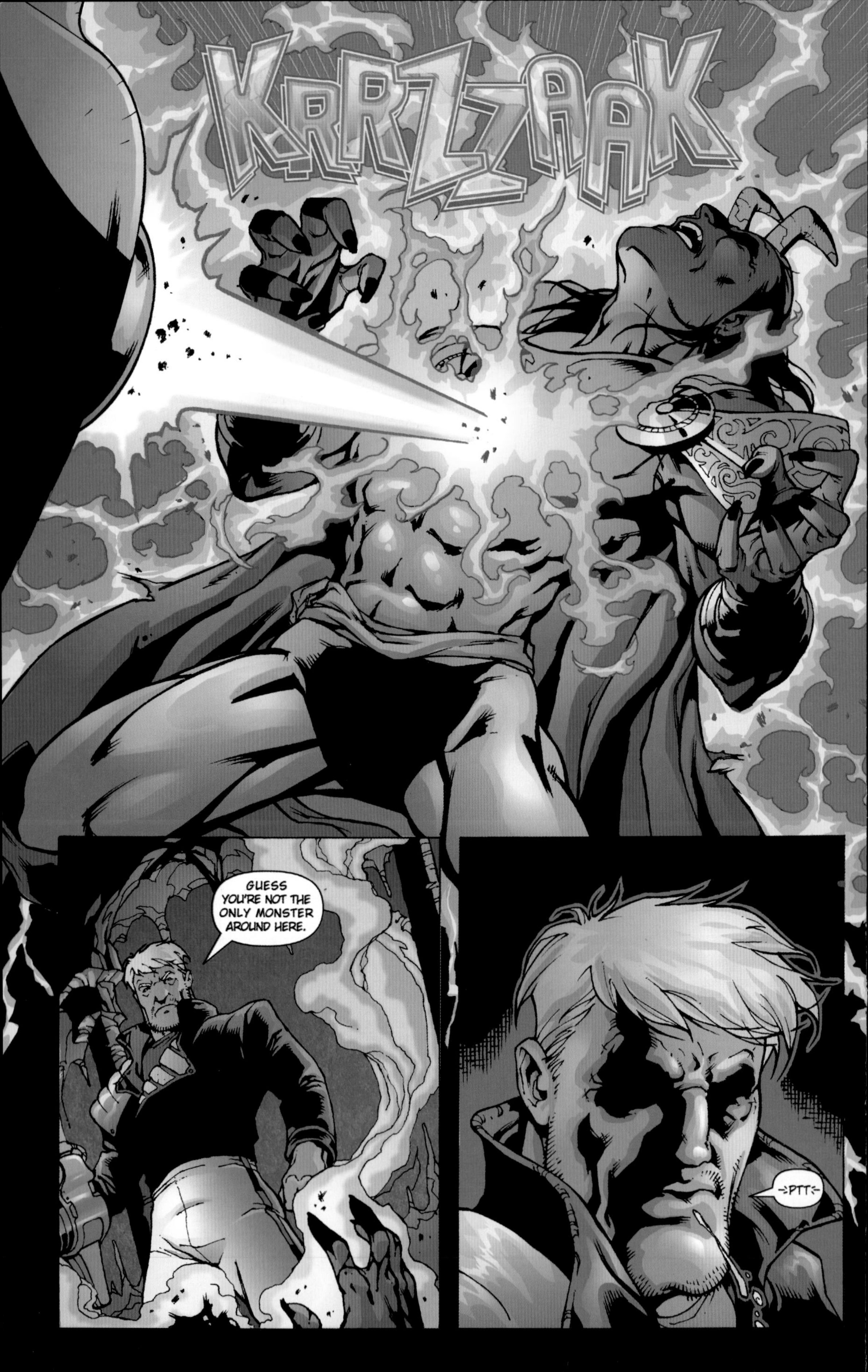
KRRZZAAK
GUESS YOU'RE NOT THE ONLY MONSTER AROUND HERE.
PTT

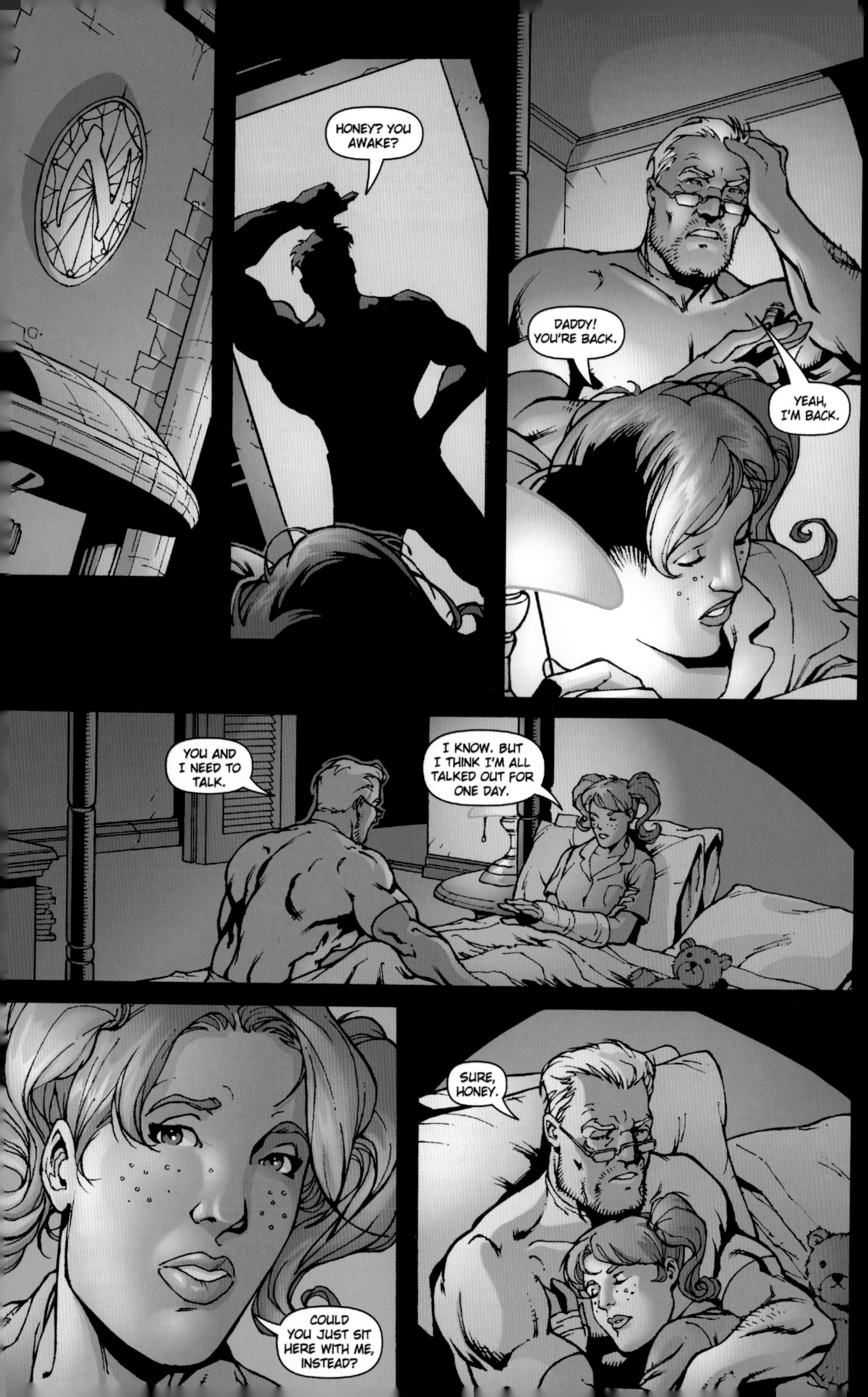

HONEY? YOU AWAKE?
DADDY! YOU'RE BACK.
YEAH, I'M BACK.
YOU AND I NEED TO TALK.
I KNOW. BUT I THINK I'M ALL TALKED OUT FOR ONE DAY.
COULD YOU JUST SIT HERE WITH ME, INSTEAD?
SURE, HONEY.

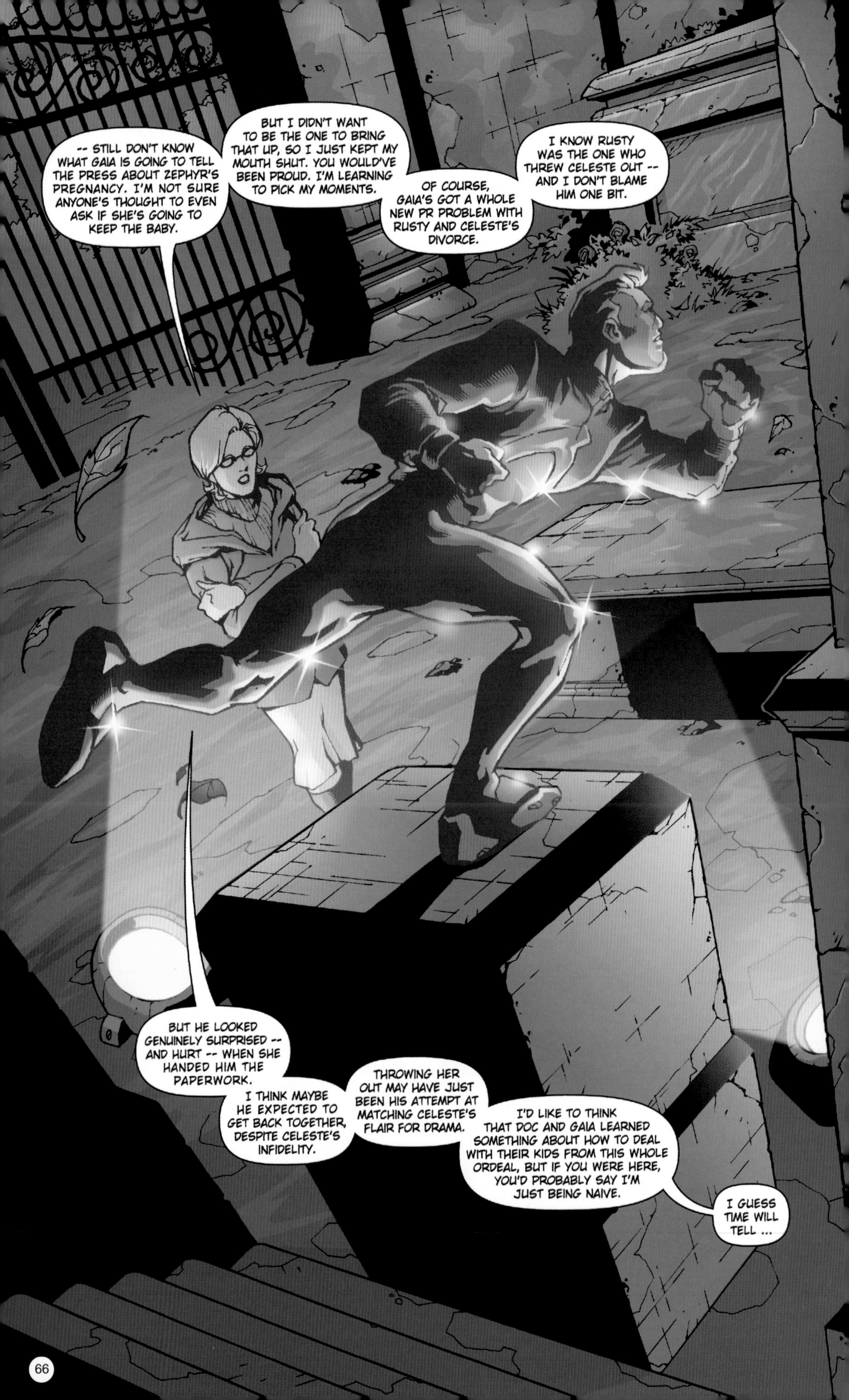
-- STILL DON'T KNOW WHAT GAIA IS GOING TO TELL THE PRESS ABOUT ZEPHYR'S PREGNANCY. I'M NOT SURE ANYONE'S THOUGHT TO EVEN ASK IF SHE'S GOING TO KEEP THE BABY.
BUT I DIDN'T WANT TO BE THE ONE TO BRING THAT UP, SO I JUST KEPT MY MOUTH SHUT. YOU WOULD'VE BEEN PROUD. I'M LEARNING TO PICK MY MOMENTS.
OF COURSE, GAIA'S GOT A WHOLE NEW PR PROBLEM WITH RUSTY AND CELESTE'S DIVORCE.
I KNOW RUSTY WAS THE ONE WHO THREW CELESTE OUT -- AND I DON'T BLAME HIM ONE BIT.
BUT HE LOOKED GENUINELY SURPRISED -- AND HURT -- WHEN SHE HANDED HIM THE PAPERWORK.
I THINK MAYBE HE EXPECTED TO GET BACK TOGETHER, DESPITE CELESTE'S INFIDELITY.
THROWING HER OUT MAY HAVE JUST BEEN HIS ATTEMPT AT MATCHING CELESTE'S FLAIR FOR DRAMA.
I'D LIKE TO THINK THAT DOC AND GAIA LEARNED SOMETHING ABOUT HOW TO DEAL WITH THEIR KIDS FROM THIS WHOLE ORDEAL, BUT IF YOU WERE HERE, YOU'D PROBABLY SAY I'M JUST BEING NAIVE.
I GUESS TIME WILL TELL ...

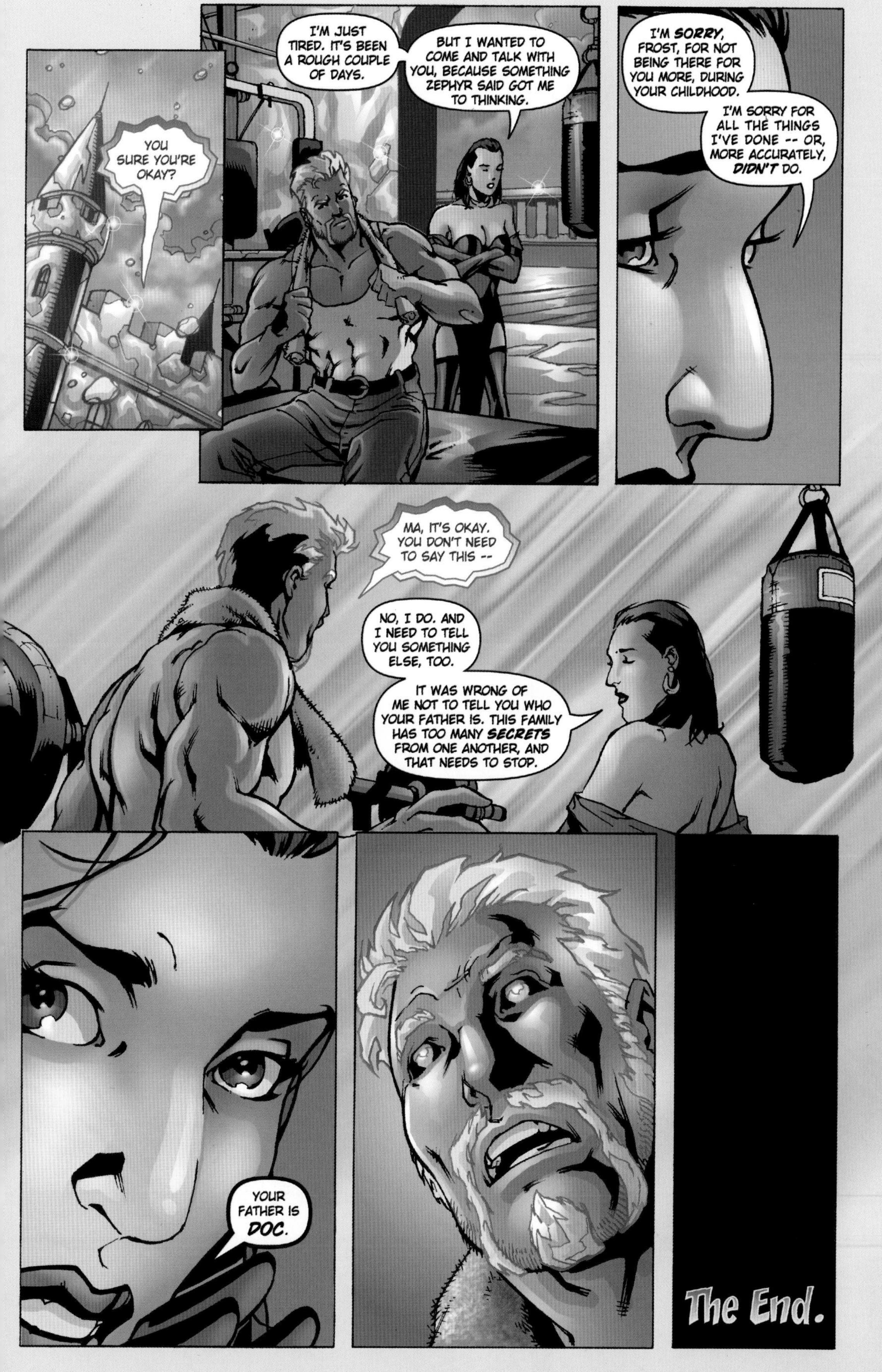
YOU SURE YOU'RE OKAY?
I'M JUST TIRED. IT'S BEEN A ROUGH COUPLE OF DAYS.
BUT I WANTED TO COME AND TALK WITH YOU, BECAUSE SOMETHING ZEPHYR SAID GOT ME TO THINKING.
I'M SORRY, FROST, FOR NOT BEING THERE FOR YOU MORE, DURING YOUR CHILDHOOD.
I'M SORRY FOR ALL THE THINGS I'VE DONE -- OR, MORE ACCURATELY, DIDN'T DO.
MA, IT'S OKAY. YOU DON'T NEED TO SAY THIS --
NO, I DO. AND I NEED TO TELL YOU SOMETHING ELSE, TOO.
IT WAS WRONG OF ME NOT TO TELL YOU WHO YOUR FATHER IS. THIS FAMILY HAS TOO MANY SECRETS FROM ONE ANOTHER, AND THAT NEEDS TO STOP.
YOUR FATHER IS DOC.
The End.

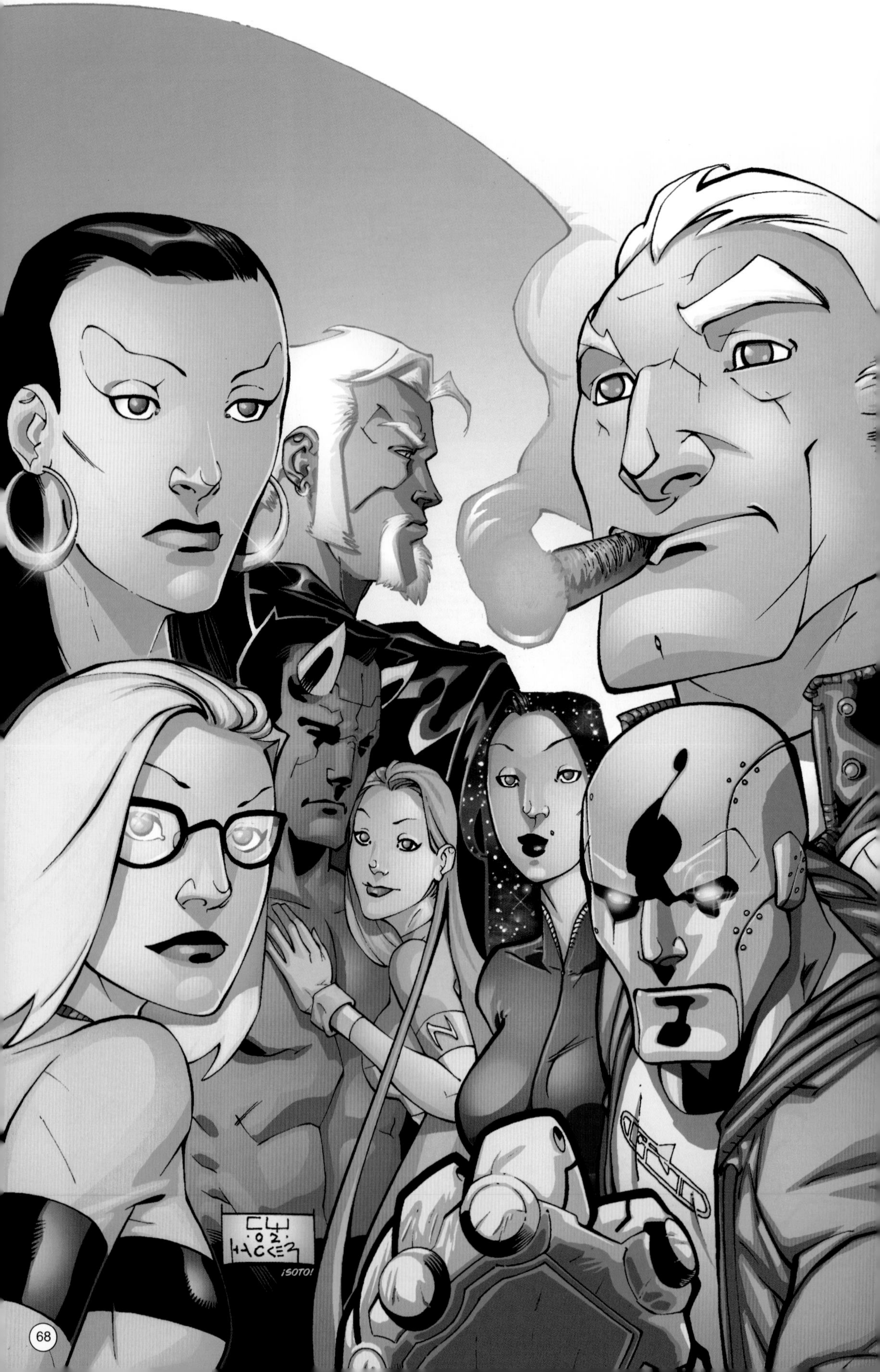
CW ·02· HACKER
¡SOTO!

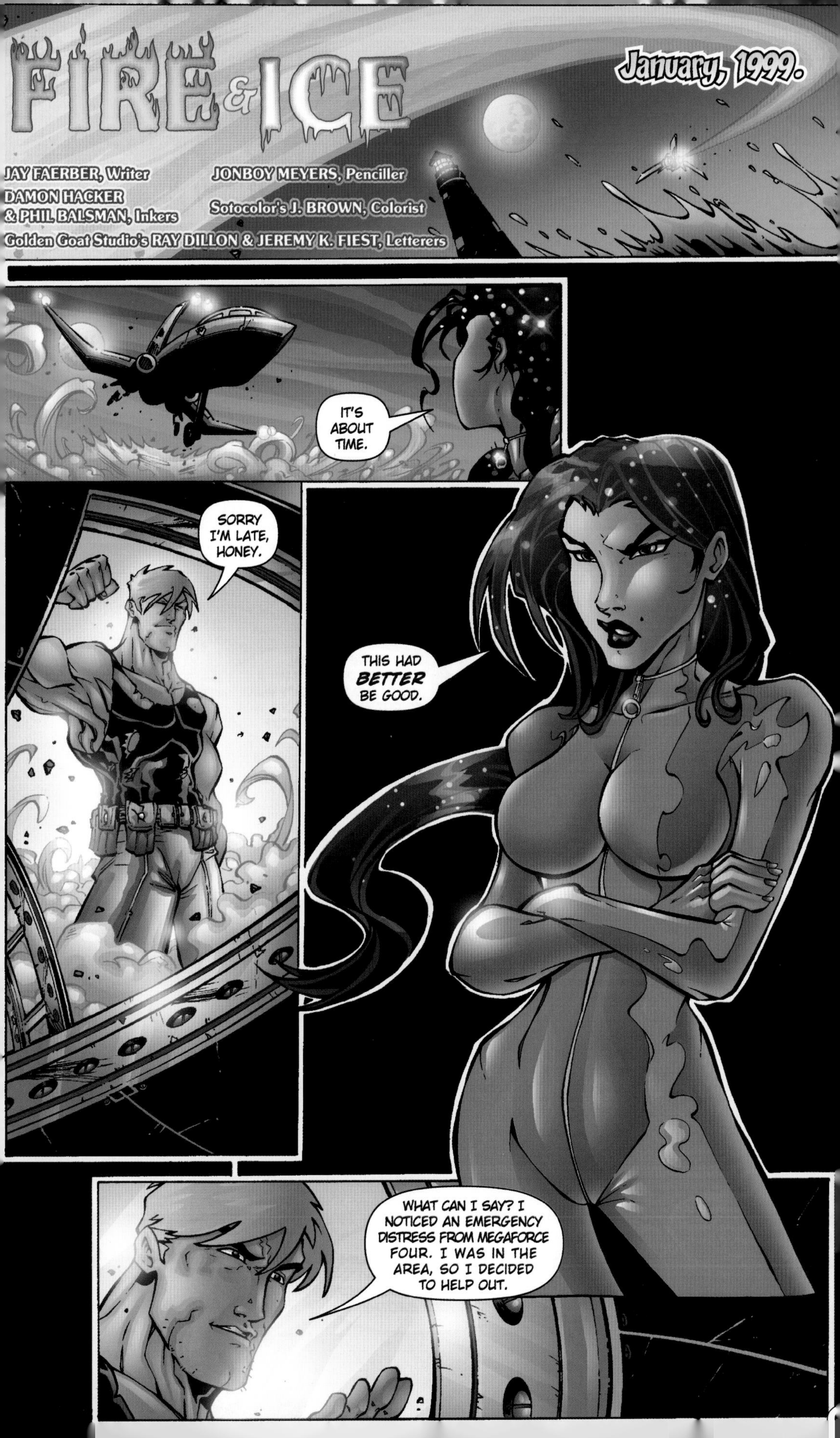
FIRE & ICE
January, 1999.
JAY FAERBER, Writer
JONBOY MEYERS, Penciller
DAMON HACKER
& PHIL BALSMAN, Inkers
Sotocolor's J. BROWN, Colorist
Golden Goat Studio's RAY DILLON & JEREMY K. FIEST, Letterers
IT'S ABOUT TIME.
SORRY I'M LATE, HONEY.
THIS HAD BETTER BE GOOD.
WHAT CAN I SAY? I NOTICED AN EMERGENCY DISTRESS FROM MEGAFORCE FOUR. I WAS IN THE AREA, SO I DECIDED TO HELP OUT.

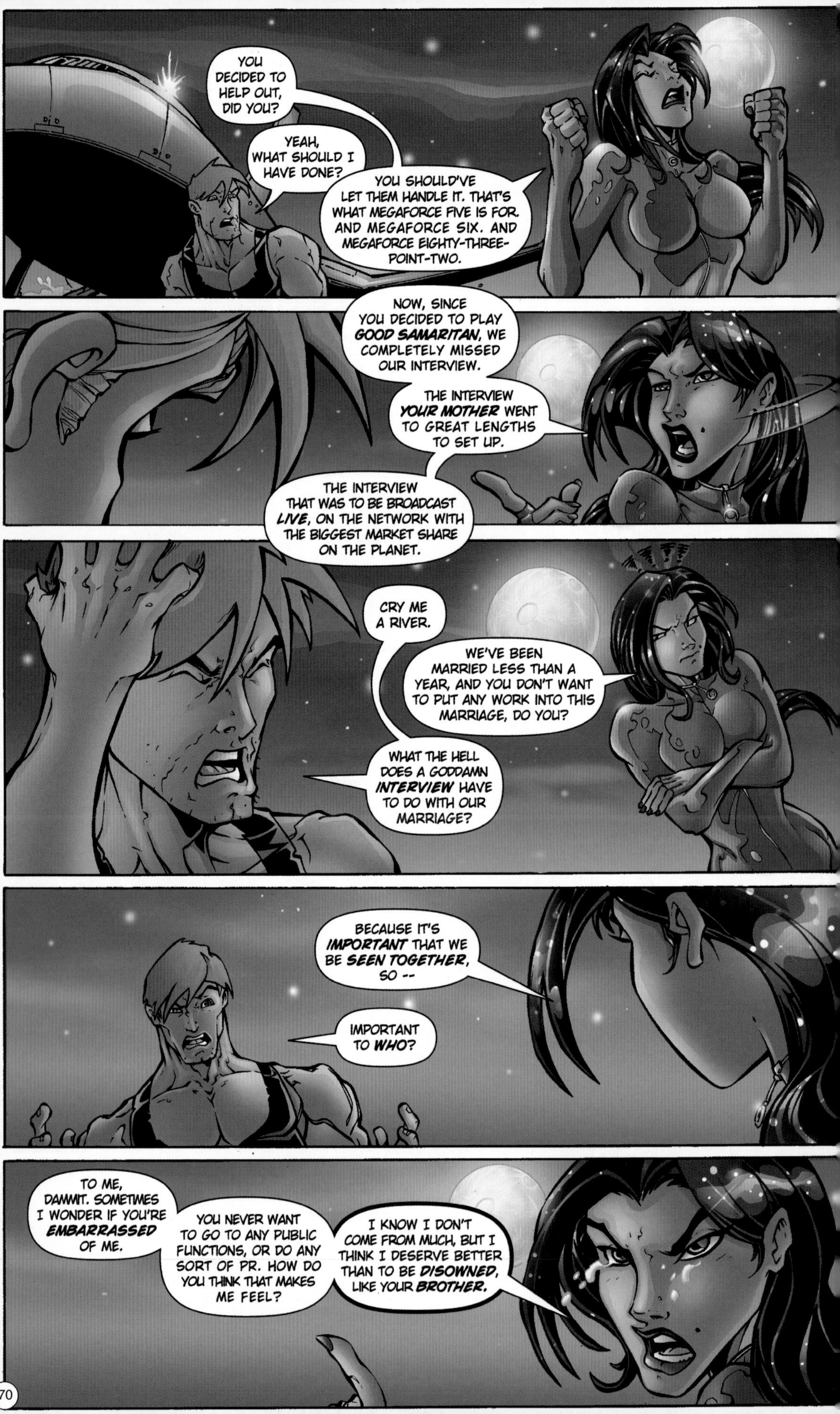
YOU DECIDED TO HELP OUT, DID YOU?
YEAH, WHAT SHOULD I HAVE DONE?
YOU SHOULD'VE LET THEM HANDLE IT. THAT'S WHAT MEGAFORCE FIVE IS FOR. AND MEGAFORCE SIX. AND MEGAFORCE EIGHTY-THREE-POINT-TWO.
NOW, SINCE YOU DECIDED TO PLAY GOOD SAMARITAN, WE COMPLETELY MISSED OUR INTERVIEW.
THE INTERVIEW YOUR MOTHER WENT TO GREAT LENGTHS TO SET UP.
THE INTERVIEW THAT WAS TO BE BROADCAST LIVE, ON THE NETWORK WITH THE BIGGEST MARKET SHARE ON THE PLANET.
CRY ME A RIVER.
WE'VE BEEN MARRIED LESS THAN A YEAR, AND YOU DON'T WANT TO PUT ANY WORK INTO THIS MARRIAGE, DO YOU?
WHAT THE HELL DOES A GODDAMN INTERVIEW HAVE TO DO WITH OUR MARRIAGE?
BECAUSE IT'S IMPORTANT THAT WE BE SEEN TOGETHER, SO --
IMPORTANT TO WHO?
TO ME, DAMMIT. SOMETIMES I WONDER IF YOU'RE EMBARRASSED OF ME.
YOU NEVER WANT TO GO TO ANY PUBLIC FUNCTIONS, OR DO ANY SORT OF PR. HOW DO YOU THINK THAT MAKES ME FEEL?
I KNOW I DON'T COME FROM MUCH, BUT I THINK I DESERVE BETTER THAN TO BE DISOWNED, LIKE YOUR BROTHER.

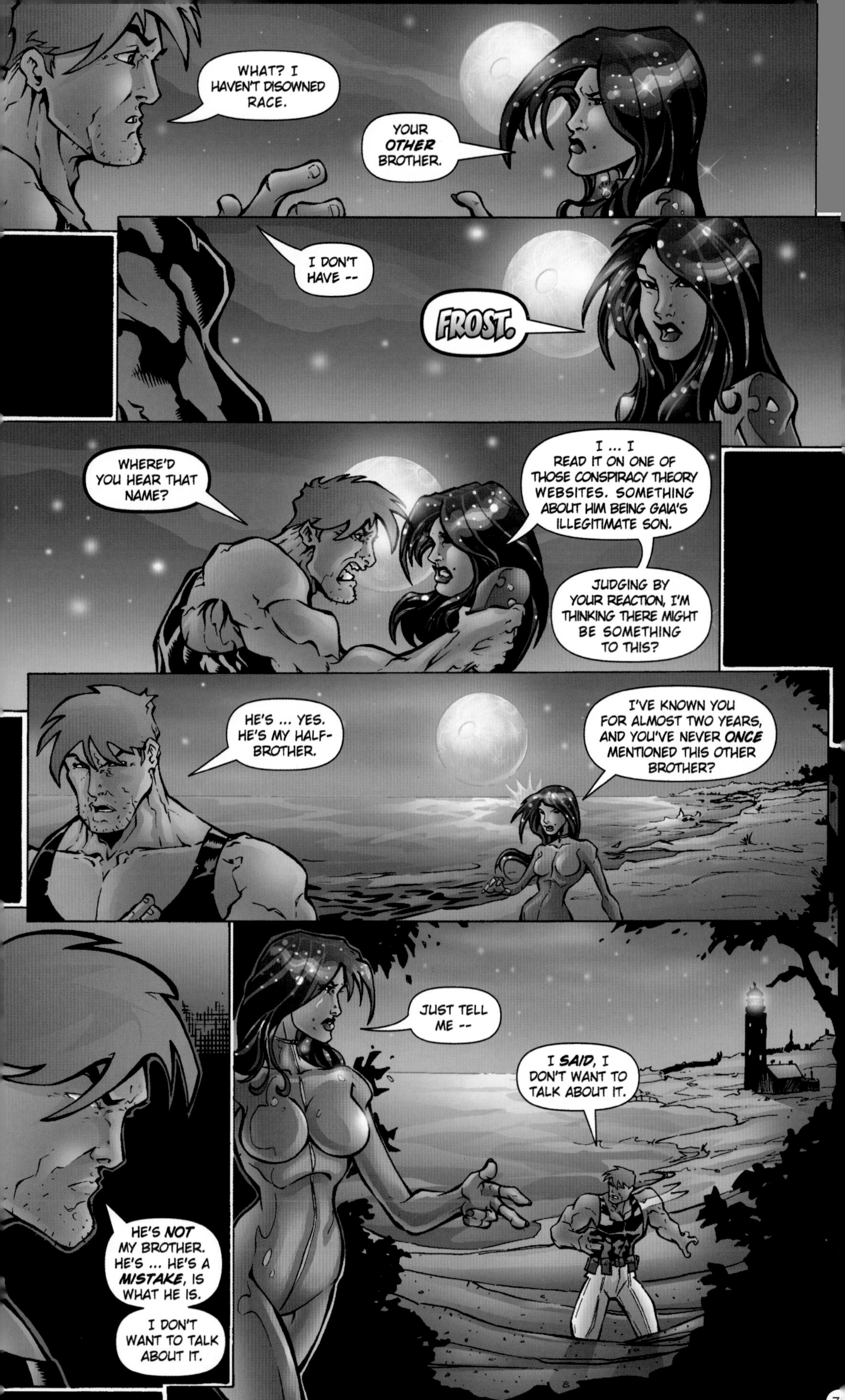

WHAT? I HAVEN'T DISOWNED RACE.
YOUR OTHER BROTHER.
I DON'T HAVE --
FROST.
WHERE'D YOU HEAR THAT NAME?
I ... I READ IT ON ONE OF THOSE CONSPIRACY THEORY WEBSITES. SOMETHING ABOUT HIM BEING GAIA'S ILLEGITIMATE SON.
JUDGING BY YOUR REACTION, I'M THINKING THERE MIGHT BE SOMETHING TO THIS?
HE'S ... YES. HE'S MY HALF-BROTHER.
I'VE KNOWN YOU FOR ALMOST TWO YEARS, AND YOU'VE NEVER ONCE MENTIONED THIS OTHER BROTHER?
HE'S NOT MY BROTHER. HE'S ... HE'S A MISTAKE, IS WHAT HE IS.
I DON'T WANT TO TALK ABOUT IT.
JUST TELL ME --
I SAID, I DON'T WANT TO TALK ABOUT IT.

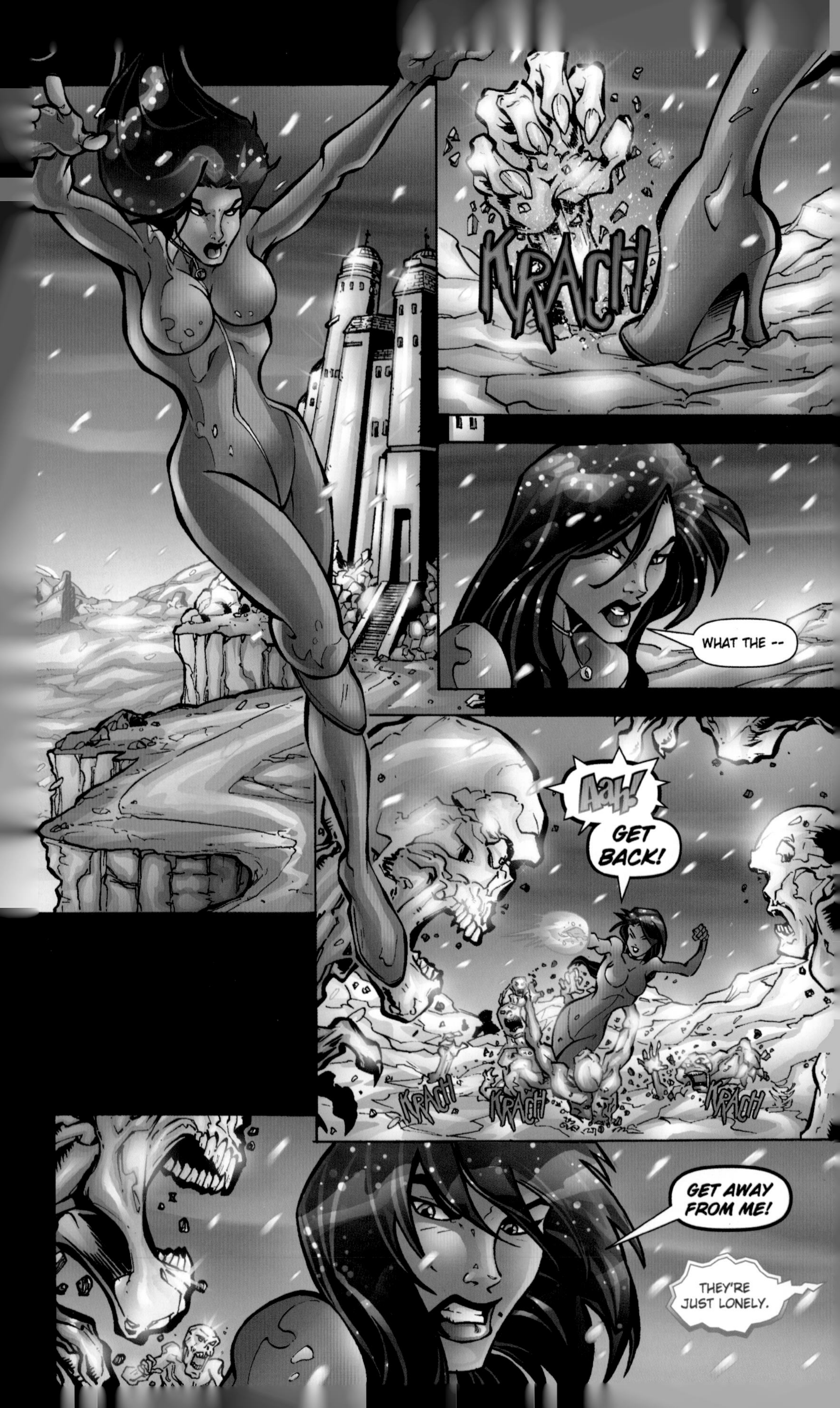
KRACH
WHAT THE --
AAH!
GET BACK!
KRACH
KRACH
KRACH
GET AWAY FROM ME!
THEY'RE JUST LONELY.

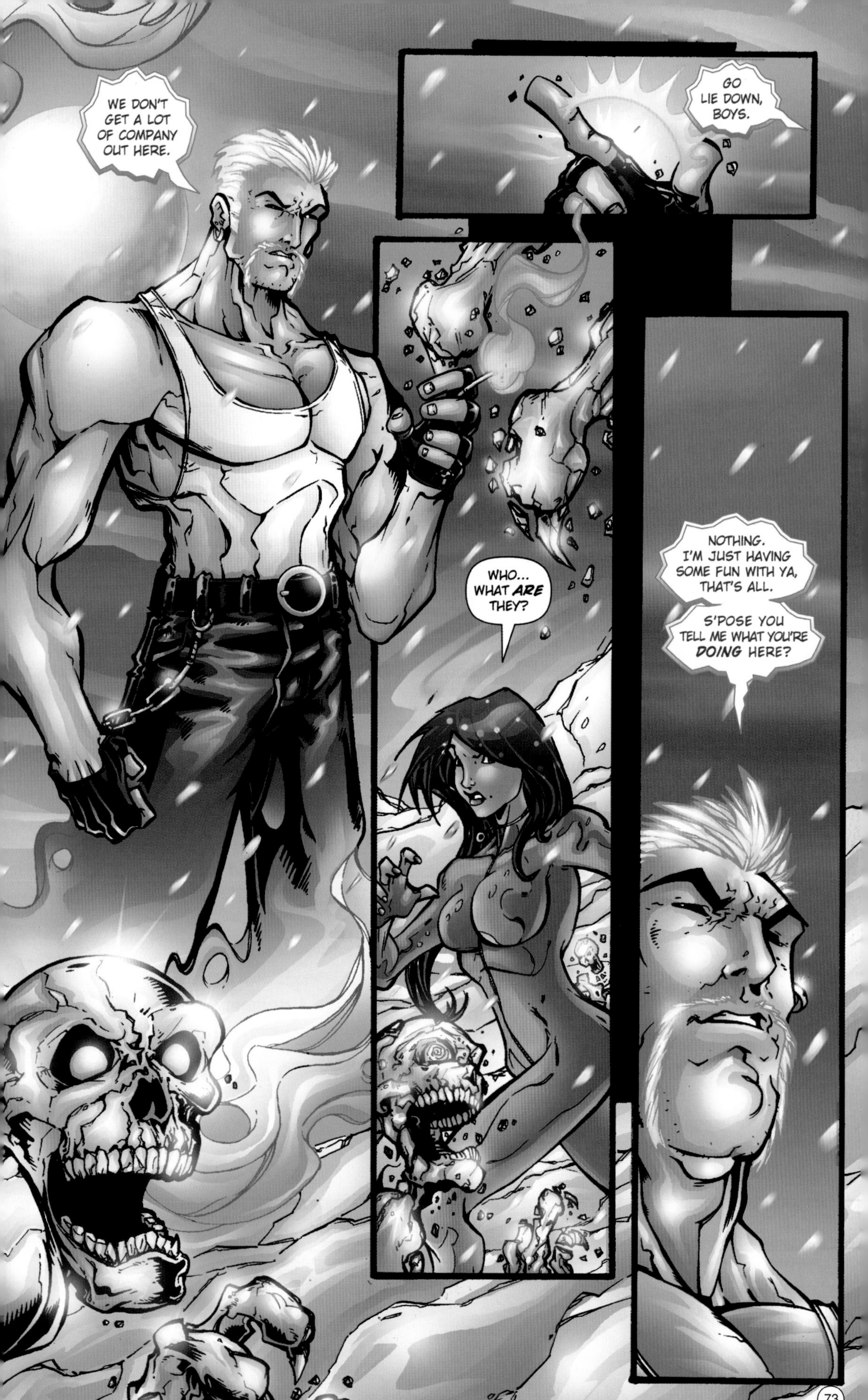
WE DON'T GET A LOT OF COMPANY OUT HERE.
GO LIE DOWN, BOYS.
WHO... WHAT **ARE** THEY?
NOTHING. I'M JUST HAVING SOME FUN WITH YA, THAT'S ALL.
S'POSE YOU TELL ME WHAT YOU'RE **DOING** HERE?

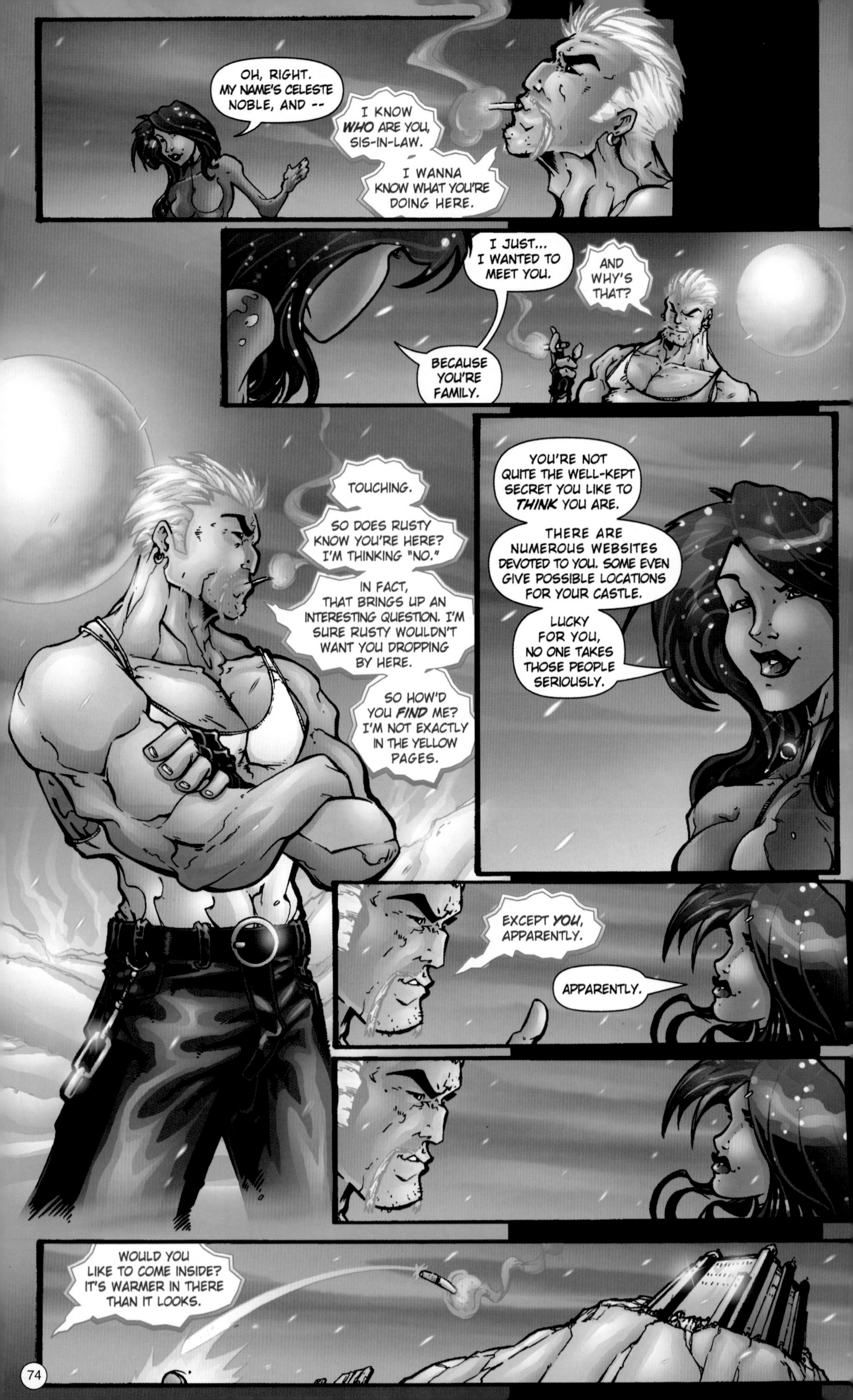
OH, RIGHT. MY NAME'S CELESTE NOBLE, AND --
I KNOW *WHO* ARE YOU, SIS-IN-LAW.
I WANNA KNOW WHAT YOU'RE DOING HERE.
I JUST... I WANTED TO MEET YOU.
AND WHY'S THAT?
BECAUSE YOU'RE FAMILY.
TOUCHING.
SO DOES RUSTY KNOW YOU'RE HERE? I'M THINKING "NO."
IN FACT, THAT BRINGS UP AN INTERESTING QUESTION. I'M SURE RUSTY WOULDN'T WANT YOU DROPPING BY HERE.
SO HOW'D YOU *FIND* ME? I'M NOT EXACTLY IN THE YELLOW PAGES.
YOU'RE NOT QUITE THE WELL-KEPT SECRET YOU LIKE TO *THINK* YOU ARE.
THERE ARE NUMEROUS WEBSITES DEVOTED TO YOU. SOME EVEN GIVE POSSIBLE LOCATIONS FOR YOUR CASTLE.
LUCKY FOR YOU, NO ONE TAKES THOSE PEOPLE SERIOUSLY.
EXCEPT *YOU*, APPARENTLY.
APPARENTLY.
WOULD YOU LIKE TO COME INSIDE? IT'S WARMER IN THERE THAN IT LOOKS.

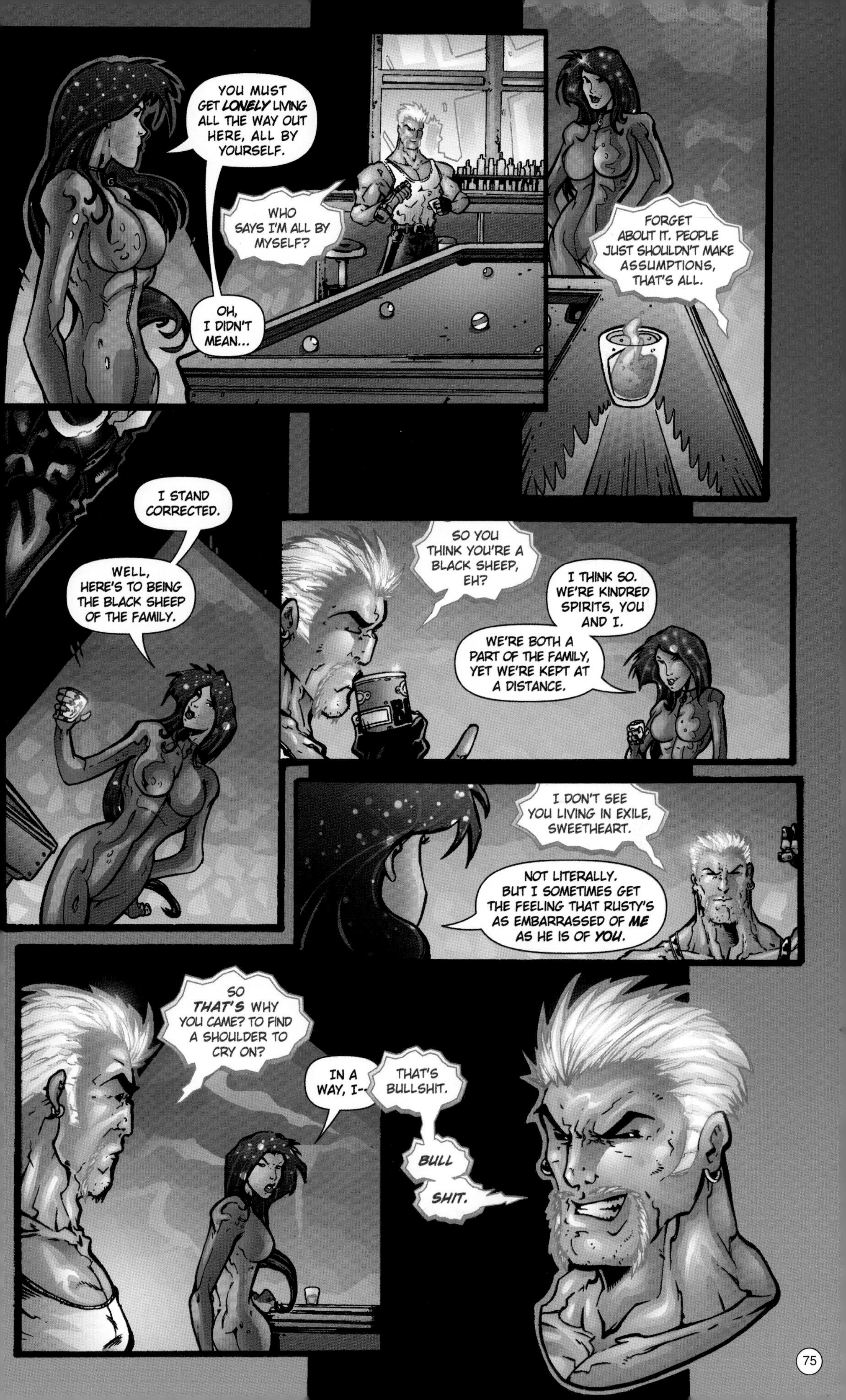
YOU MUST GET LONELY LIVING ALL THE WAY OUT HERE, ALL BY YOURSELF.
WHO SAYS I'M ALL BY MYSELF?
OH, I DIDN'T MEAN...
FORGET ABOUT IT. PEOPLE JUST SHOULDN'T MAKE ASSUMPTIONS, THAT'S ALL.
I STAND CORRECTED.
WELL, HERE'S TO BEING THE BLACK SHEEP OF THE FAMILY.
SO YOU THINK YOU'RE A BLACK SHEEP, EH?
I THINK SO. WE'RE KINDRED SPIRITS, YOU AND I.
WE'RE BOTH A PART OF THE FAMILY, YET WE'RE KEPT AT A DISTANCE.
I DON'T SEE YOU LIVING IN EXILE, SWEETHEART.
NOT LITERALLY. BUT I SOMETIMES GET THE FEELING THAT RUSTY'S AS EMBARRASSED OF ME AS HE IS OF YOU.
SO THAT'S WHY YOU CAME? TO FIND A SHOULDER TO CRY ON?
IN A WAY, I--
THAT'S BULLSHIT.
BULL
SHIT.

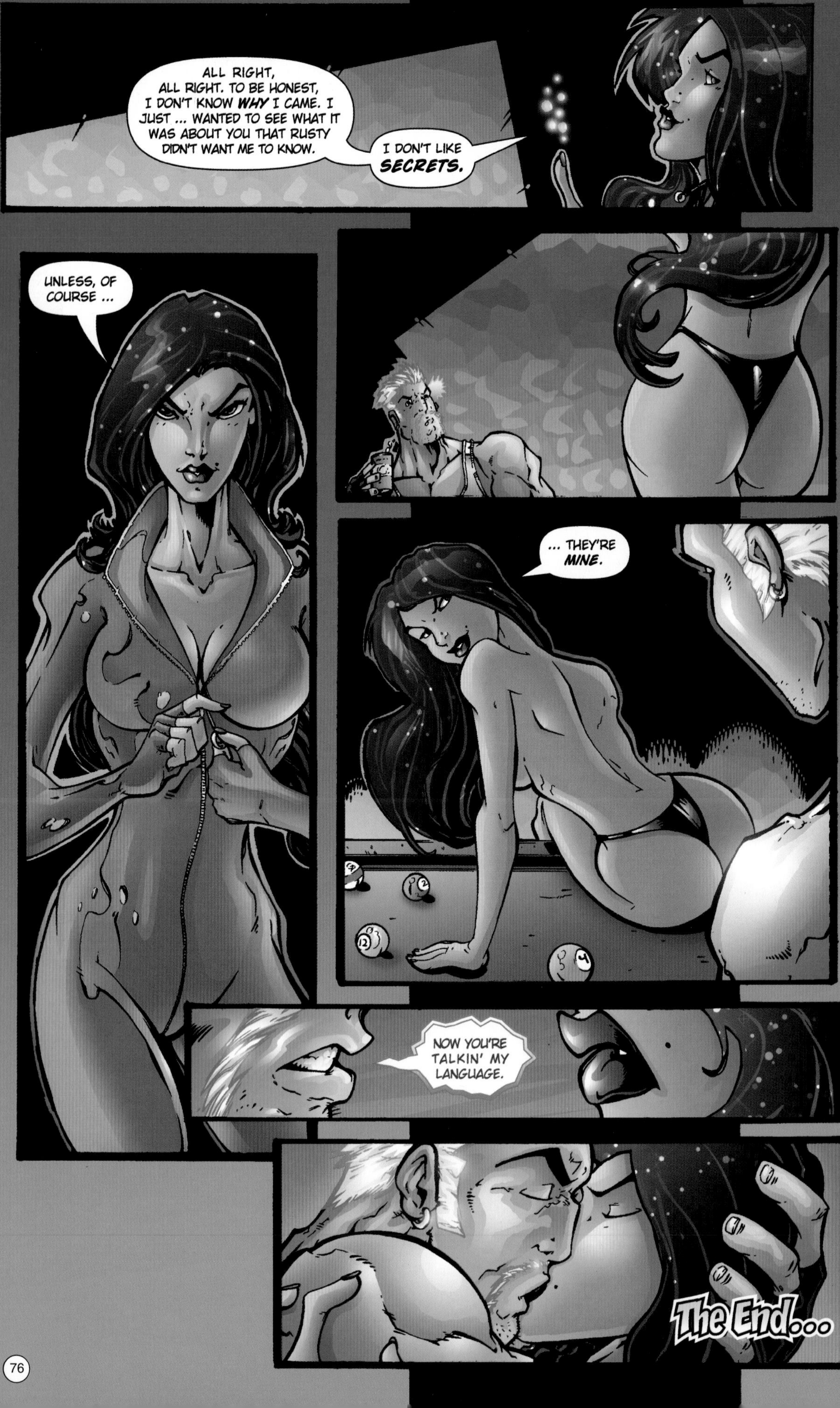
ALL RIGHT, ALL RIGHT. TO BE HONEST, I DON'T KNOW WHY I CAME. I JUST ... WANTED TO SEE WHAT IT WAS ABOUT YOU THAT RUSTY DIDN'T WANT ME TO KNOW.
I DON'T LIKE SECRETS.
UNLESS, OF COURSE ...
... THEY'RE MINE.
NOW YOU'RE TALKIN' MY LANGUAGE.
The End...

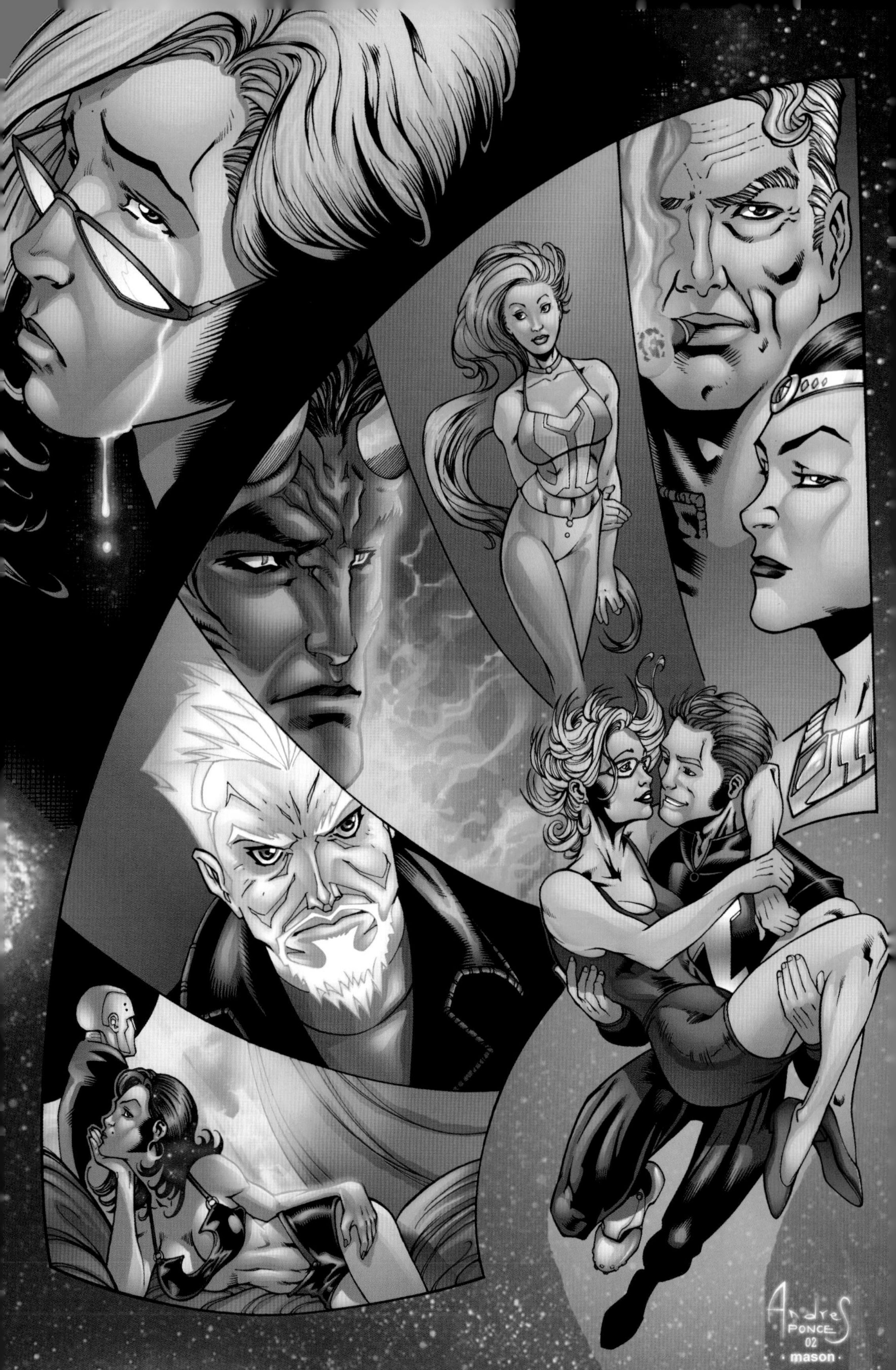
Andres
PONCE
02
mason

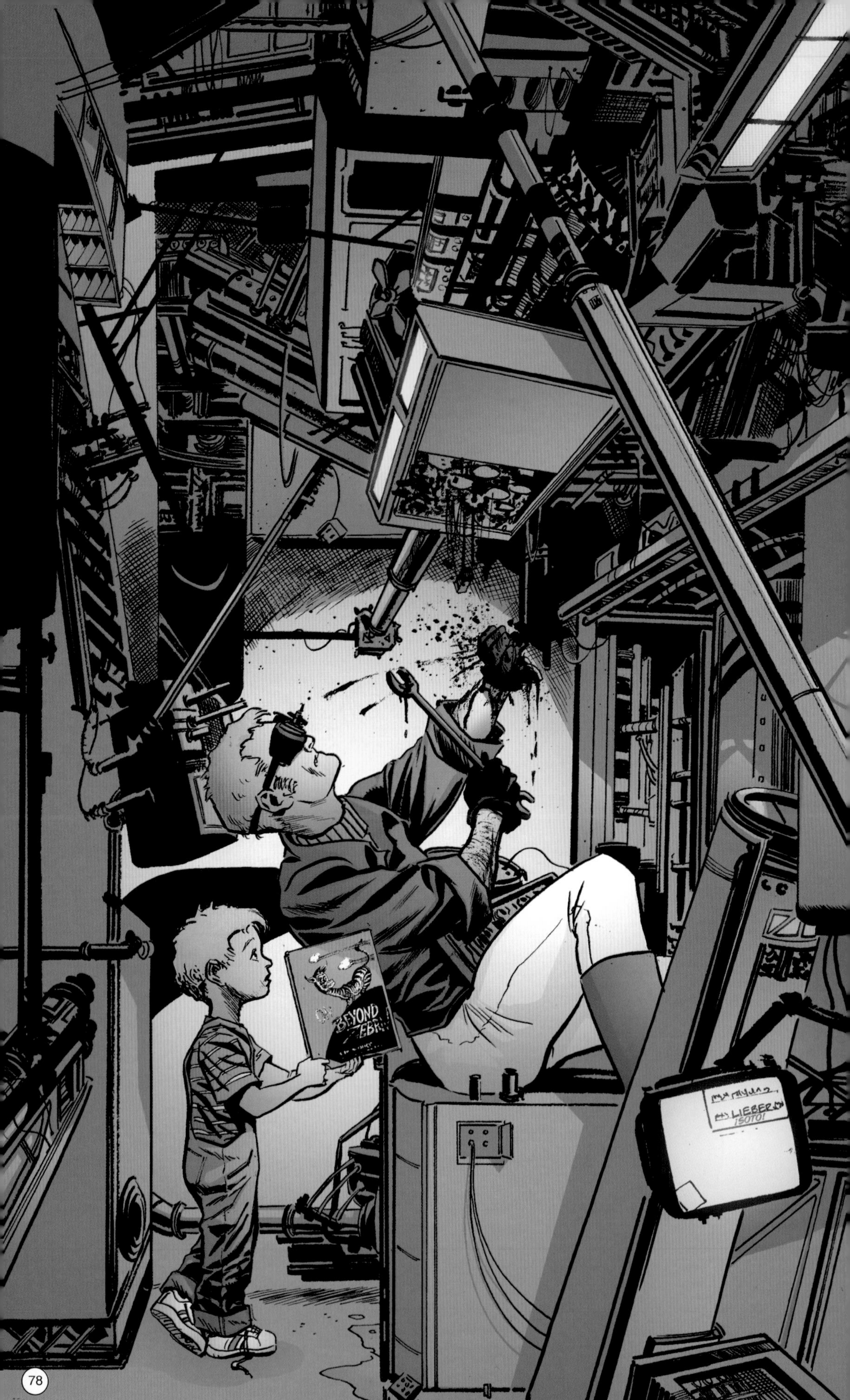
BEYOND
LIEBER
¡SOTO!

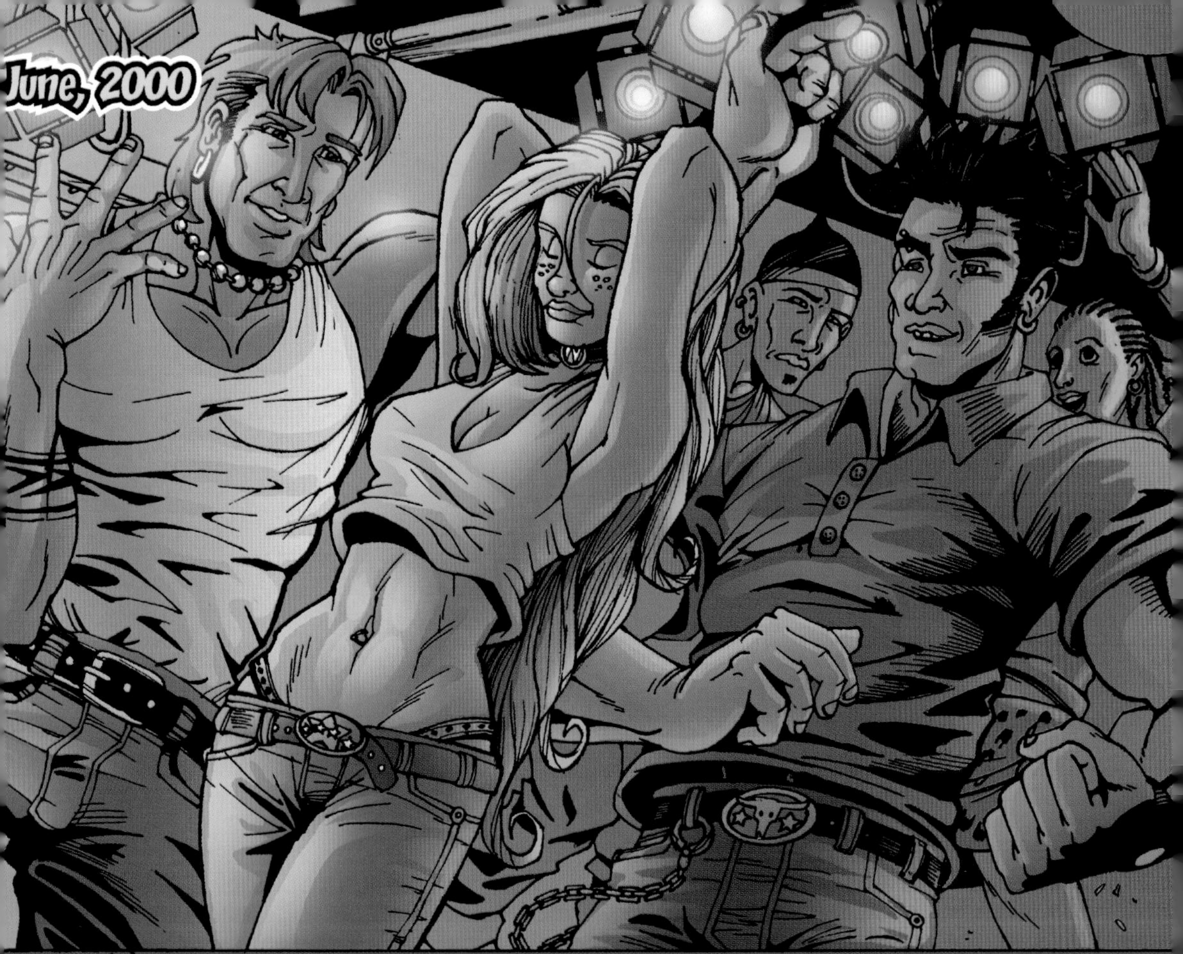
June, 2000

Unrequited

JAY FAERBER Writer
MATT WENDT Penciller
ED HERRERA Inker
J. BROWN Colorist
Sotocolor Graphics
RAY DILLON Letterer
Golden Goat Studios

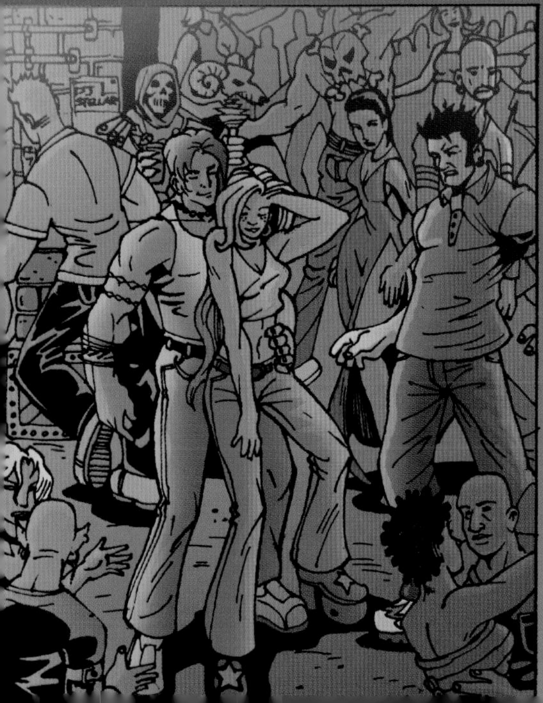

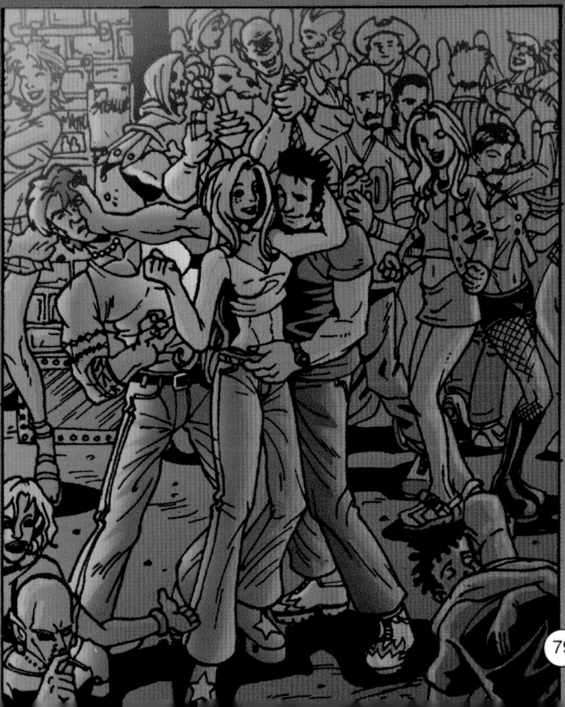

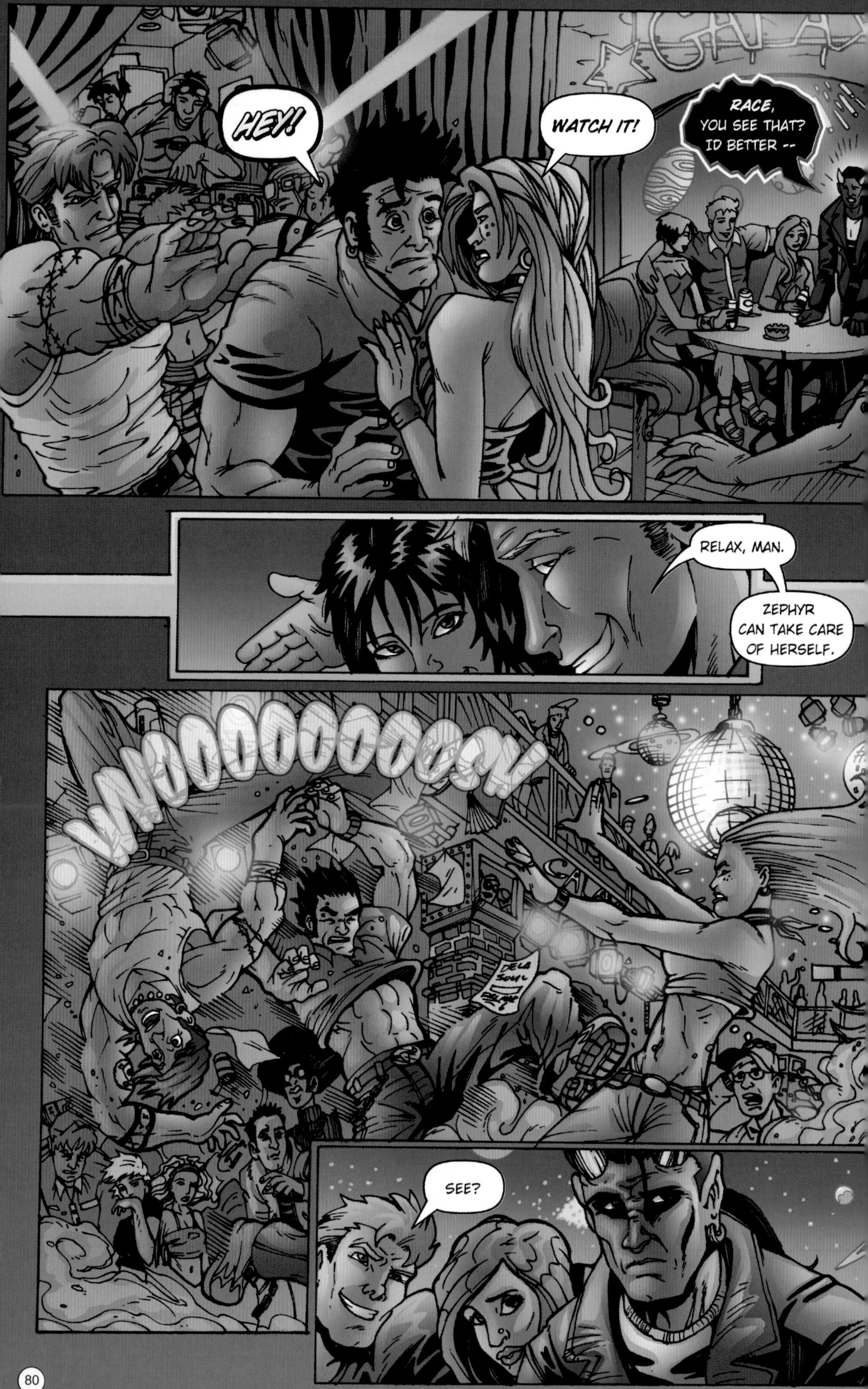
HEY!
WATCH IT!
RACE, YOU SEE THAT? ID BETTER --
RELAX, MAN.
ZEPHYR CAN TAKE CARE OF HERSELF.
WHOOOOOOOOOSH!
SEE?

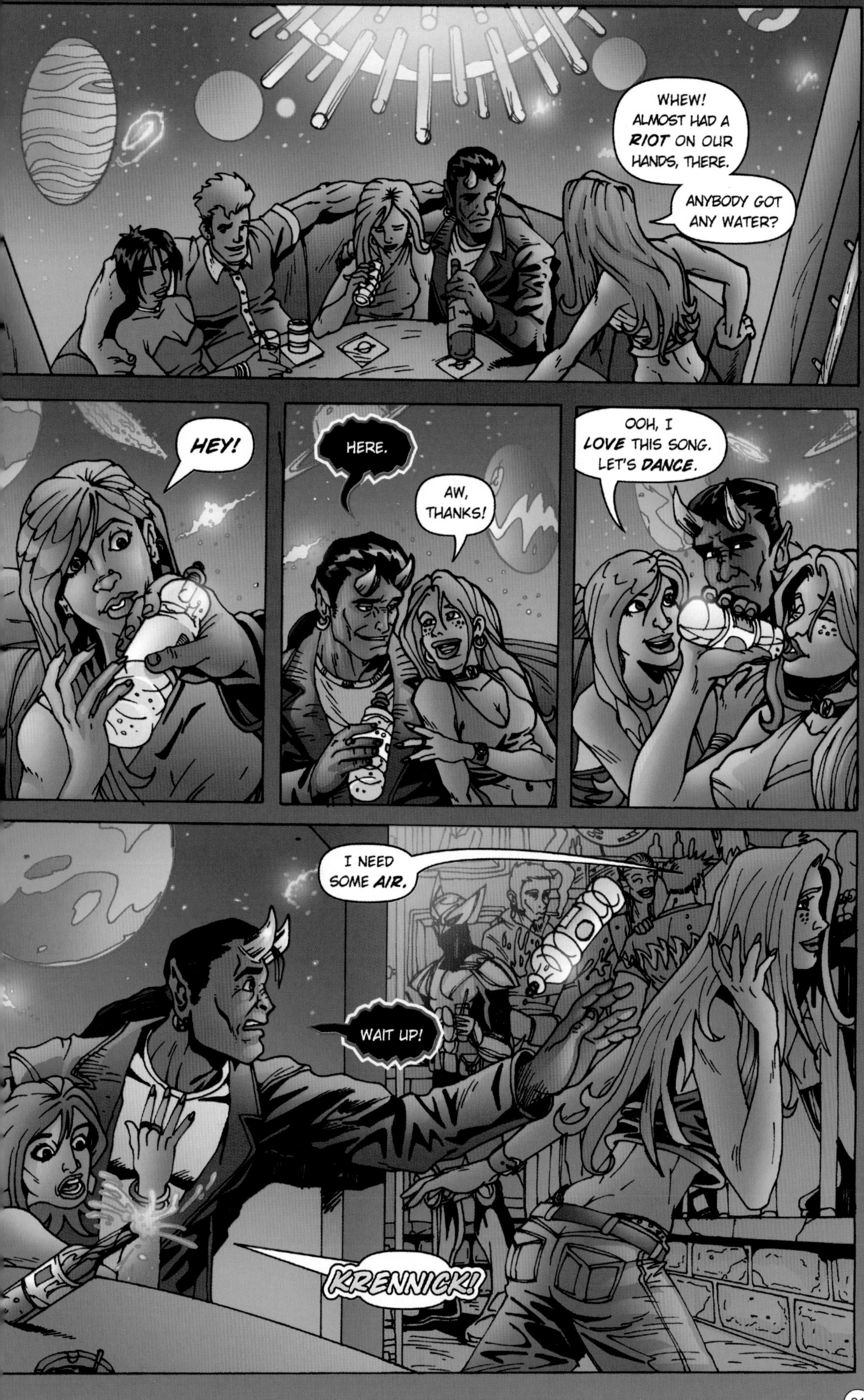
WHEW! ALMOST HAD A RIOT ON OUR HANDS, THERE.
ANYBODY GOT ANY WATER?
HEY!
HERE.
AW, THANKS!
OOH, I LOVE THIS SONG. LET'S DANCE.
I NEED SOME AIR.
WAIT UP!
KRENNICK!

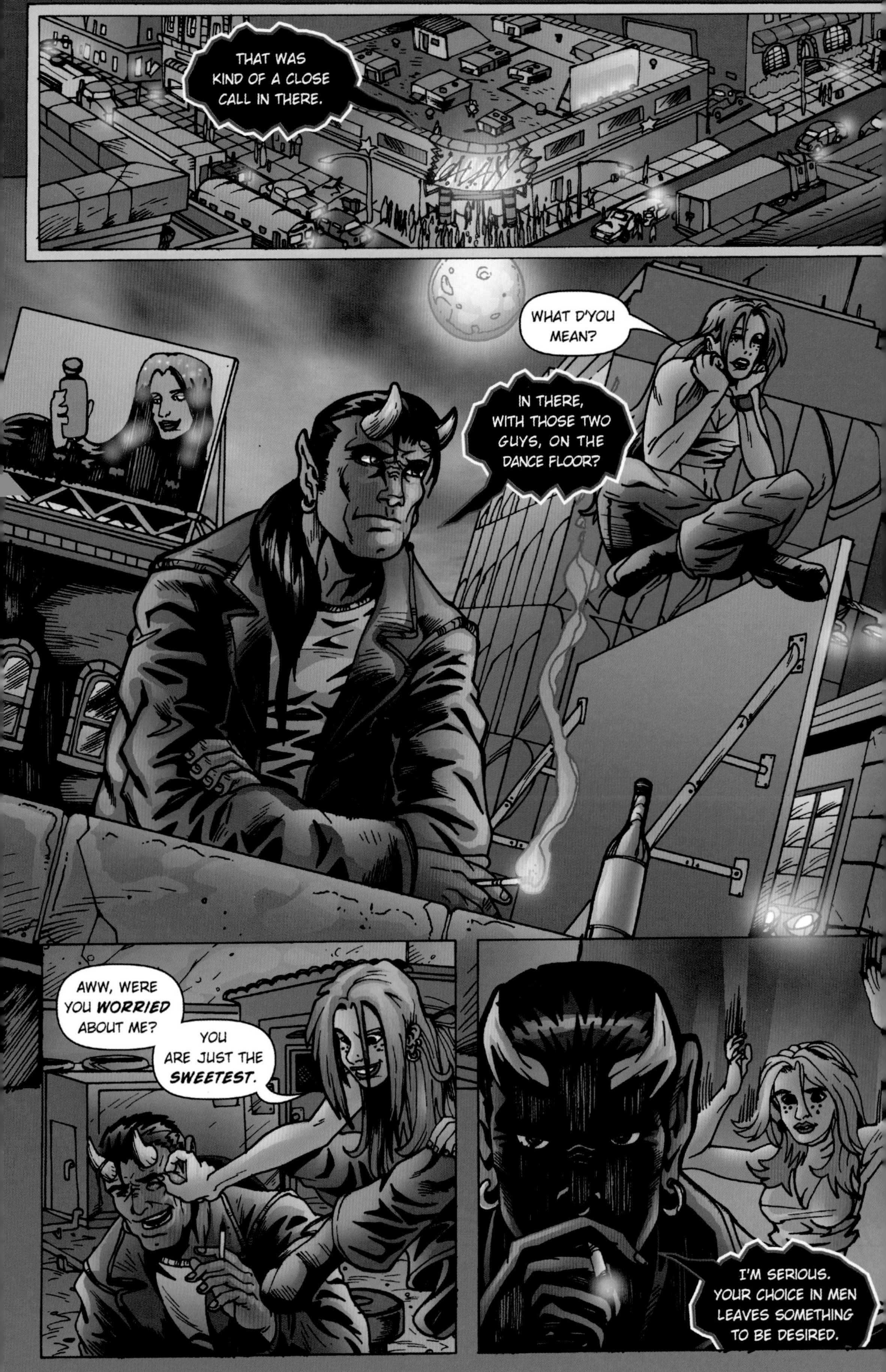
THAT WAS KIND OF A CLOSE CALL IN THERE.
WHAT D'YOU MEAN?
IN THERE, WITH THOSE TWO GUYS, ON THE DANCE FLOOR?
AWW, WERE YOU **WORRIED** ABOUT ME?
YOU ARE JUST THE **SWEETEST**.
I'M SERIOUS. YOUR CHOICE IN MEN LEAVES SOMETHING TO BE DESIRED.

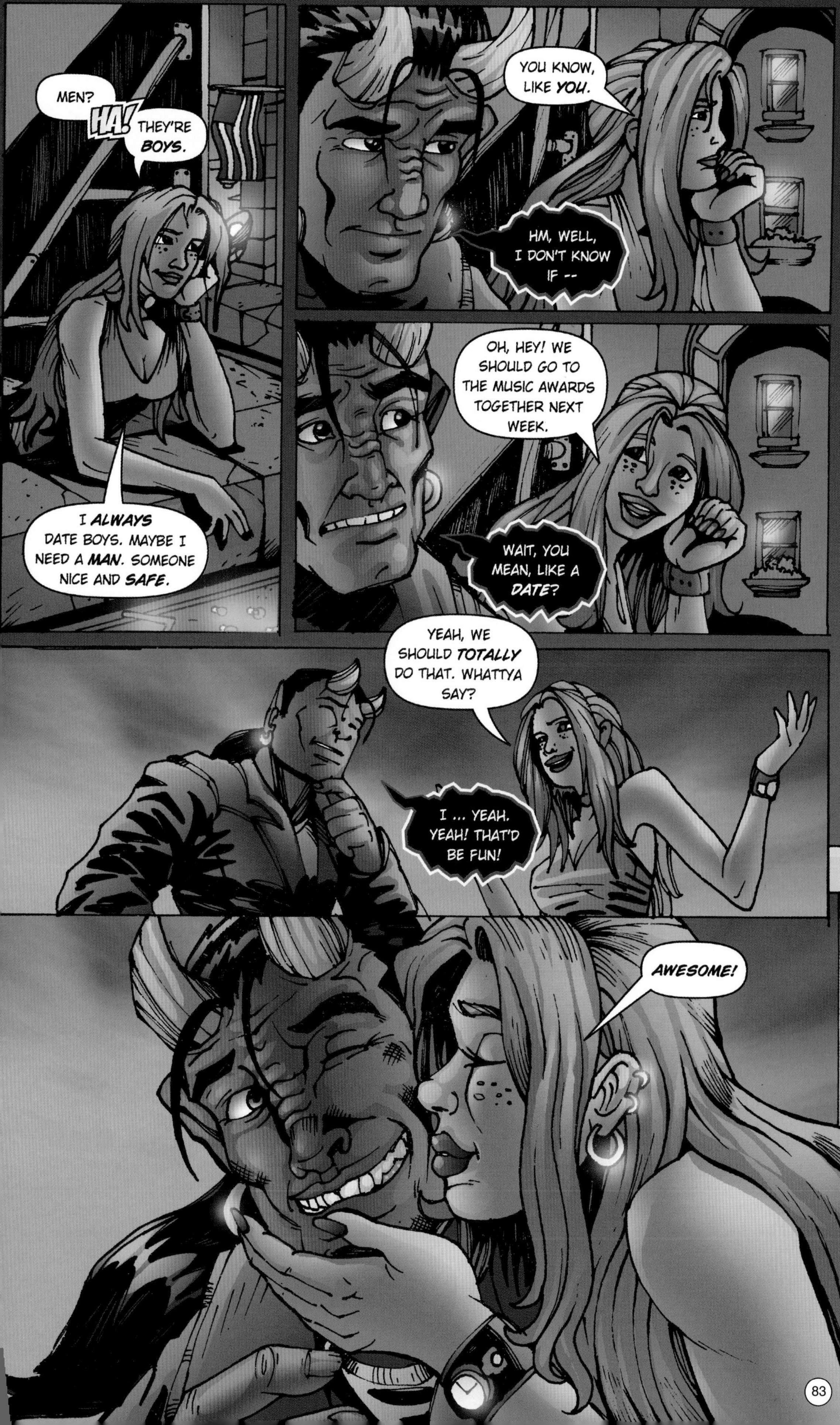
MEN?
HA!
THEY'RE BOYS.
I ALWAYS DATE BOYS. MAYBE I NEED A MAN. SOMEONE NICE AND SAFE.
YOU KNOW, LIKE YOU.
HM, WELL, I DON'T KNOW IF --
OH, HEY! WE SHOULD GO TO THE MUSIC AWARDS TOGETHER NEXT WEEK.
WAIT, YOU MEAN, LIKE A DATE?
YEAH, WE SHOULD TOTALLY DO THAT. WHATTYA SAY?
I ... YEAH. YEAH! THAT'D BE FUN!
AWESOME!

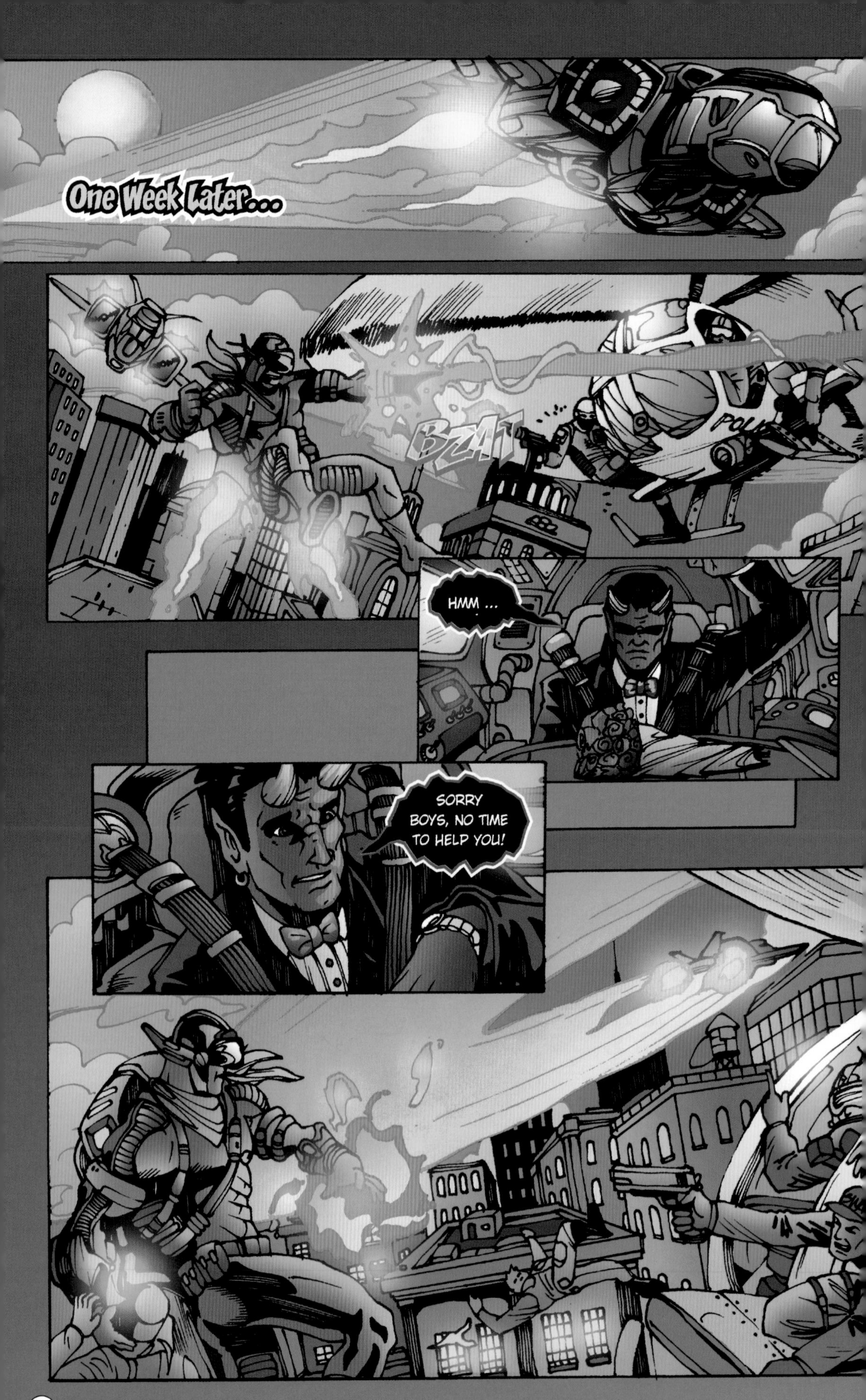
One Week Later...
BZAT
HMM ...
SORRY BOYS, NO TIME TO HELP YOU!

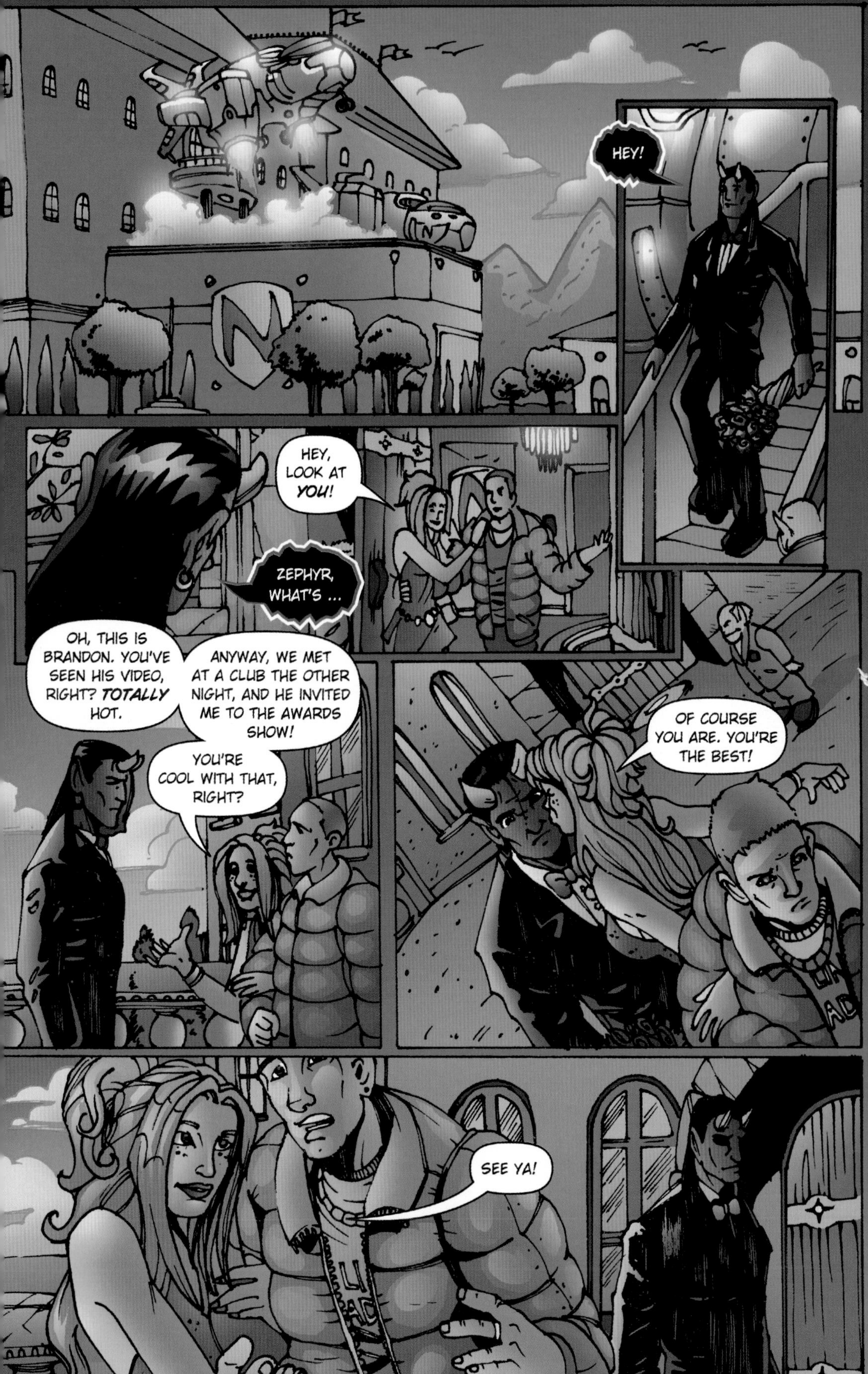
HEY!
HEY, LOOK AT *YOU!*
ZEPHYR, WHAT'S ...
OH, THIS IS BRANDON. YOU'VE SEEN HIS VIDEO, RIGHT? *TOTALLY* HOT.
ANYWAY, WE MET AT A CLUB THE OTHER NIGHT, AND HE INVITED ME TO THE AWARDS SHOW!
YOU'RE COOL WITH THAT, RIGHT?
OF COURSE YOU ARE. YOU'RE THE BEST!
SEE YA!

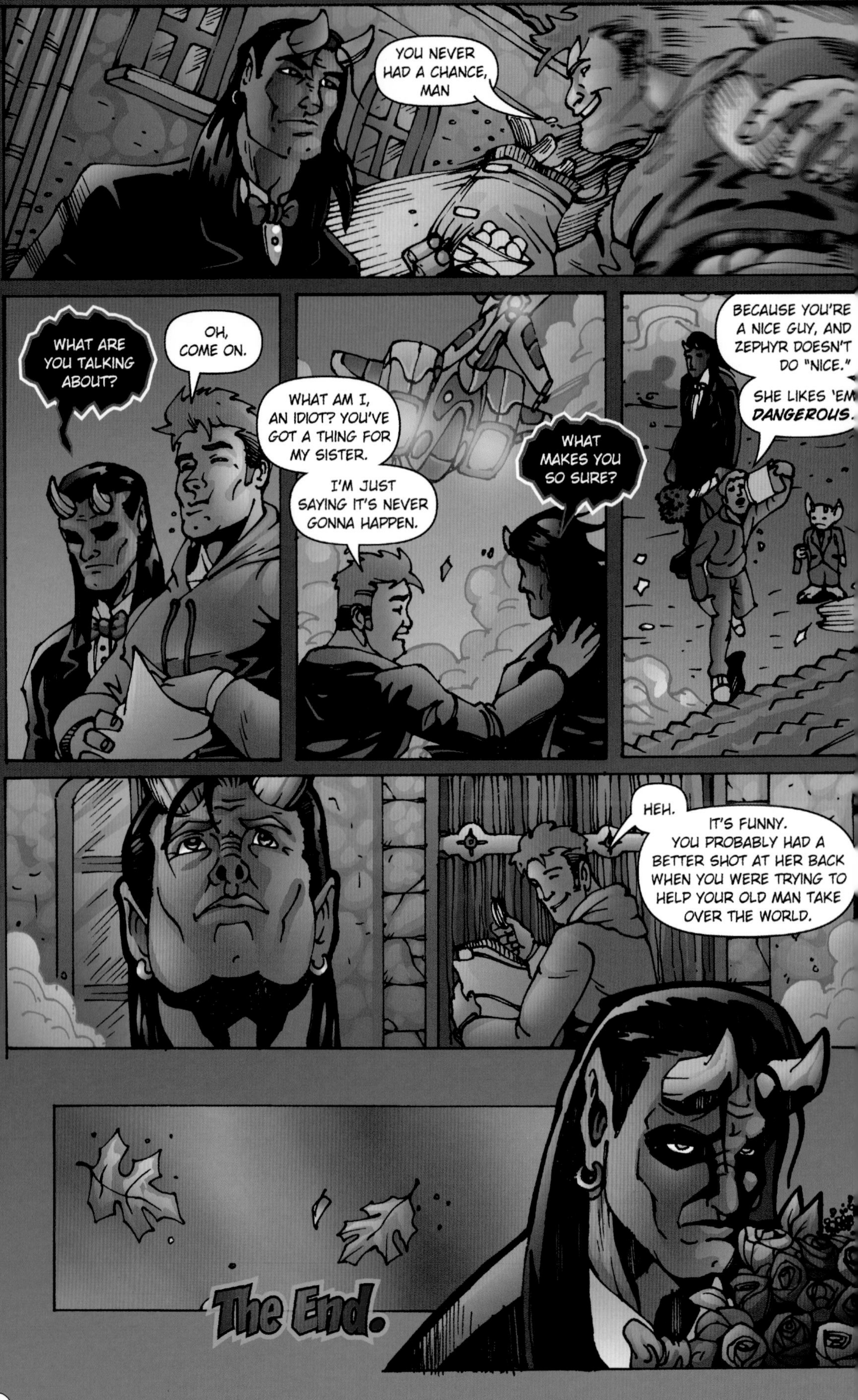
YOU NEVER HAD A CHANCE, MAN
WHAT ARE YOU TALKING ABOUT?
OH, COME ON.
WHAT AM I, AN IDIOT? YOU'VE GOT A THING FOR MY SISTER.
I'M JUST SAYING IT'S NEVER GONNA HAPPEN.
WHAT MAKES YOU SO SURE?
BECAUSE YOU'RE A NICE GUY, AND ZEPHYR DOESN'T DO "NICE."
SHE LIKES 'EM DANGEROUS.
HEH.
IT'S FUNNY. YOU PROBABLY HAD A BETTER SHOT AT HER BACK WHEN YOU WERE TRYING TO HELP YOUR OLD MAN TAKE OVER THE WORLD.
The End.

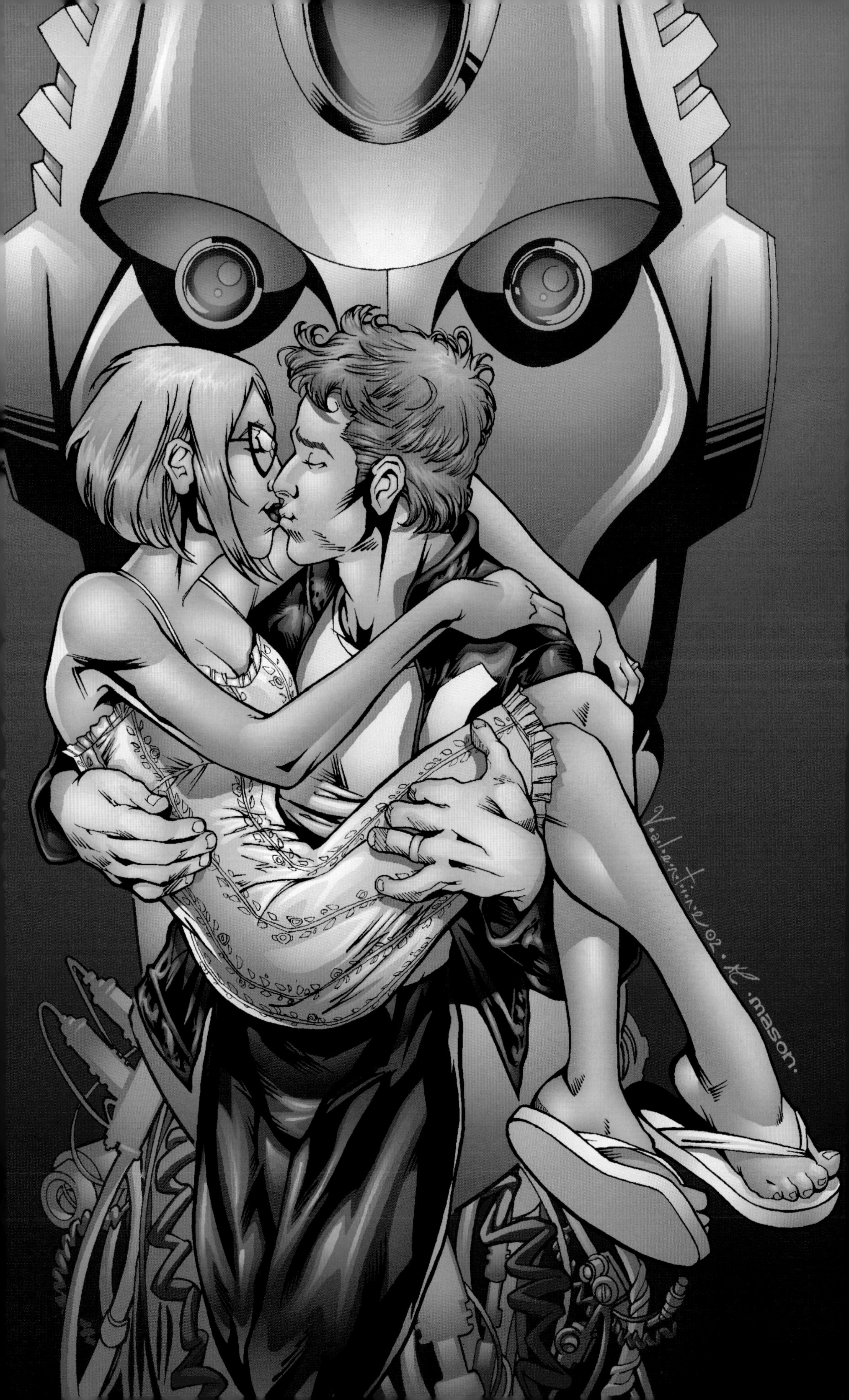
valentine 02
.mason.

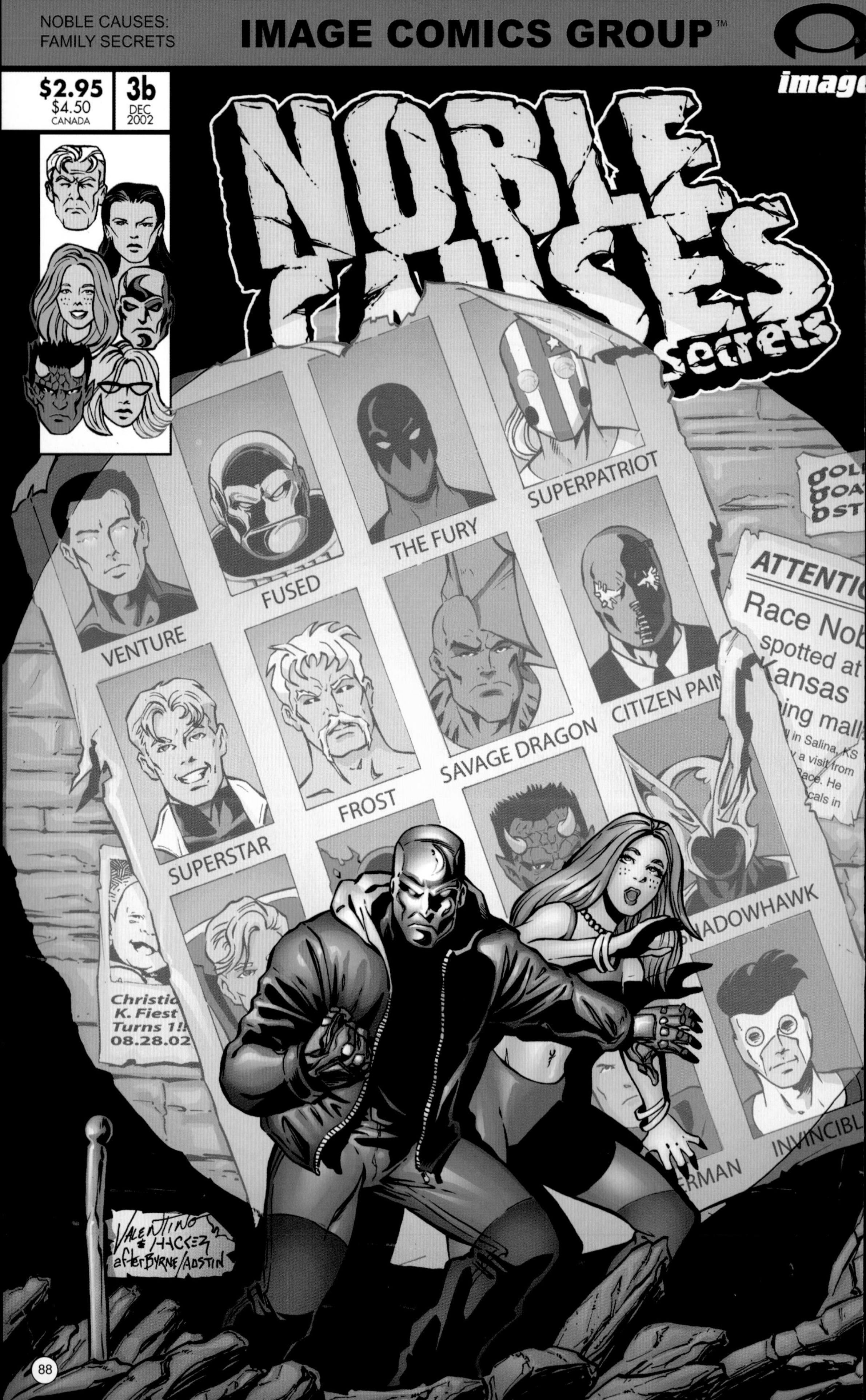
NOBLE CAUSES:
FAMILY SECRETS
IMAGE COMICS GROUP™
$2.95
$4.50 CANADA
3b
DEC 2002
image
NOBLE CAUSES
Secrets
VENTURE
FUSED
THE FURY
SUPERPATRIOT
SUPERSTAR
FROST
SAVAGE DRAGON
ATTENTION
Race
Kansas
Turns 1!!
08.28.02
Valentino & Hacker after Byrne/Austin

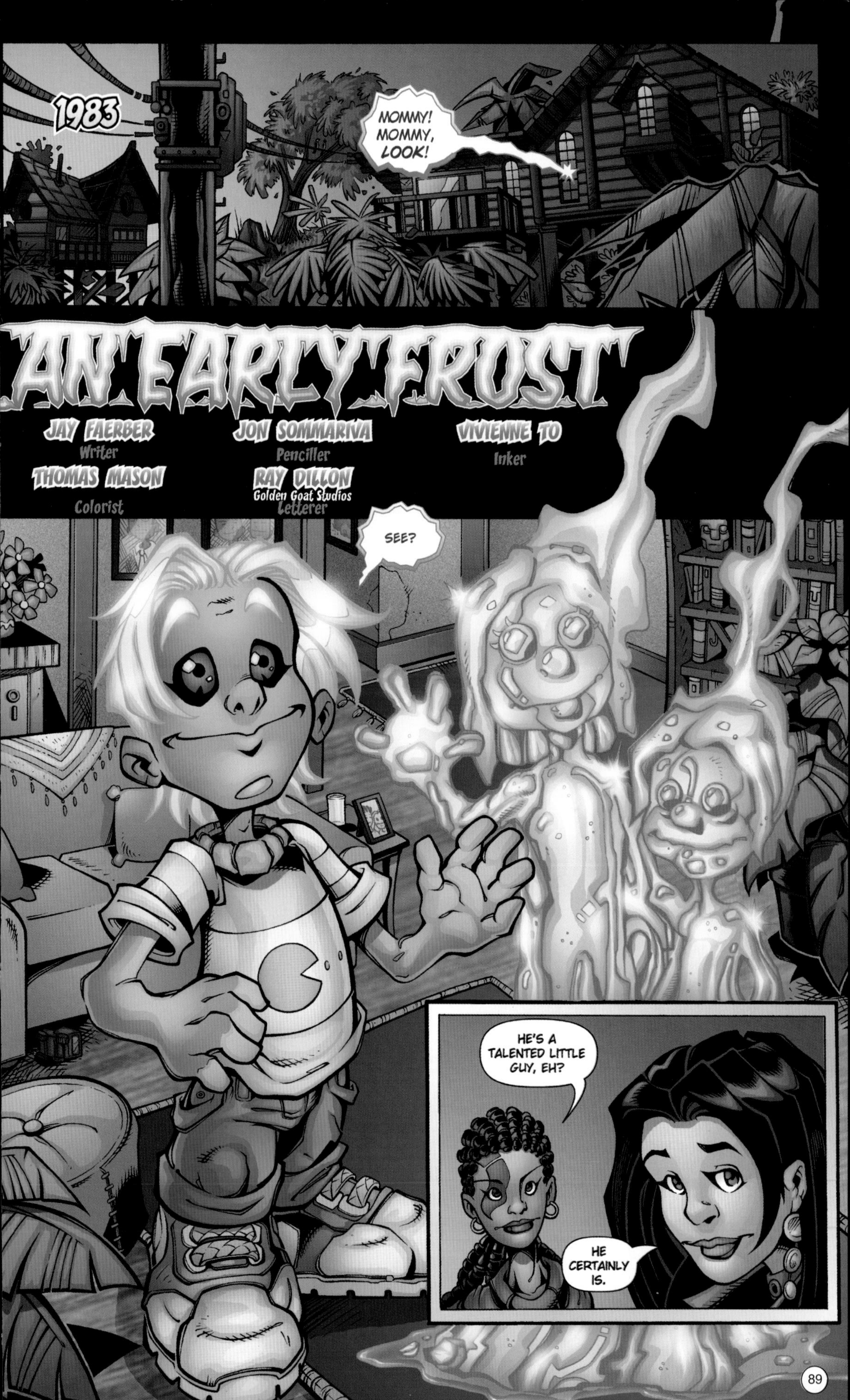
1983
MOMMY! MOMMY, LOOK!
AN EARLY FROST
JAY FAERBER
Writer
JON SOMMARIVA
Penciller
VIVIENNE TO
Inker
THOMAS MASON
Colorist
RAY DILLON
Golden Goat Studios
Letterer
SEE?
HE'S A TALENTED LITTLE GUY, EH?
HE CERTAINLY IS.

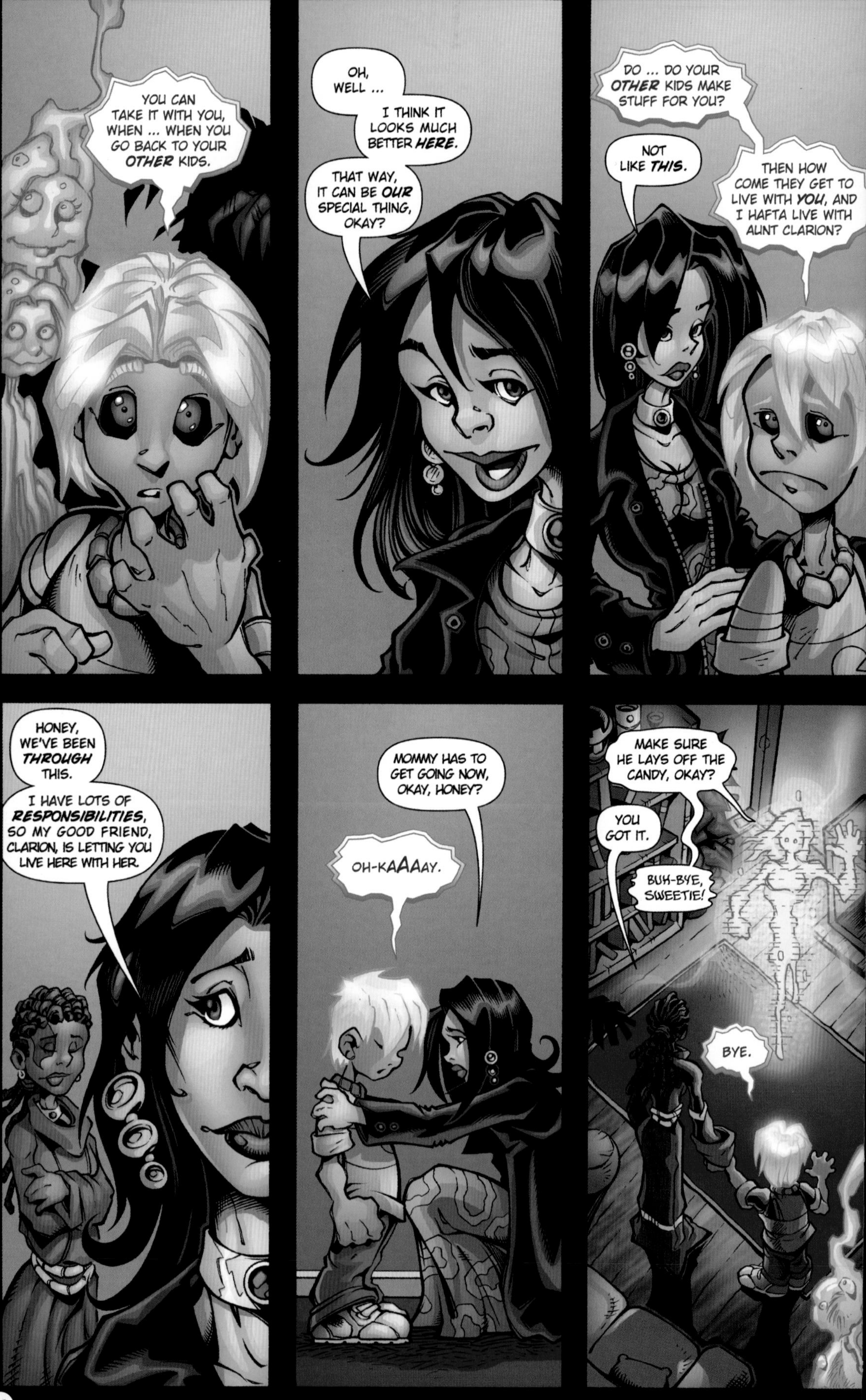
YOU CAN TAKE IT WITH YOU, WHEN ... WHEN YOU GO BACK TO YOUR OTHER KIDS.
OH, WELL ...
I THINK IT LOOKS MUCH BETTER HERE.
THAT WAY, IT CAN BE OUR SPECIAL THING, OKAY?
DO ... DO YOUR OTHER KIDS MAKE STUFF FOR YOU?
NOT LIKE THIS.
THEN HOW COME THEY GET TO LIVE WITH YOU, AND I HAFTA LIVE WITH AUNT CLARION?
HONEY, WE'VE BEEN THROUGH THIS.
I HAVE LOTS OF RESPONSIBILITIES, SO MY GOOD FRIEND, CLARION, IS LETTING YOU LIVE HERE WITH HER.
MOMMY HAS TO GET GOING NOW, OKAY, HONEY?
OH-KAAAAY.
MAKE SURE HE LAYS OFF THE CANDY, OKAY?
YOU GOT IT.
BUH-BYE, SWEETIE!
BYE.

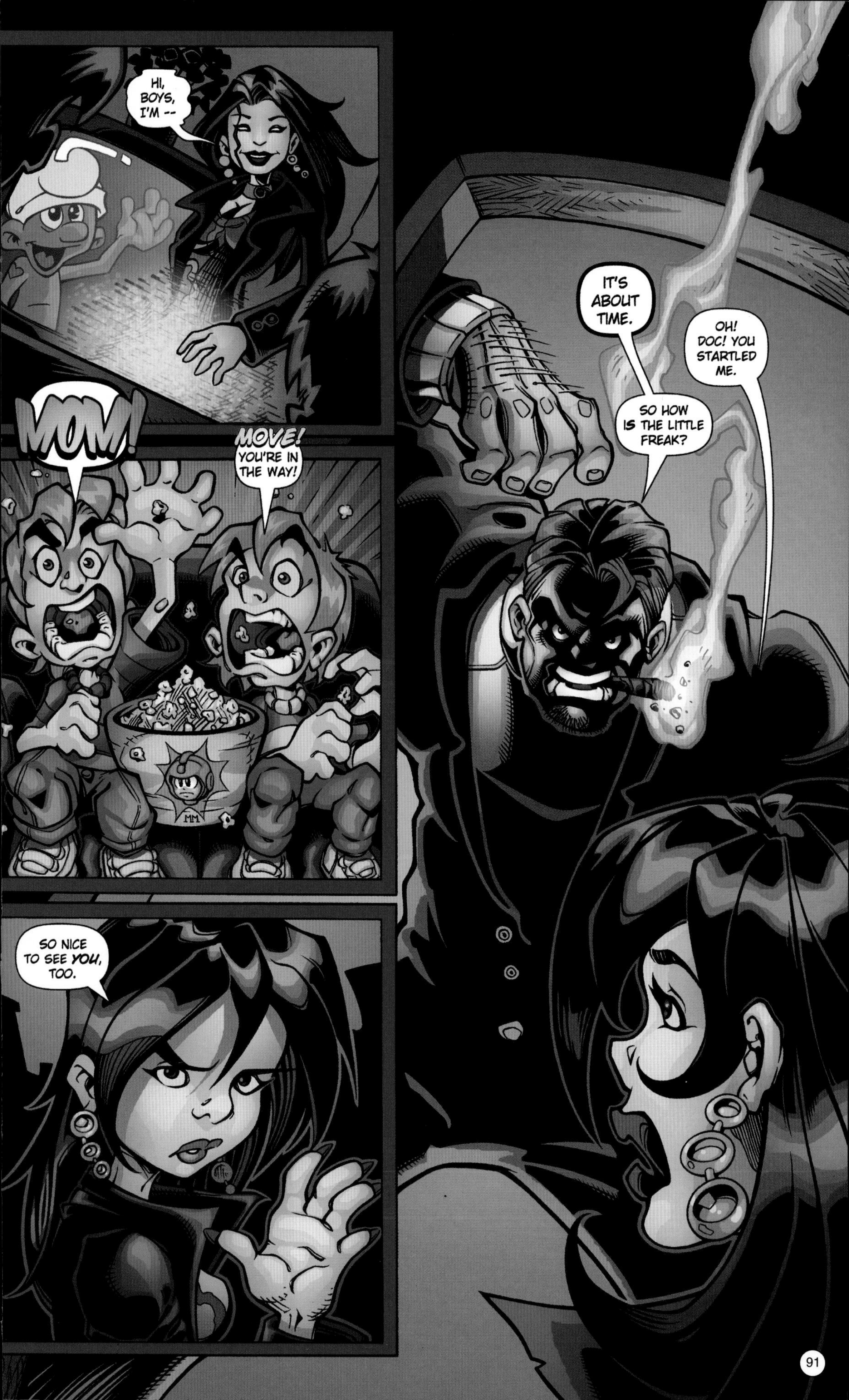
HI, BOYS, I'M --
MOM!
MOVE! YOU'RE IN THE WAY!
SO NICE TO SEE YOU, TOO.
IT'S ABOUT TIME.
OH! DOC! YOU STARTLED ME.
SO HOW IS THE LITTLE FREAK?

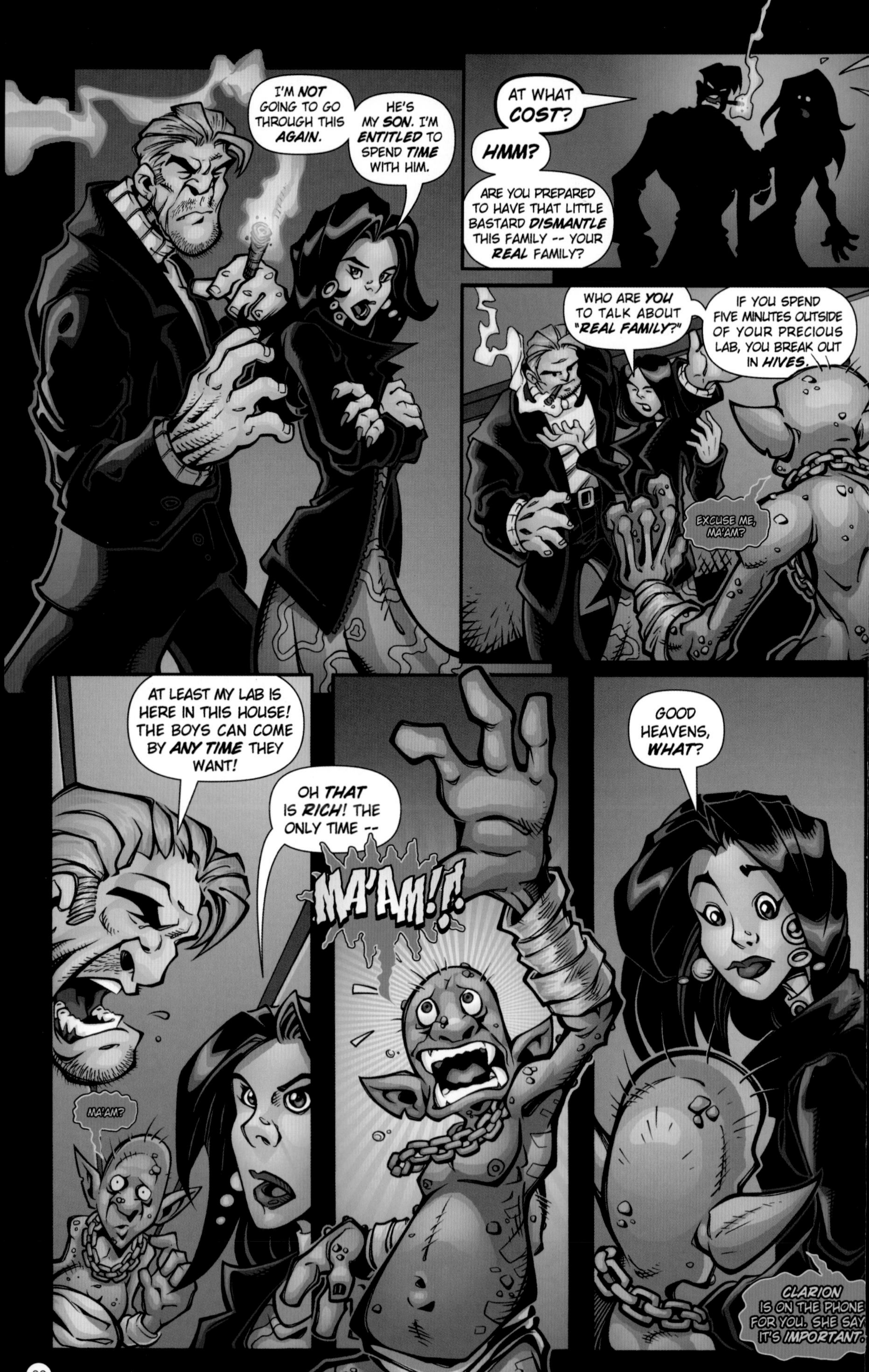

I'M NOT GOING TO GO THROUGH THIS AGAIN.
HE'S MY SON. I'M ENTITLED TO SPEND TIME WITH HIM.
AT WHAT COST?
HMM?
ARE YOU PREPARED TO HAVE THAT LITTLE BASTARD DISMANTLE THIS FAMILY -- YOUR REAL FAMILY?
WHO ARE YOU TO TALK ABOUT "REAL FAMILY?"
IF YOU SPEND FIVE MINUTES OUTSIDE OF YOUR PRECIOUS LAB, YOU BREAK OUT IN HIVES.
EXCUSE ME, MA'AM?
AT LEAST MY LAB IS HERE IN THIS HOUSE! THE BOYS CAN COME BY ANY TIME THEY WANT!
MA'AM?
OH THAT IS RICH! THE ONLY TIME --
MA'AM!?!
GOOD HEAVENS, WHAT?
CLARION IS ON THE PHONE FOR YOU. SHE SAY IT'S IMPORTANT.

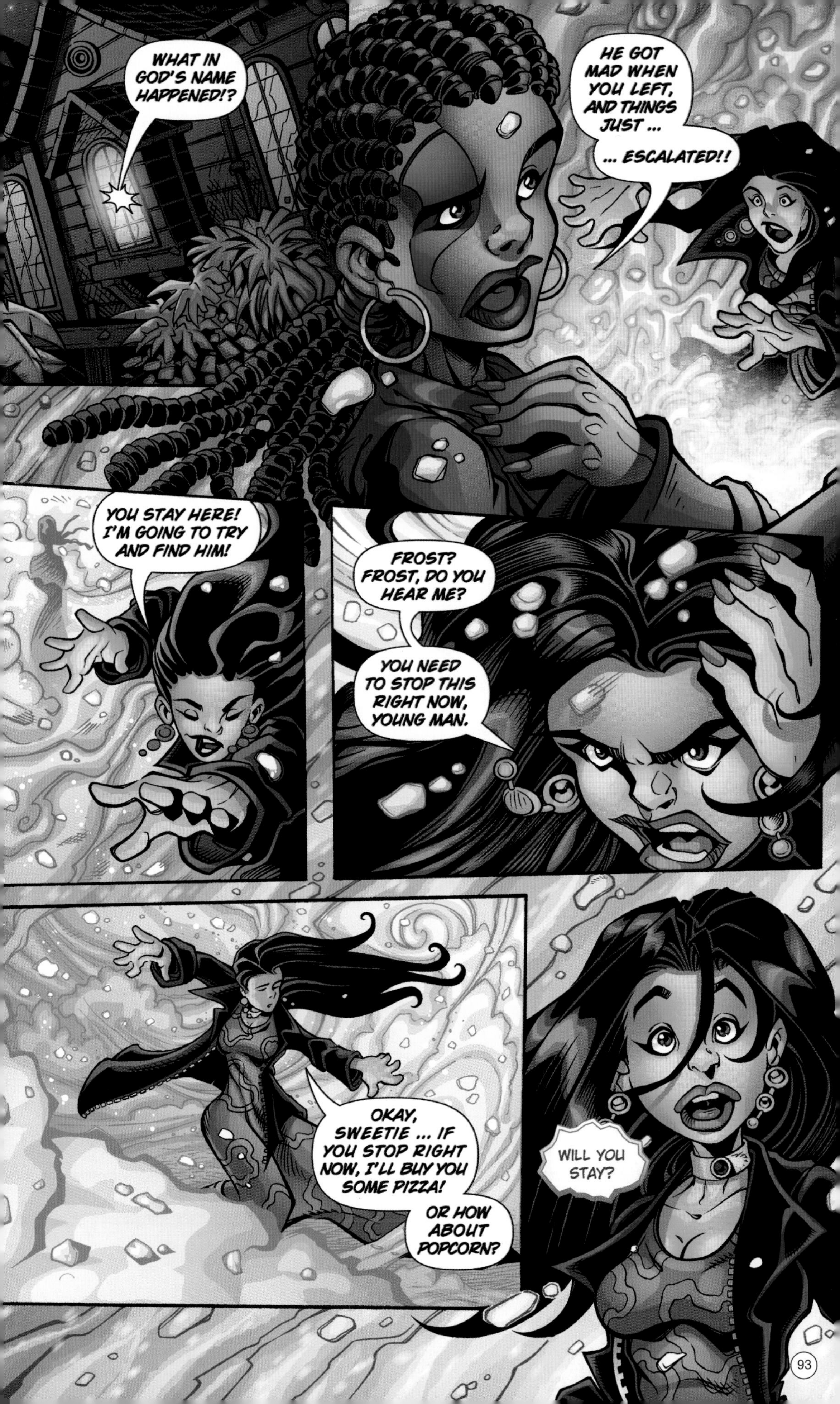
WHAT IN GOD'S NAME HAPPENED!?
HE GOT MAD WHEN YOU LEFT, AND THINGS JUST ...
... ESCALATED!!
YOU STAY HERE! I'M GOING TO TRY AND FIND HIM!
FROST? FROST, DO YOU HEAR ME?
YOU NEED TO STOP THIS RIGHT NOW, YOUNG MAN.
OKAY, SWEETIE ... IF YOU STOP RIGHT NOW, I'LL BUY YOU SOME PIZZA!
OR HOW ABOUT POPCORN?
WILL YOU STAY?

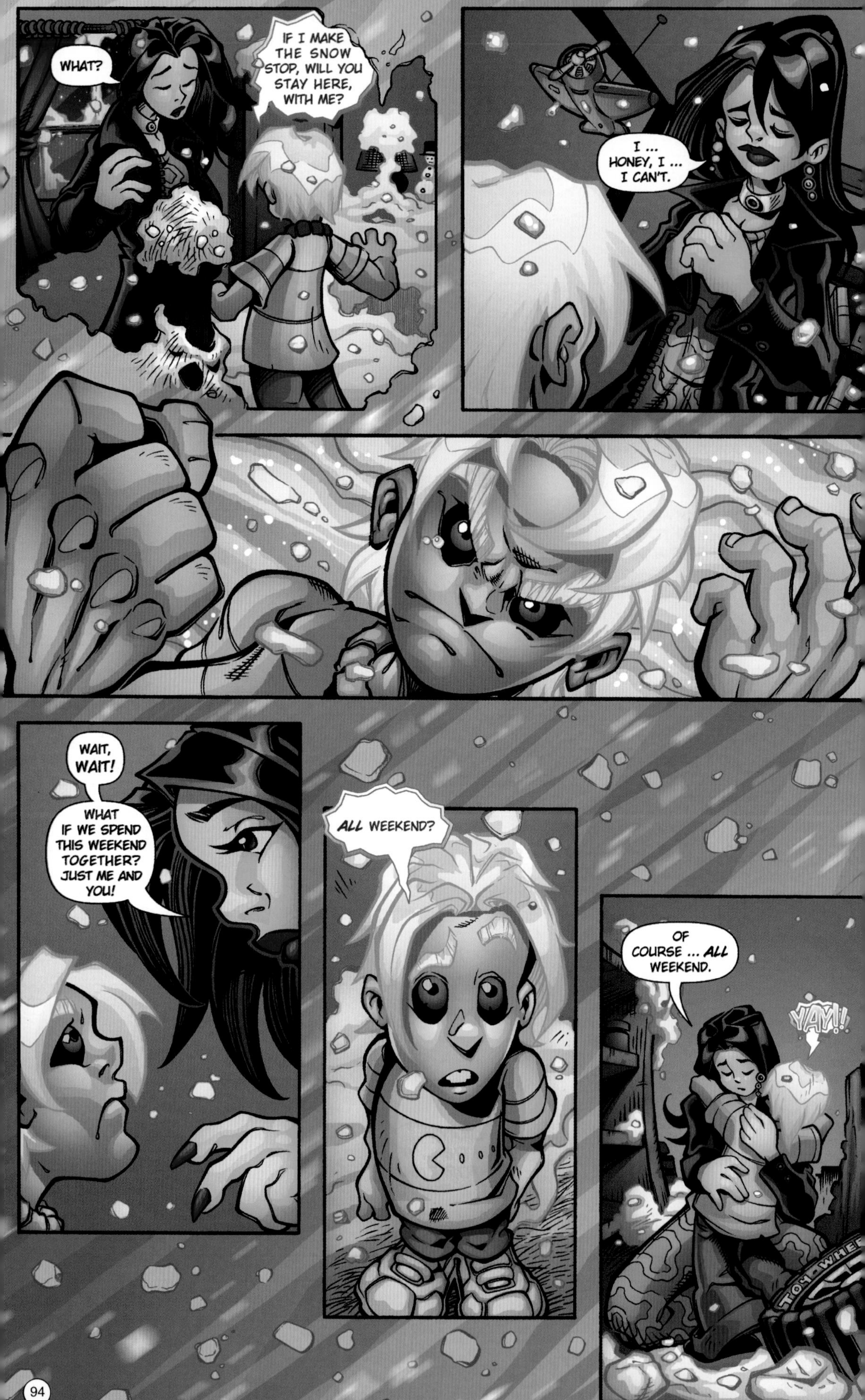

WHAT?
IF I MAKE THE SNOW STOP, WILL YOU STAY HERE, WITH ME?
I ... HONEY, I ... I CAN'T.
WAIT, WAIT!
WHAT IF WE SPEND THIS WEEKEND TOGETHER? JUST ME AND YOU!
ALL WEEKEND?
OF COURSE ... ALL WEEKEND.
YAY!!

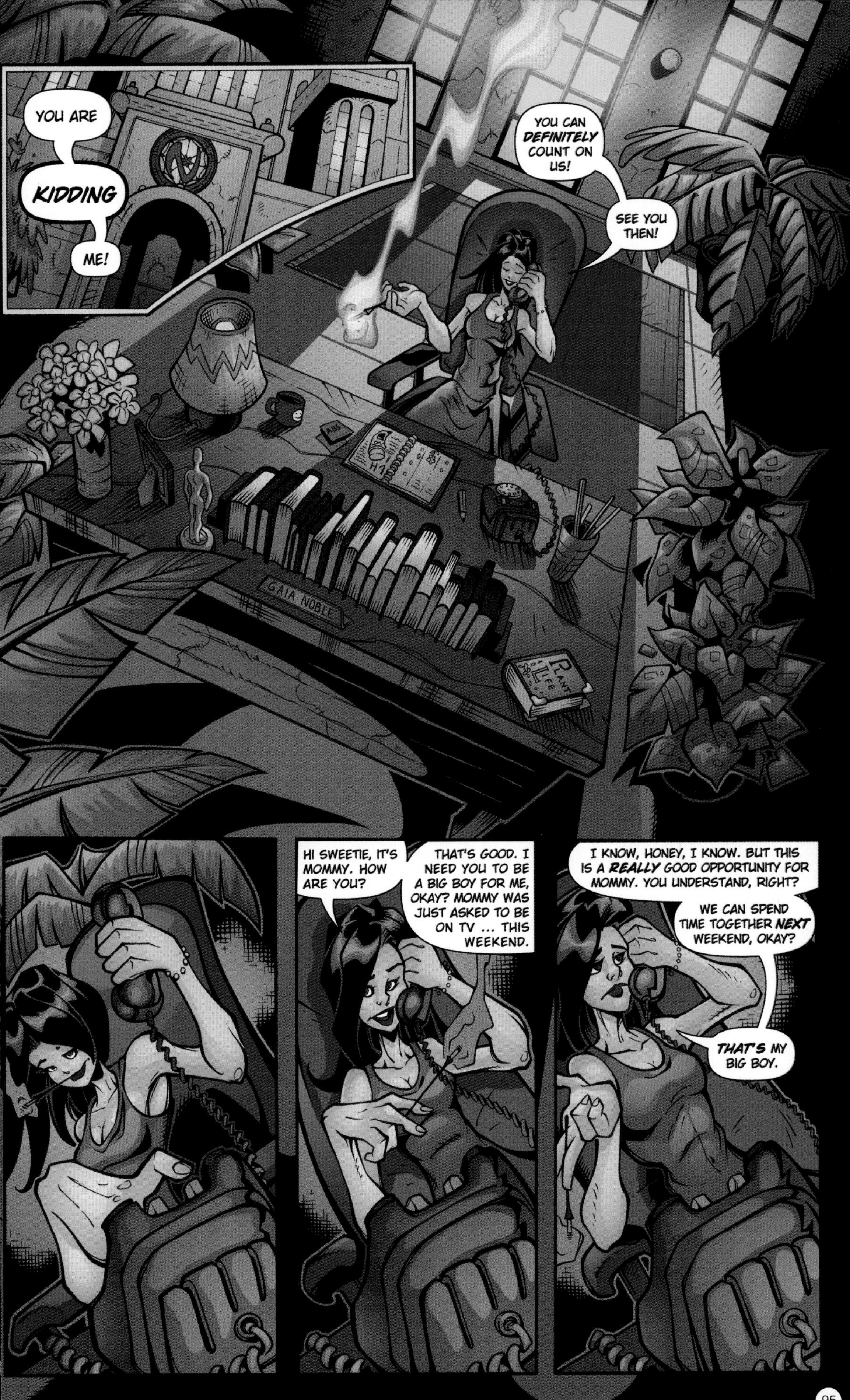
YOU ARE
KIDDING
ME!
YOU CAN *DEFINITELY* COUNT ON US!
SEE YOU THEN!
GAIA NOBLE
PLANT LIFE
HI SWEETIE, IT'S MOMMY. HOW ARE YOU?
THAT'S GOOD. I NEED YOU TO BE A BIG BOY FOR ME, OKAY? MOMMY WAS JUST ASKED TO BE ON TV ... THIS WEEKEND.
I KNOW, HONEY, I KNOW. BUT THIS IS A *REALLY* GOOD OPPORTUNITY FOR MOMMY. YOU UNDERSTAND, RIGHT?
WE CAN SPEND TIME TOGETHER *NEXT* WEEKEND, OKAY?
THAT'S MY BIG BOY.

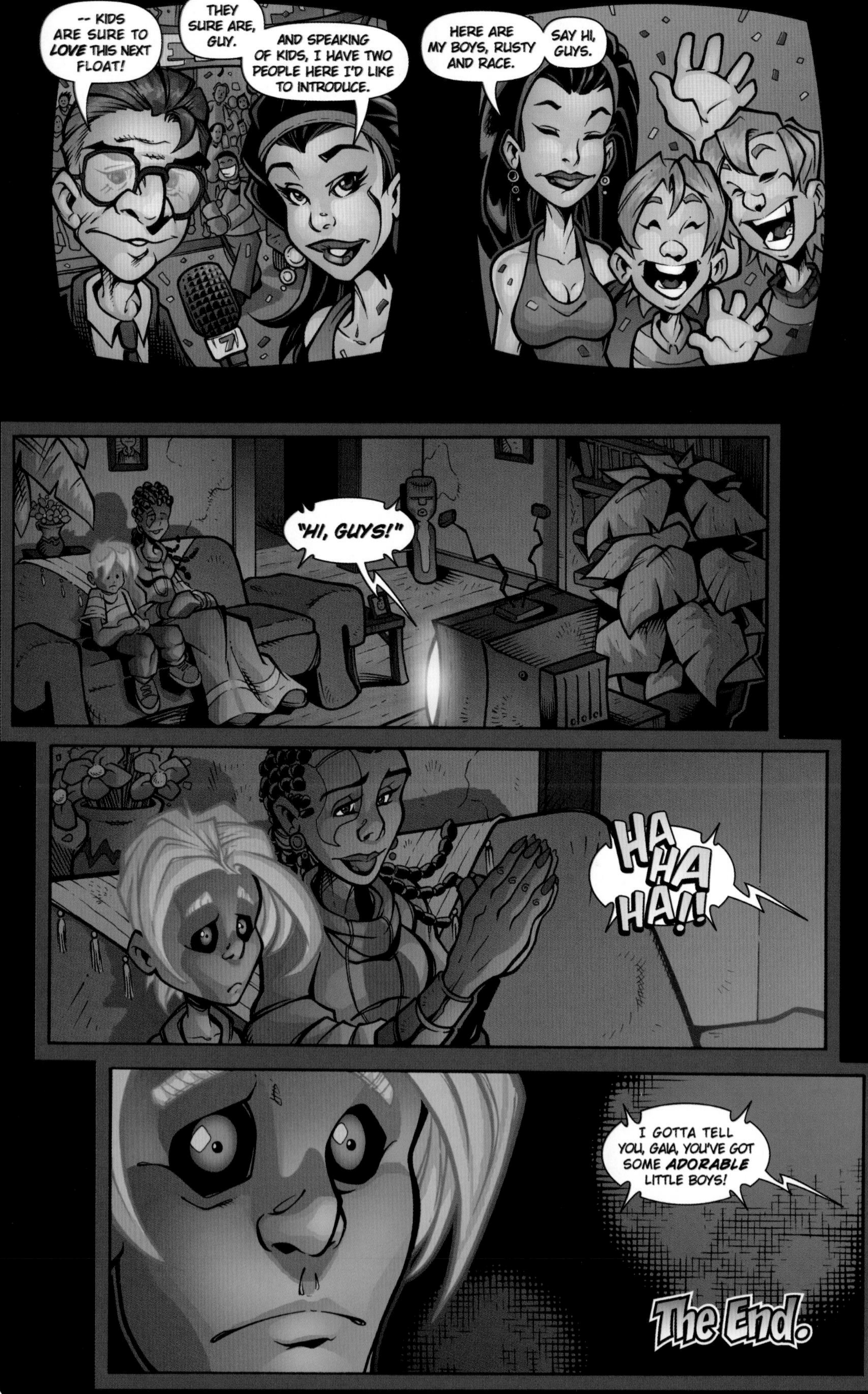
-- KIDS ARE SURE TO *LOVE* THIS NEXT FLOAT!
THEY SURE ARE, GUY.
AND SPEAKING OF KIDS, I HAVE TWO PEOPLE HERE I'D LIKE TO INTRODUCE.
HERE ARE MY BOYS, RUSTY AND RACE.
SAY HI, GUYS.
"HI, GUYS!"
HA HA HA!!
I GOTTA TELL YOU, GAIA, YOU'VE GOT SOME *ADORABLE* LITTLE BOYS!
The End.

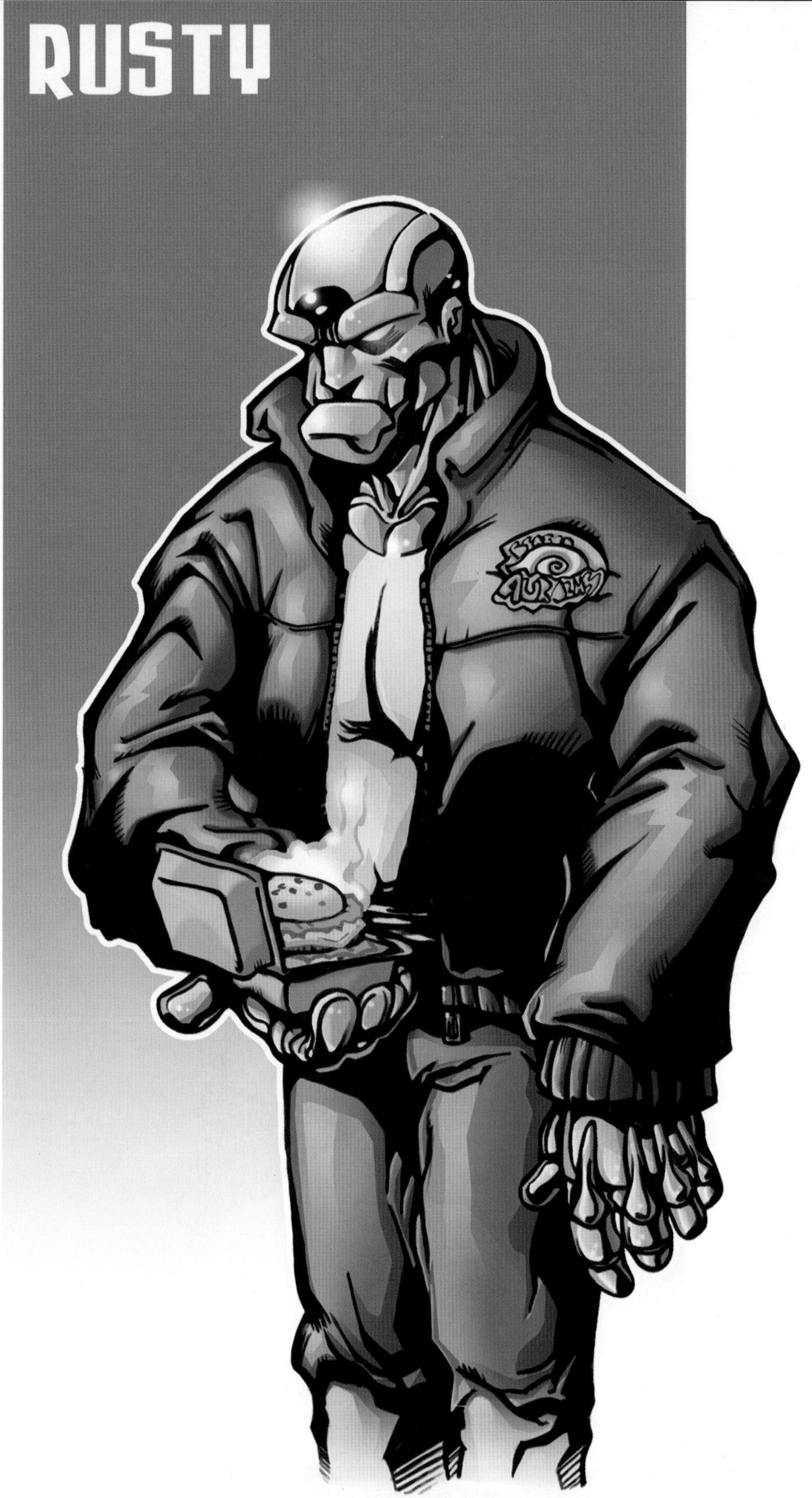
RUSTY

Rusty Noble

art & color by
Pedro Potier

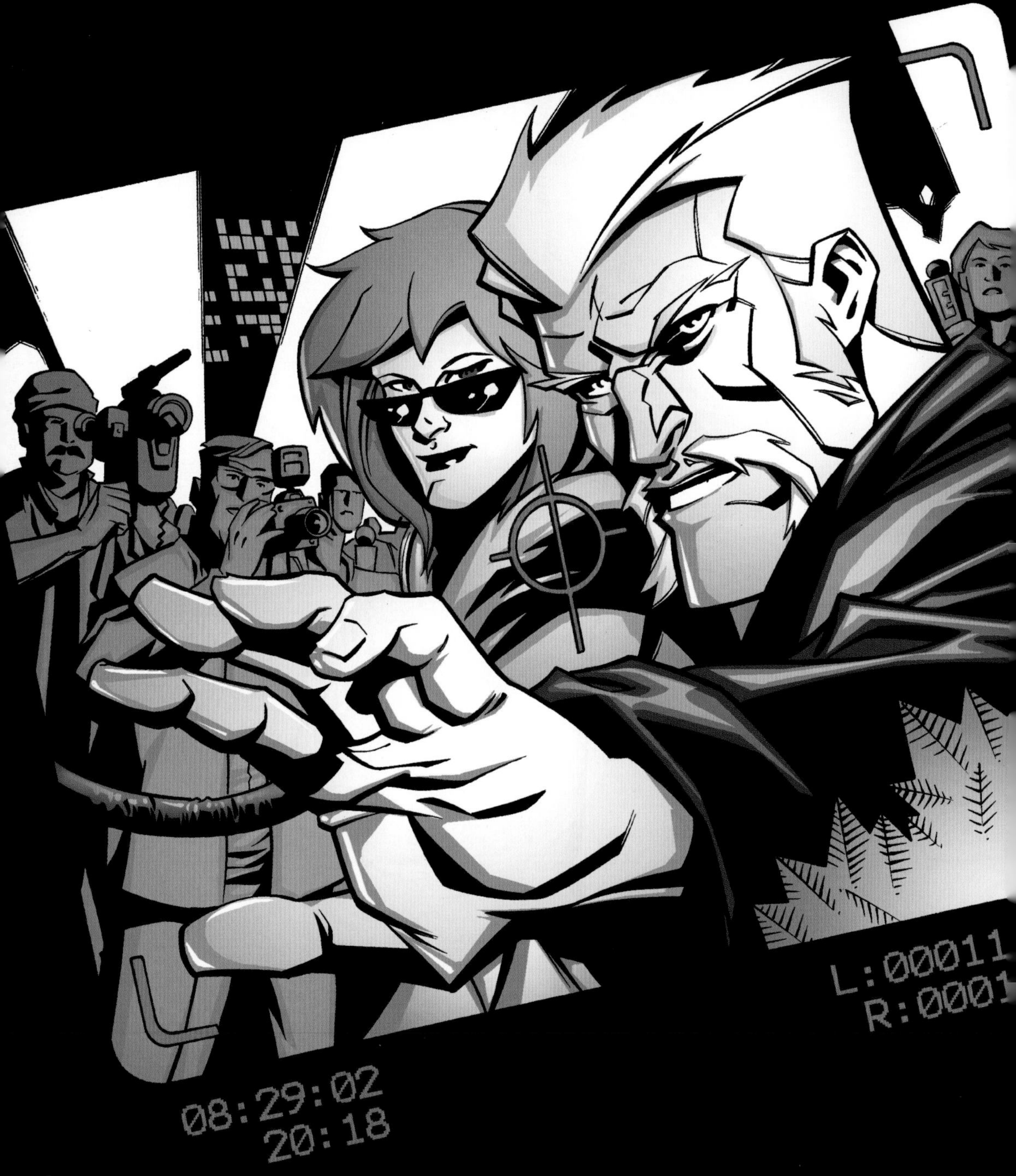
L:00011
R:0001
08:29:02
20:18

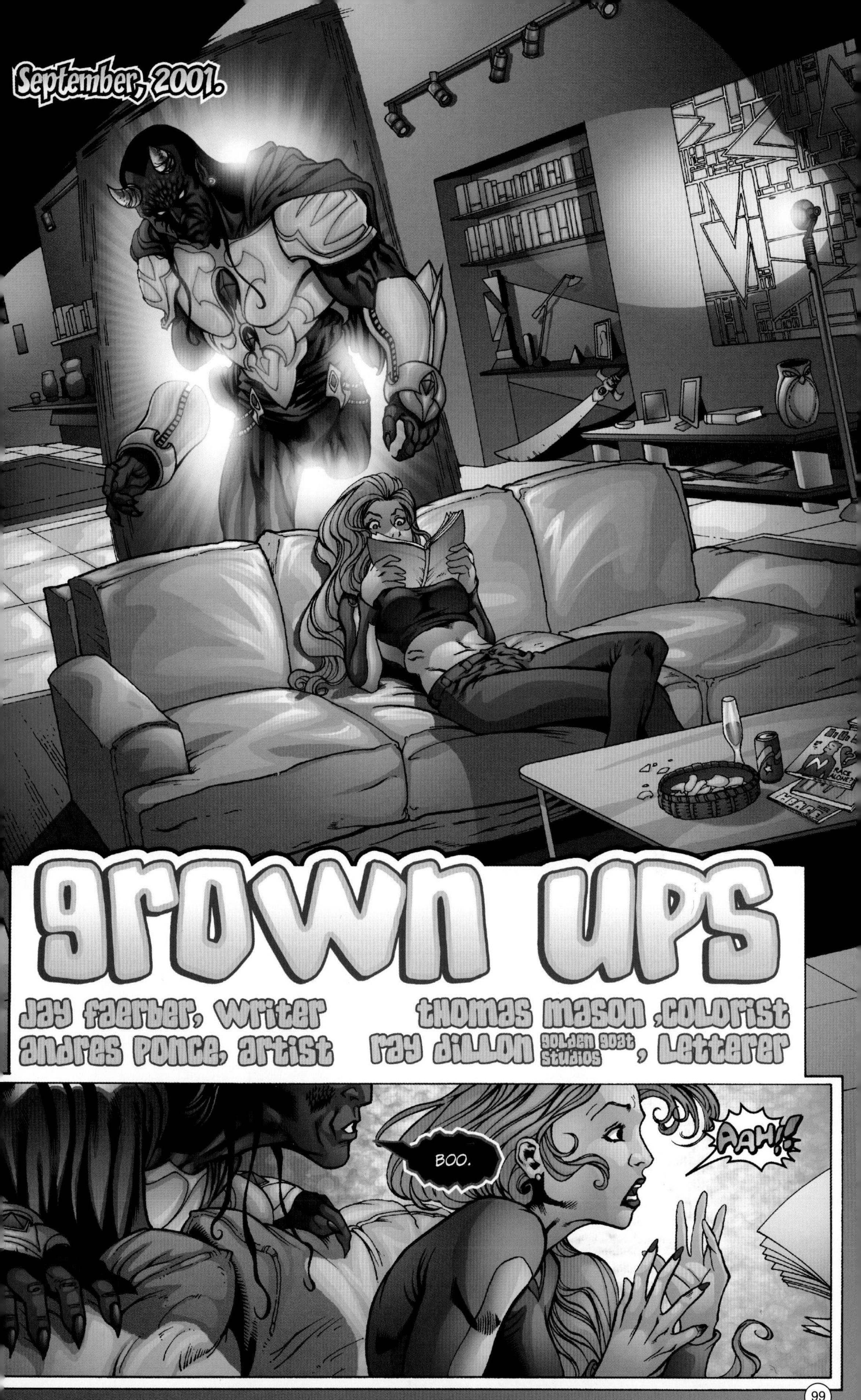

September, 2001.
RACE ALONE?
grown ups
Jay Faerber, writer
Andres Ponce, artist
Thomas Mason, colorist
Ray Dillon golden goat studios, letterer
BOO.
AAH!!

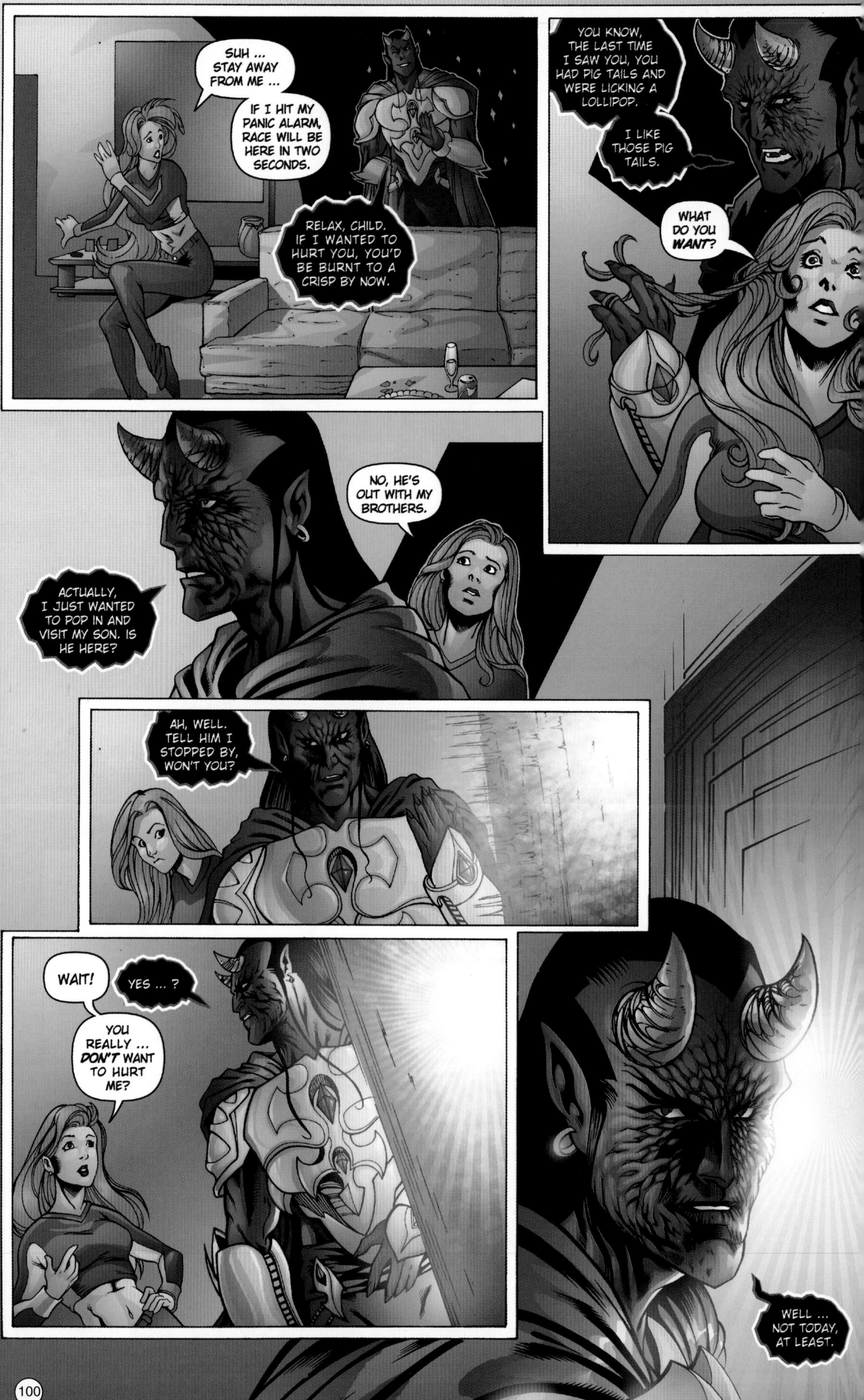

SUH ... STAY AWAY FROM ME ...
IF I HIT MY PANIC ALARM, RACE WILL BE HERE IN TWO SECONDS.
RELAX, CHILD. IF I WANTED TO HURT YOU, YOU'D BE BURNT TO A CRISP BY NOW.
YOU KNOW, THE LAST TIME I SAW YOU, YOU HAD PIG TAILS AND WERE LICKING A LOLLIPOP.
I LIKE THOSE PIG TAILS.
WHAT DO YOU *WANT*?
ACTUALLY, I JUST WANTED TO POP IN AND VISIT MY SON. IS HE HERE?
NO, HE'S OUT WITH MY BROTHERS.
AH, WELL. TELL HIM I STOPPED BY, WON'T YOU?
WAIT!
YES ... ?
YOU REALLY ... ***DON'T*** WANT TO HURT ME?
WELL ... NOT TODAY, AT LEAST.

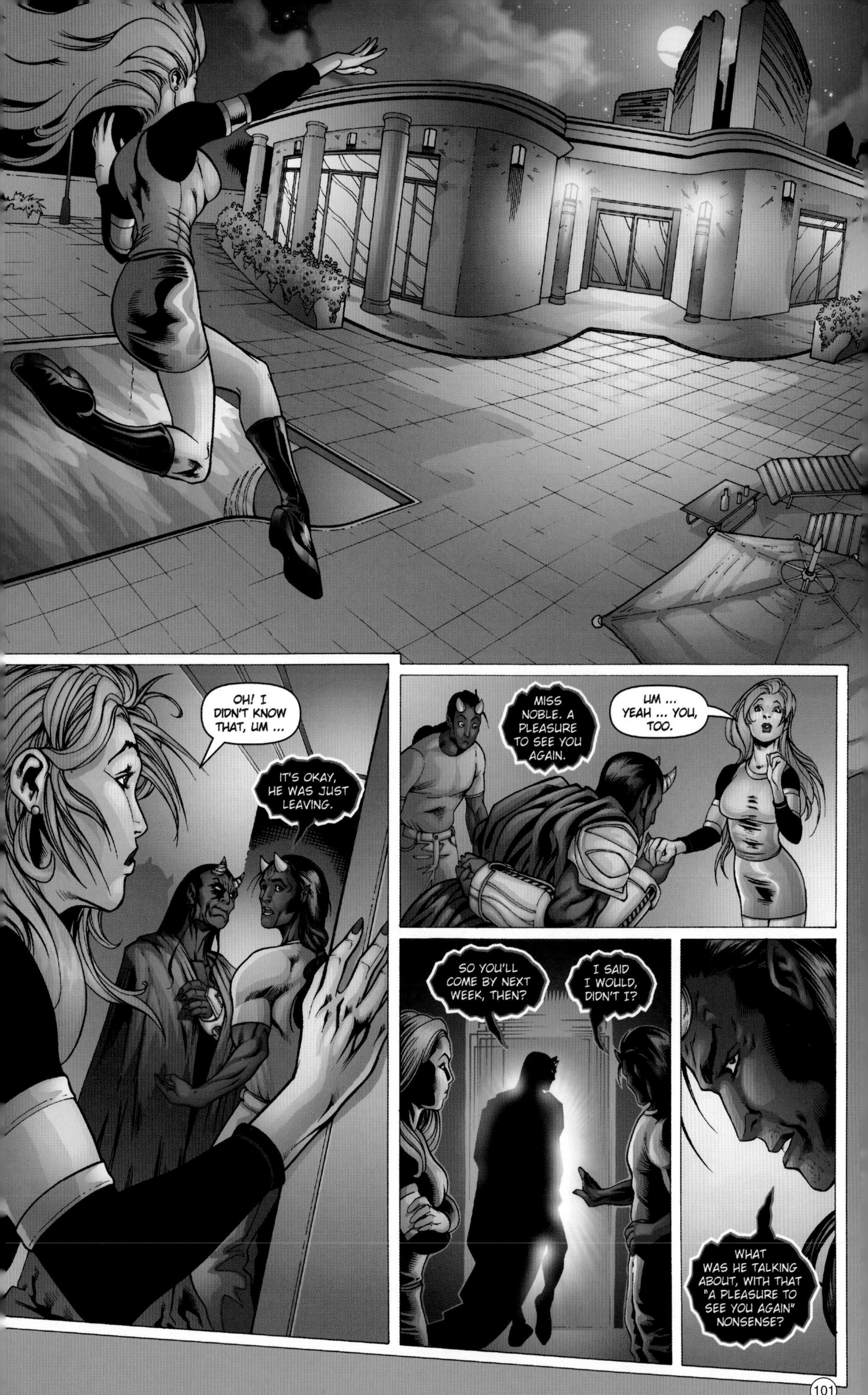
OH! I DIDN'T KNOW THAT, UM ...
IT'S OKAY, HE WAS JUST LEAVING.
MISS NOBLE. A PLEASURE TO SEE YOU AGAIN.
UM ... YEAH ... YOU, TOO.
SO YOU'LL COME BY NEXT WEEK, THEN?
I SAID I WOULD, DIDN'T I?
WHAT WAS HE TALKING ABOUT, WITH THAT "A PLEASURE TO SEE YOU AGAIN" NONSENSE?

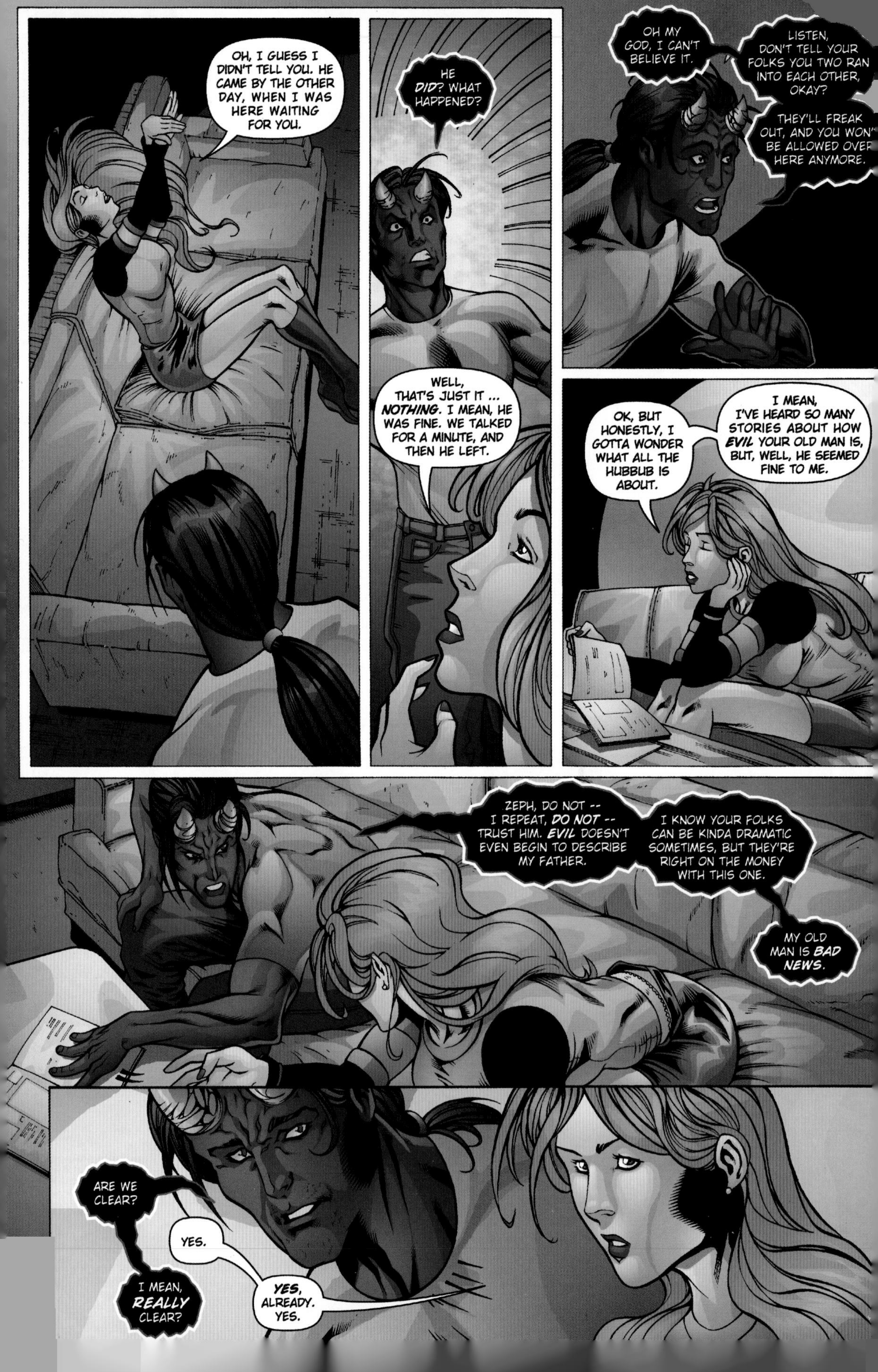
OH, I GUESS I DIDN'T TELL YOU. HE CAME BY THE OTHER DAY, WHEN I WAS HERE WAITING FOR YOU.
HE DID? WHAT HAPPENED?
WELL, THAT'S JUST IT ... NOTHING. I MEAN, HE WAS FINE. WE TALKED FOR A MINUTE, AND THEN HE LEFT.
OH MY GOD, I CAN'T BELIEVE IT.
LISTEN, DON'T TELL YOUR FOLKS YOU TWO RAN INTO EACH OTHER, OKAY?
THEY'LL FREAK OUT, AND YOU WON'T BE ALLOWED OVER HERE ANYMORE.
OK, BUT HONESTLY, I GOTTA WONDER WHAT ALL THE HUBBUB IS ABOUT.
I MEAN, I'VE HEARD SO MANY STORIES ABOUT HOW EVIL YOUR OLD MAN IS, BUT, WELL, HE SEEMED FINE TO ME.
ZEPH, DO NOT -- I REPEAT, DO NOT -- TRUST HIM. EVIL DOESN'T EVEN BEGIN TO DESCRIBE MY FATHER.
I KNOW YOUR FOLKS CAN BE KINDA DRAMATIC SOMETIMES, BUT THEY'RE RIGHT ON THE MONEY WITH THIS ONE.
MY OLD MAN IS BAD NEWS.
ARE WE CLEAR?
YES.
I MEAN, REALLY CLEAR?
YES, ALREADY. YES.

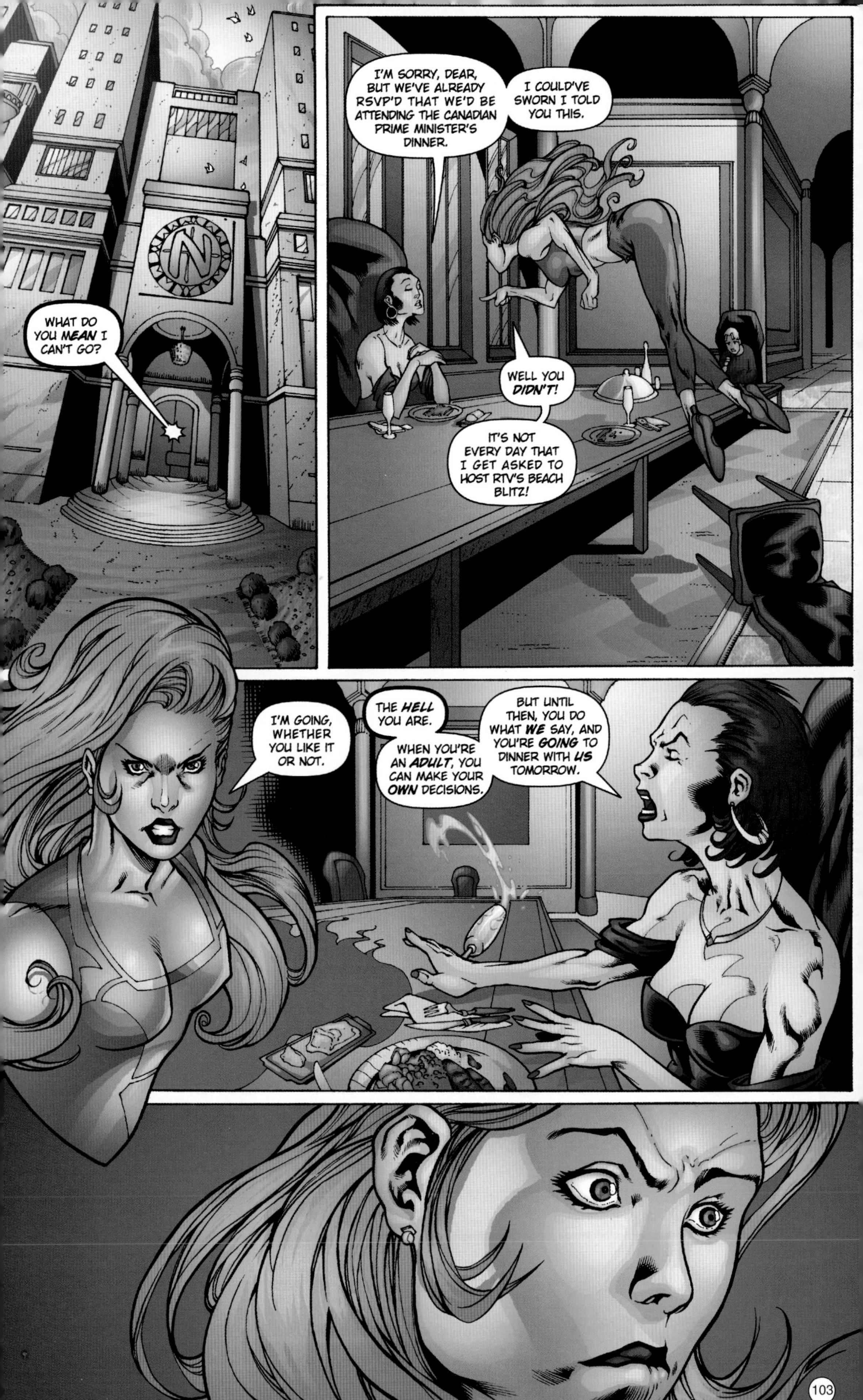
WHAT DO YOU MEAN I CAN'T GO?
I'M SORRY, DEAR, BUT WE'VE ALREADY RSVP'D THAT WE'D BE ATTENDING THE CANADIAN PRIME MINISTER'S DINNER.
I COULD'VE SWORN I TOLD YOU THIS.
WELL YOU DIDN'T!
IT'S NOT EVERY DAY THAT I GET ASKED TO HOST RTV'S BEACH BLITZ!
I'M GOING, WHETHER YOU LIKE IT OR NOT.
THE HELL YOU ARE.
WHEN YOU'RE AN ADULT, YOU CAN MAKE YOUR OWN DECISIONS.
BUT UNTIL THEN, YOU DO WHAT WE SAY, AND YOU'RE GOING TO DINNER WITH US TOMORROW.

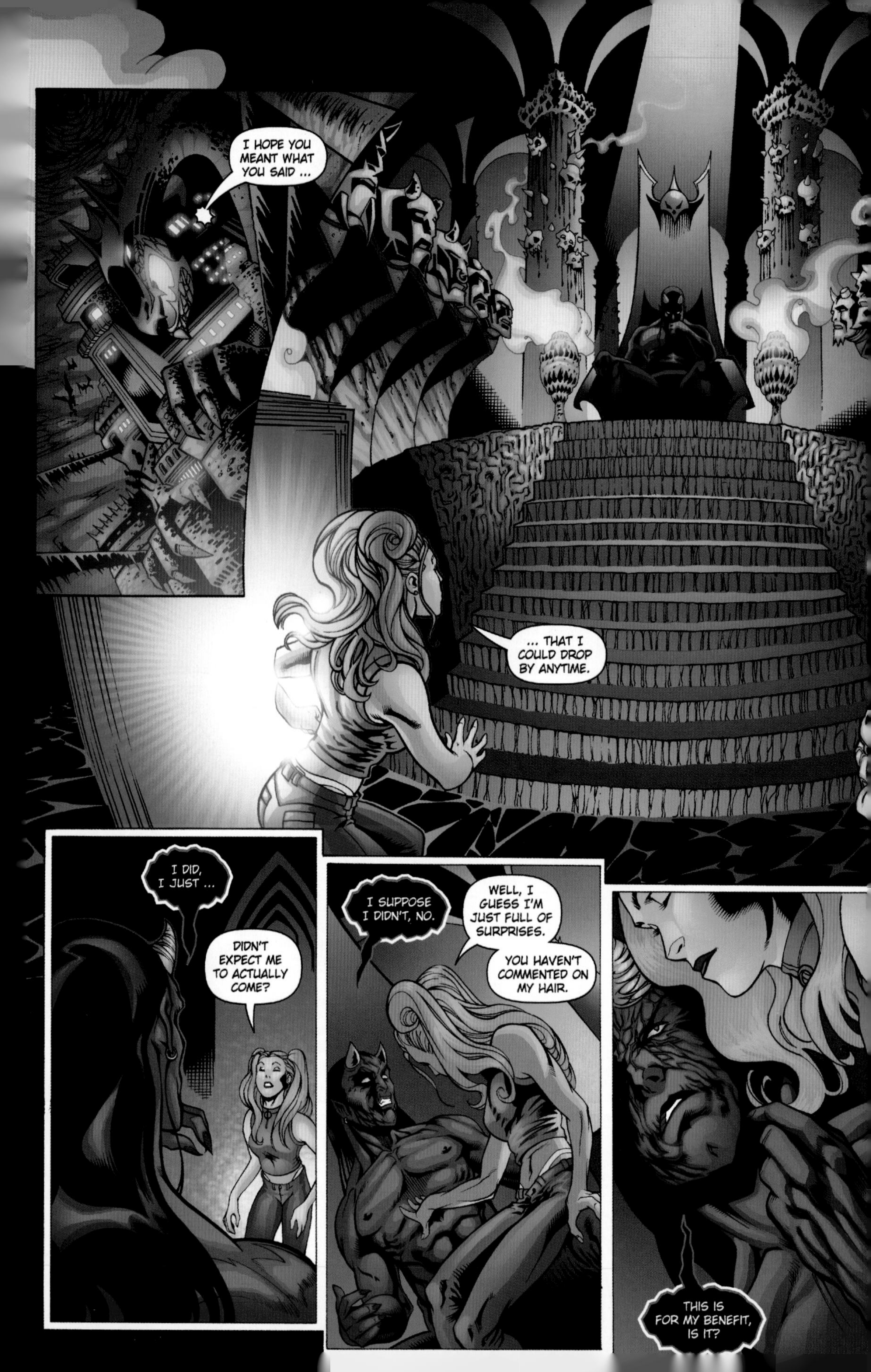
I HOPE YOU MEANT WHAT YOU SAID ...
... THAT I COULD DROP BY ANYTIME.
I DID, I JUST ...
DIDN'T EXPECT ME TO ACTUALLY COME?
I SUPPOSE I DIDN'T, NO.
WELL, I GUESS I'M JUST FULL OF SURPRISES.
YOU HAVEN'T COMMENTED ON MY HAIR.
THIS IS FOR MY BENEFIT, IS IT?

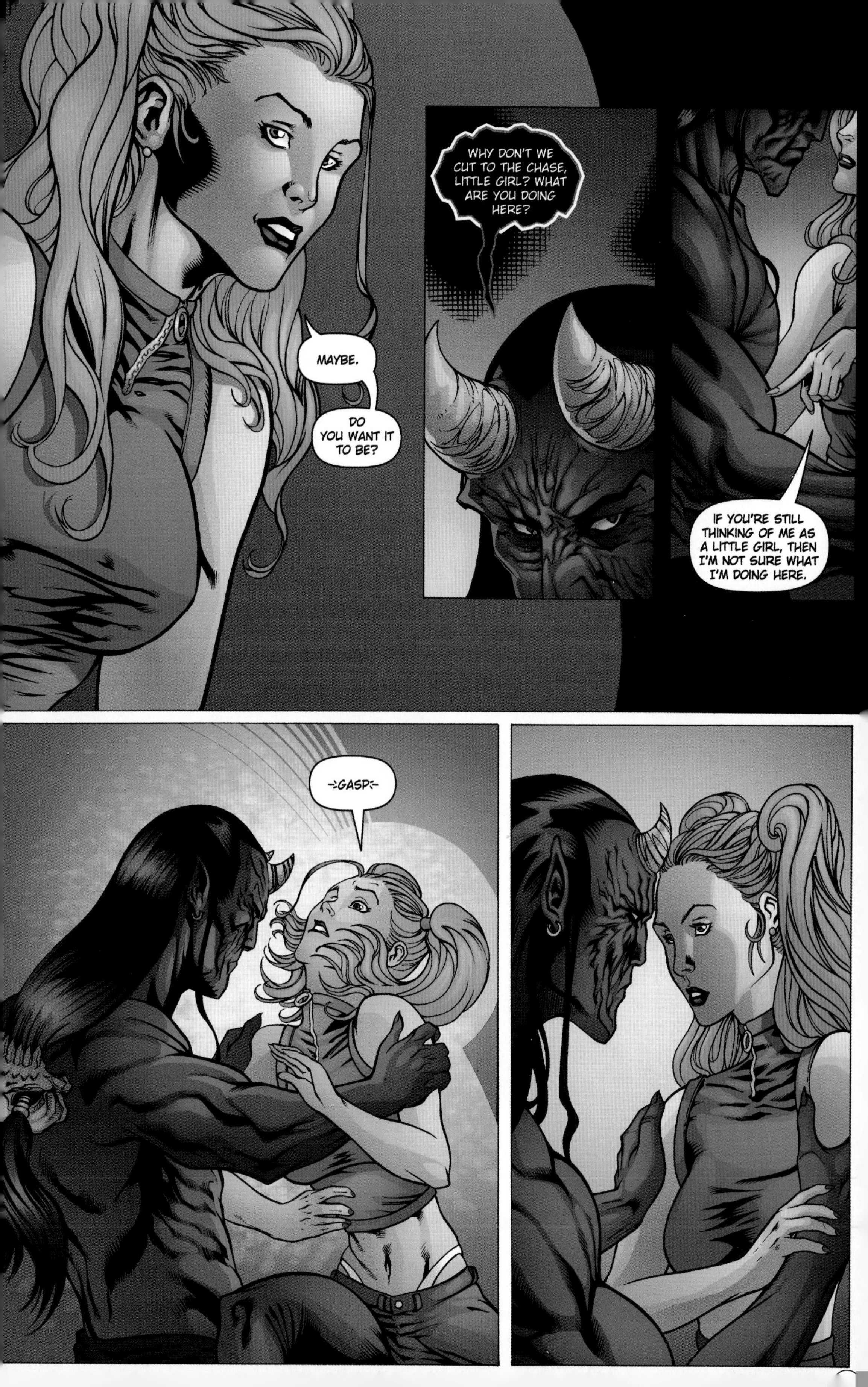
MAYBE.
DO YOU WANT IT TO BE?
WHY DON'T WE CUT TO THE CHASE, LITTLE GIRL? WHAT ARE YOU DOING HERE?
IF YOU'RE STILL THINKING OF ME AS A LITTLE GIRL, THEN I'M NOT SURE WHAT I'M DOING HERE.
-GASP-

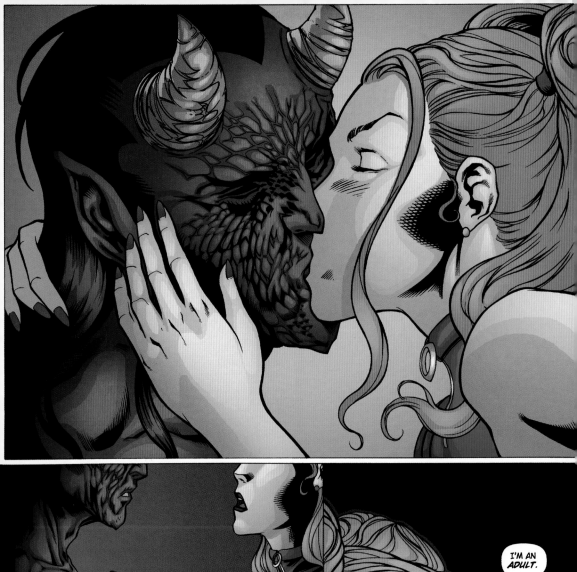

IS THIS SOME PLOY TO GET BACK AT MOMMY AND DADDY FOR SENDING YOU TO BED WITHOUT DINNER?

OF COURSE NOT.

I'M AN *ADULT*.

I MAKE MY *OWN* DECISIONS.

The End.

We're always in search of more promotion, so we sent along a little piece to the guys at Wizard, hoping maybe we'd get some more coverage in their magazine. Ian drew a scene that showed the Nobles anxiously flipping through the latest Wizard, to see if they were featured within it. Our little ploy didn't work, and our shameless bribe never landed us any extra promotion. And don't ask me what Rusty's doing with his hands. I don't want to know.

My first idea for the cover of this trade paperback was a shot of the Noble family on the steps in front of some impressive-looking building, complete with Greek pillars, and maybe a stone lion or two. Ian's first attempt was good, but we both agreed it lacked a certain "majesty," so he agreed to start over, and push in closer on the characters, which resulted in the second cover of this book, which was even used as an ad in a few Image comics. But the more we thought about it, the more we thought we could come up with something stronger, so Ian went back to work yet again, resulting in the final cover.

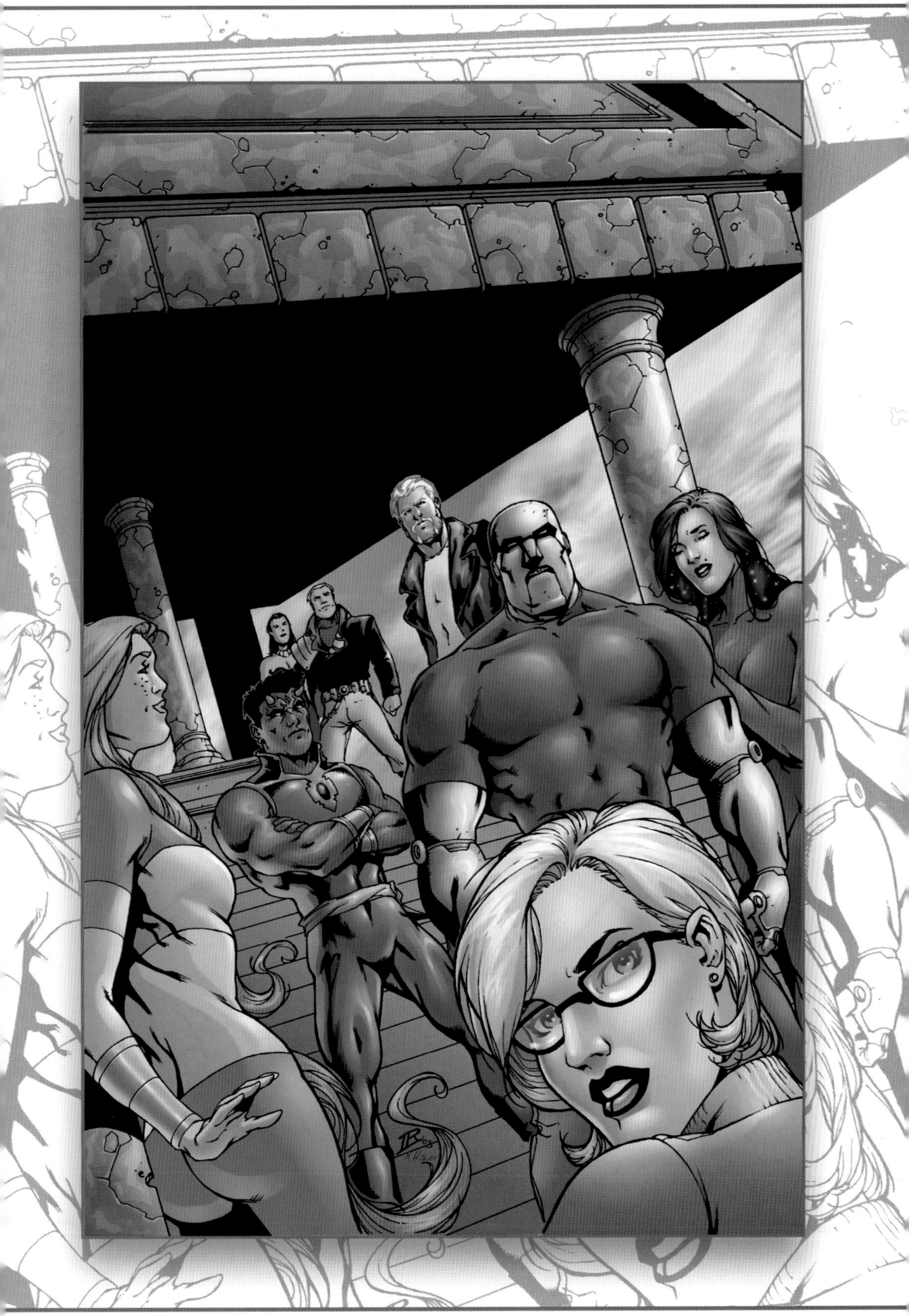

In addition to writing Noble Causes, I also wrote an Image series called Venture, which was drawn and co-created by Jamal Igle. Had the book not been cancelled, issue #5 would have featured a guest appearance by Rusty Noble, and Ian and Jamal agreed to each do a cover for this issue, depicting Rusty and Venture about to fight.

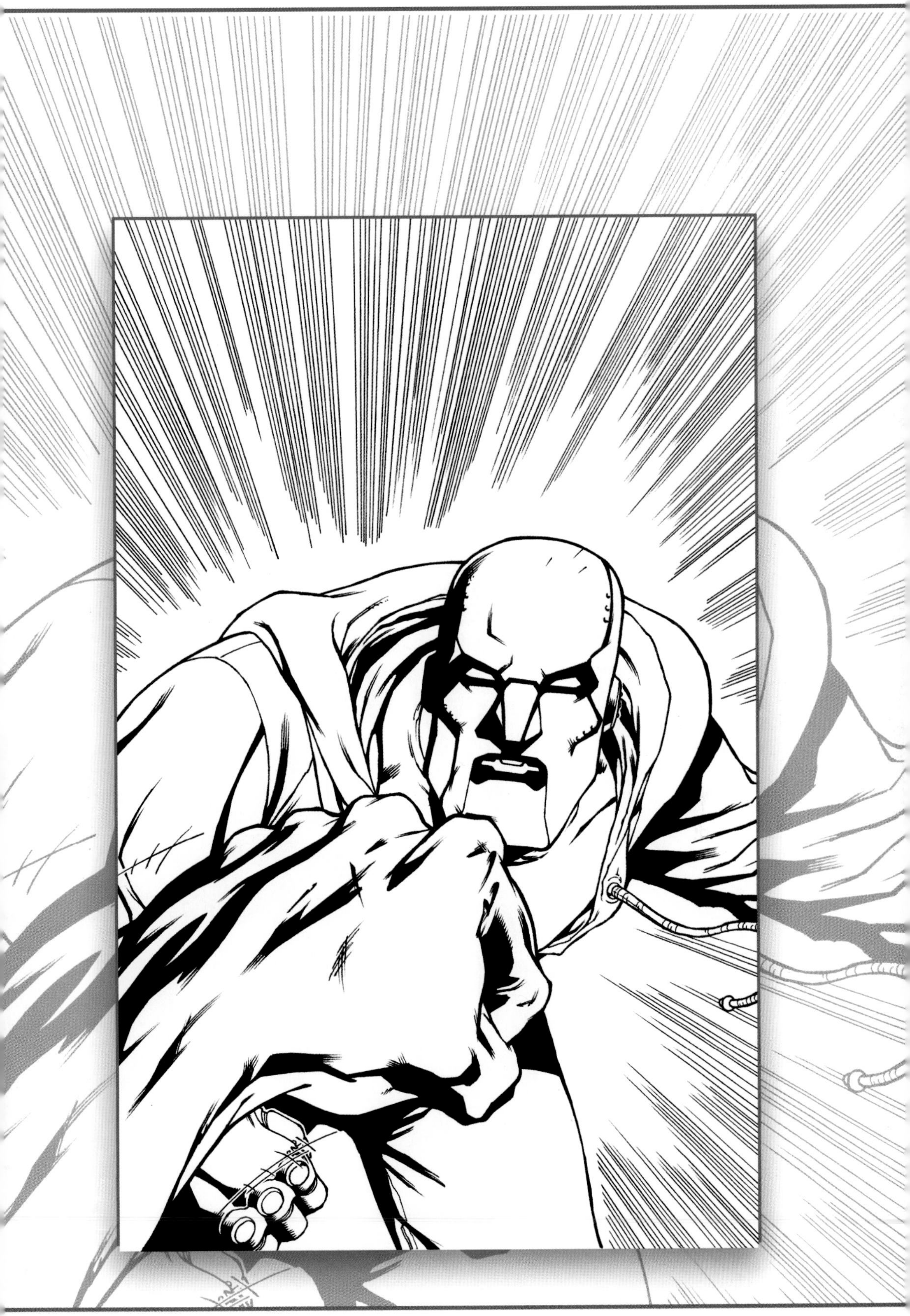

I first came across Ian's artwork in a feature in an online comic book magazine called Borderline, wherein Ian was the subject of a regular piece about new talent. I liked Ian's samples enough to ask the Borderline guys for his contact info, and got him to tryout for Noble Causes.

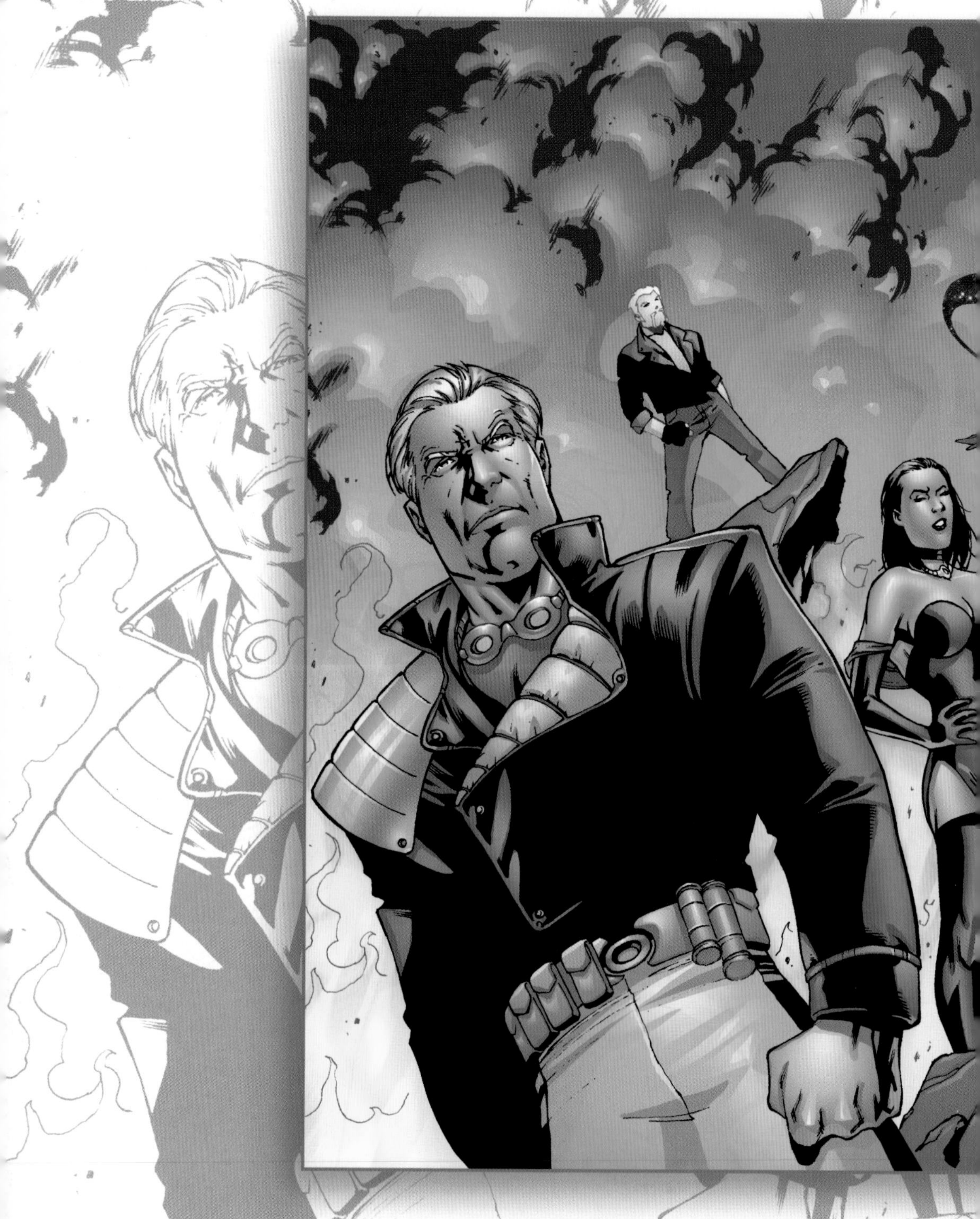

After Ian had gotten the gig, and we were launching Noble Causes: Family Secrets, I thought it only fitting that we do something nice for Borderline, so Ian contributed this cover for them.

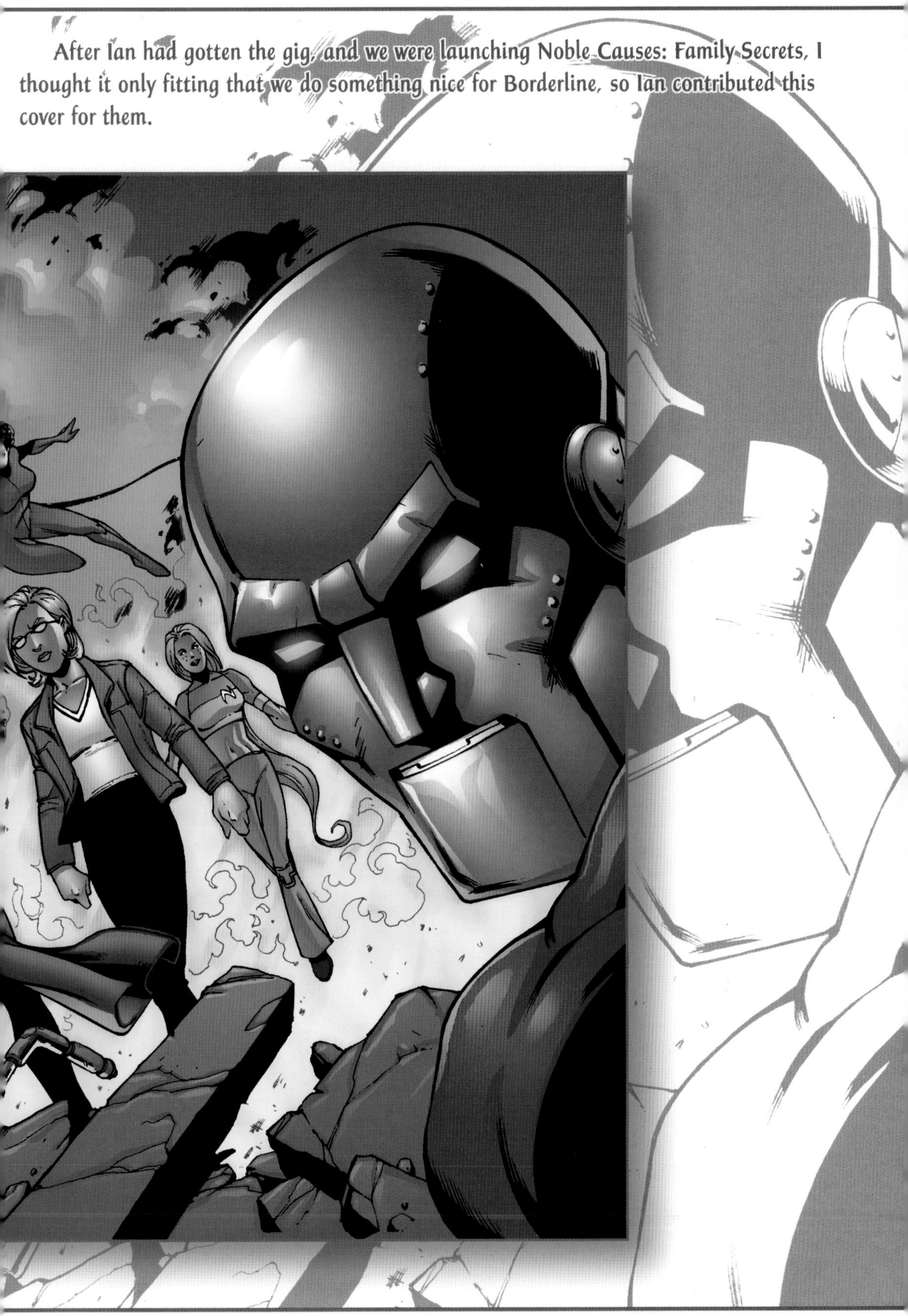

In order to make sure Ian was right for this book, I asked him to draw a few pages from an old Noble Causes script. In fact, this is the same script sequence that I used to try out Pat Gleason and John Wycough on the previous series. I chose this bit because it features pretty much the whole cast, and has a nice mix of character interaction and fight scenes. It's pretty cool to see how Ian's art has evolved since this tryout. Not only has he gotten even better, but he changed his take on some of the characters.

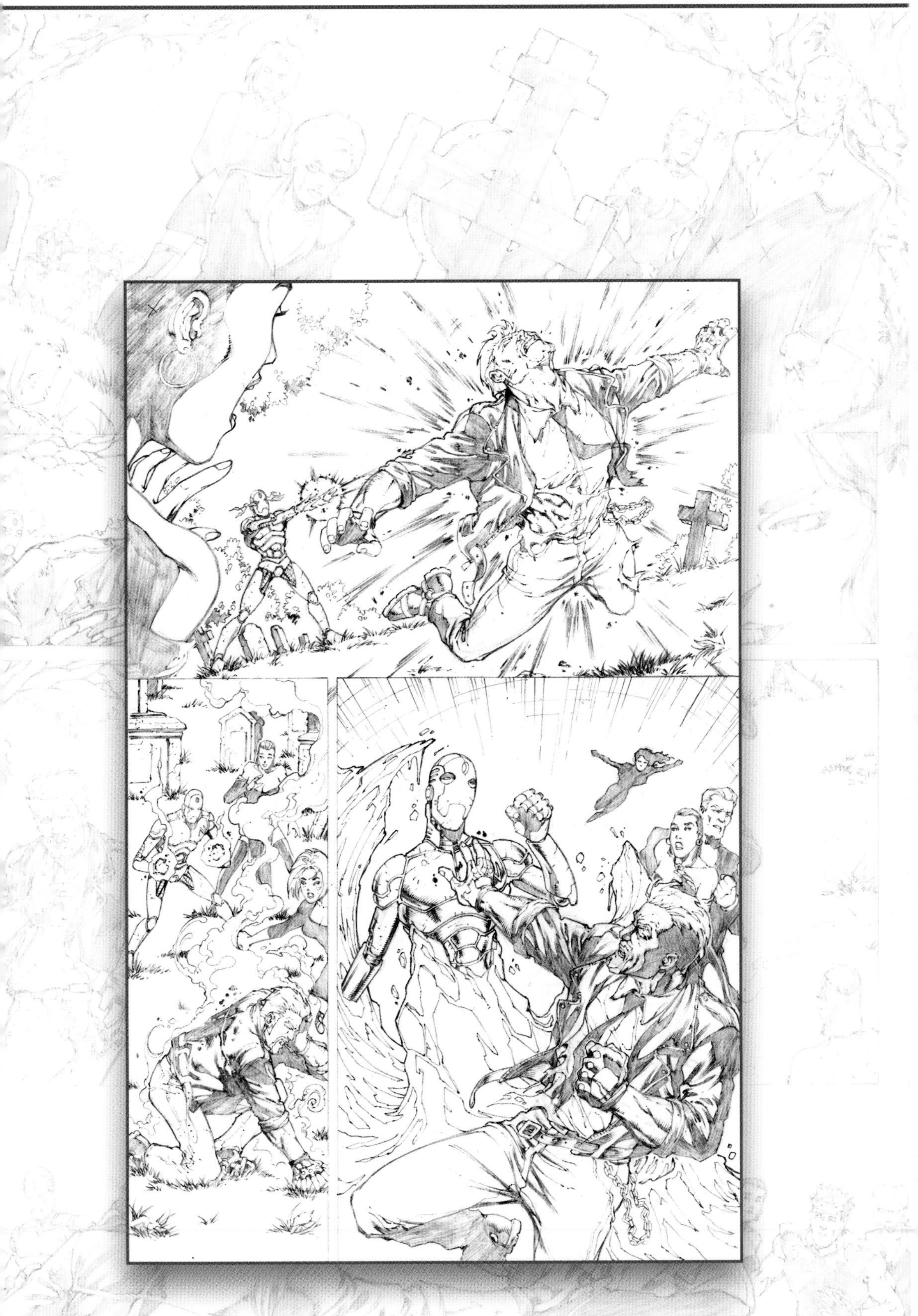

I was getting ready to go to Wizard World East, in Philadelphia, the summer before Noble Causes: Family Secrets was released, and Ian and I wanted to have something to show the fans, so he came up with this family portrait, which we used as a watermark image on the inside front covers of the series.

As part of the launch of Image's wave of superhero books in 2003, all the creators of these books contributed to a jam illustration that was used on the cover of the Westfield comic book subscription service's catalog.

Although Noble Causes was a pre-existing book, and not technically part of the "launch," we were included in this universe, so we took part in the jam piece.

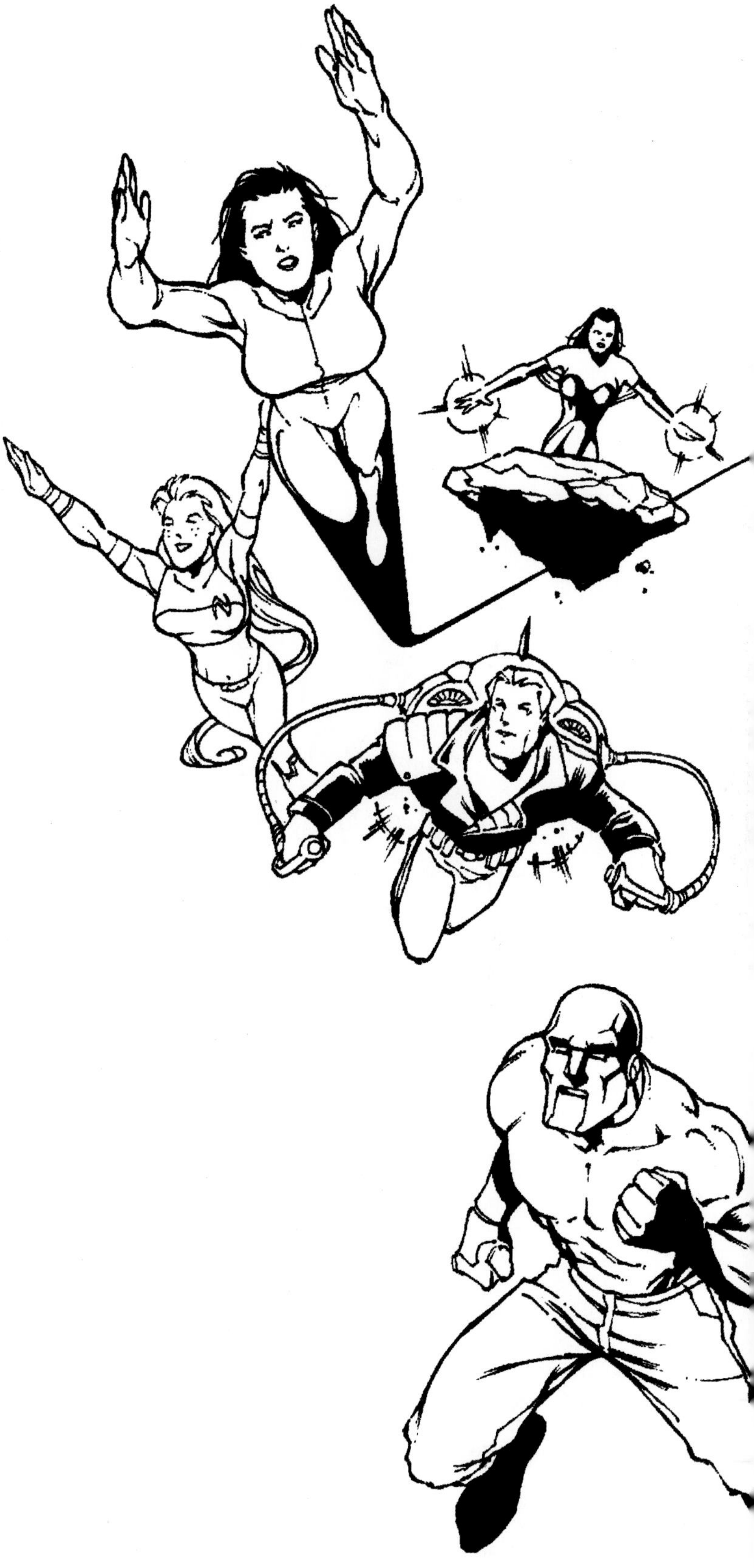

Artist Jon Sommariva produced these character concept sketches as he prepared to draw his back-up story, which featured Rusty, Frost, and Race as young boys, and also introduced the new character of Clarion.

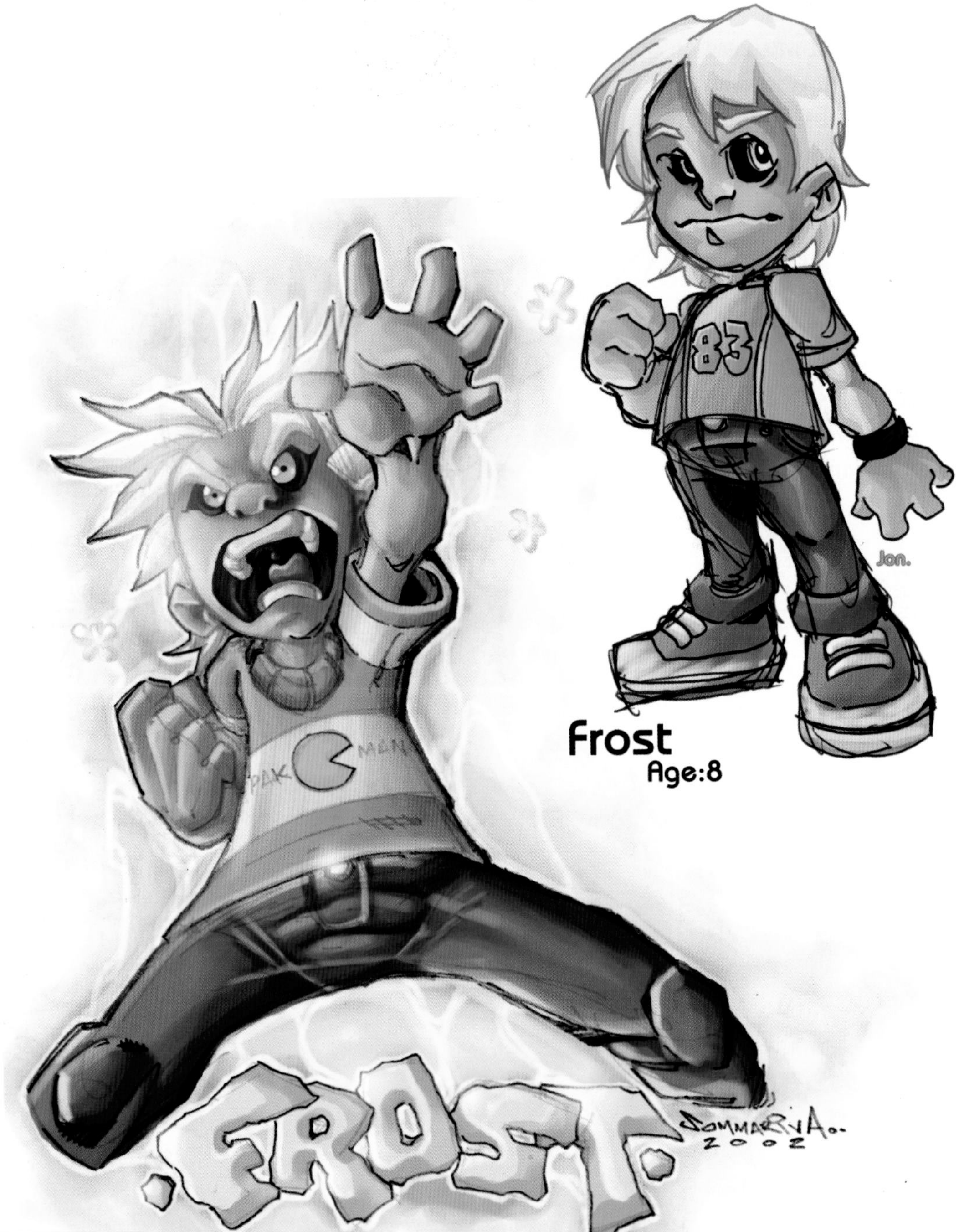
83
Jon.
Frost
Age:8
PAK
MAN
FROST
SOMMARIVA
2002

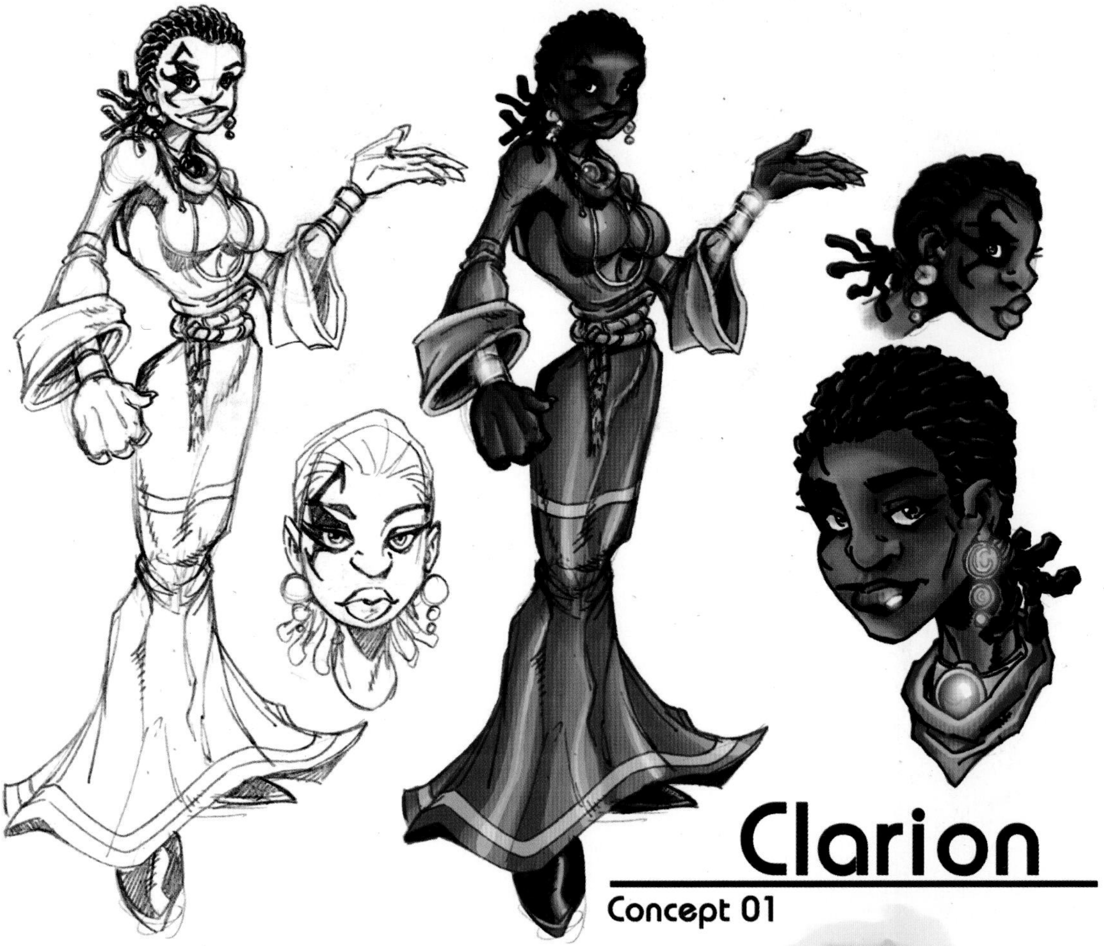
Clarion
Concept 01

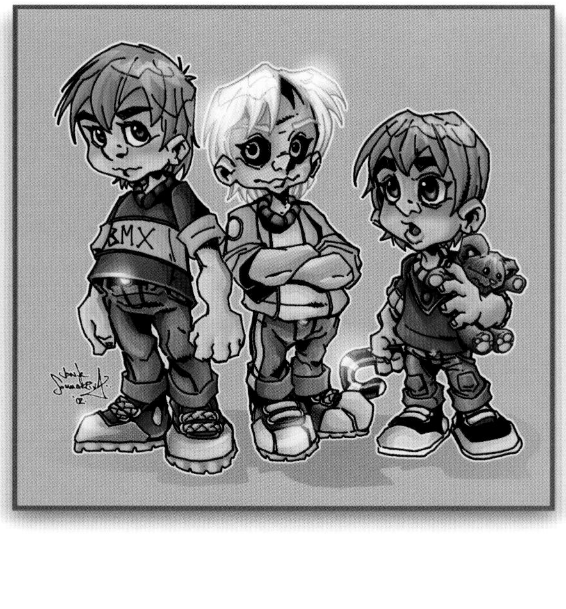
BMX

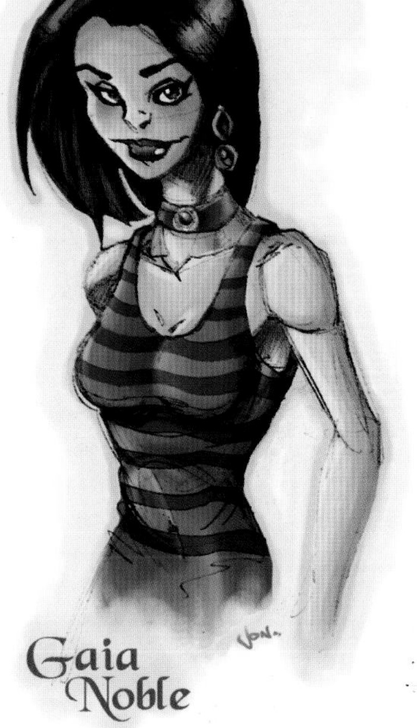
Gaia Noble

MORE GREAT TITLES FROM IMAGE

A DISTANT SOIL VOL I
THE GATHERING
ISBN: 1-887259-51-2
STAR07382

AGE OF BRONZE VOL I
A THOUSAND SHIPS
ISBN: 1-58240-2000
STAR13458

ARIA VOL I
THE MAGIC OF ARIA
ISBN: 1-58240-139-X
STAR11559

AVIGON
ISBN: 1-58240-182-9
STAR11946

BLUNTMAN AND CHRONIC
1-58240-208-6
STAR13070

BULLETPROOF MONK
ISBN: 1-58240-244-2
STAR16331

CHASING DOGMA
ISBN: 1-58240-206-X
STAR13071

CLERKS
THE COMIC BOOKS
ISBN: 1-58240-209-4
STAR13071

DARKNESS VOL I
COMING OF AGE
ISBN: 1-58240-032-6
STAR08526

DAWN VOL II
RETURN OF THE GODDESS
ISBN: 1-58240-242-6
STAR15771

DELICATE CREATURES
ISBN: 1-58240-225-6
STAR14906

E.V.E. PROTOMECHA VOL I
SINS OF THE DAUGHTER
ISBN: 1-58240-214-0
STAR13075

FATHOM VOL I
ISBN: 1-58240-210-8
STAR15804

G.I. JOE VOL I
REINSTATED
ISBN: 1-58240-252-3
STAR16642

GOLDFISH
THE DEFINITIVE COLLECTION
ISBN: 1-58240-195-0
STAR13576

JINX
THE DEFINITIVE COLLECTION
ISBN: 1-58240-179-9
STAR13039

KABUKI VOL I
CIRCLE OF BLOOD
ISBN: 1-88727-9-806
STAR12480

KIN VOL I
DESCENT OF MAN
ISBN: 1-58240-224-8
STAR15032

LAZARUS CHURCHYARD
THE FINAL CUT
ISBN: 1-58240-180-2
STAR12720

LEAVE IT TO CHANCE VOL I
SHAMAN'S RAIN
ISBN: 1-58240-253-1
STAR16641

LIBERTY MEADOWS VOL I
EDEN
ISBN: 1-58240-260-4
STAR16143

MAGDALENA VOL I
BLOOD DIVINE
ISBN: 1-58240-215-9
STAR15519

MAGE:
THE HERO DEFINED VOL I
ISBN: 1-58240-012-1
STAR08160

NOWHERESVILLE
ISBN: 1-58240-241-8
STAR15904

OBERGEIST VOL I
THE DIRECTOR'S CUT
ISBN: 1-58240-243-4
STAR15853

POWERS VOL I
WHO KILLED RETRO GIRL?
ISBN: 1-58240-223-X
STAR12482

RISING STARS VOL I
BORN IN FIRE
ISBN: 1-58240-172-1
STAR12207

SAVAGE DRAGON VOL I
BAPTISM OF FIRE
ISBN: 1-58240-165-9
STAR13080

TELLOS VOL I
RELUCTANT HEROES
ISBN: 1-58240-186-1
STAR12831

TOMB RAIDER VOL I
SAGA OF THE MEDUSA MASK
ISBN: 1-58240-164-0
STAR03000

TORSO
THE DEFINITIVE COLLECTION
ISBN: 1-58240-174-8
STAR12688

VIOLENT MESSIAHS VOL I
THE BOOK OF JOB
ISBN: 1-58240-236-1
STAR160053

WITCHBLADE VOL I
ORIGINS
ISBN: 1-887279-65-2
STAR07991

ZORRO
THE COMPLETE ALEX TOTH
ISBN: 1-58240-090-3
STAR14527